AMBASSADOR EXTRAORDINAIRE
Daniel O'Daly, 1595–1662

The person believed to be Daniel O'Daly
courtesy of the Library of Corpo Santo

Margaret Mac Curtain

AMBASSADOR EXTRAORDINAIRE
Daniel O'Daly, 1595–1662

ARLEN
HOUSE

Ambassador Extraordinaire:
Daniel O'Daly, 1595–1662

is published in 2017 by
ARLEN HOUSE
42 Grange Abbey Road
Baldoyle
Dublin 13
Ireland
Phone: +353 85 7695697
Email: arlenhouse@gmail.com

ISBN 978–1–85132–190–2, paperback

International distribution by
SYRACUSE UNIVERSITY PRESS
621 Skytop Road, Suite 110
Syracuse, New York
USA 13244–5290
Phone: 315–443–5534/Fax: 315–443–5545
Email: supress@syr.edu
www.syracuseuniversitypress.syr.edu

Typesetting by Arlen House

Cover image:
Hippolyte (Paul) Delaroche, 'Cardinal Mazarin's Last Sickness'
copyright The Wallace Collection

CONTENTS

ACKNOWLEDGEMENTS

This book owes its publication to the commitment of Alan Hayes of Arlen House and the urging of Professor Maureen Murphy of Hofstra University, Long Island; both had faith in the project.

Many of those whom I thanked in the original doctoral thesis are dead, but the various archives they serviced are welcoming places to the many researchers whom they assist. The Dominican archivists, Fr Luke Taheny, O.P., provincial archivist of the Irish Dominicans, and Fr Godfrey Anstruther, O.P., of the general archives of the Dominican order in Rome, gave me invaluable support. Fr Leonard Boyle, O.P., prefect of the Vatican library, introduced me to the treasures of the Vatican archives and library. The archivists of the Spanish archives in Simancas Castle in Valladolid unravelled complex documents in seventeenth-century Spanish. Mother Cecelia Murray, archivist of Bom Sucesso convent in Lisbon, kept intact the records of that historic convent. The courtesy of the librarians in the National Library in Dublin and that of Séamus Helferty of the University College, Dublin archives in Belfield deserve my appreciation. For the supervisors of my master's thesis, Professor Dudley Edwards, and of my doctoral thesis, Professor T.D. Williams, I retain immense respect for their role in advancing the study of Irish history in Ireland and abroad. The Kerry Archaeological and Historical Society and its former president, Gerry O'Leary, and Fr Pat Sugrue placed a memorial gravestone to the memory of Fr Dominic O'Daly in the Kilsarkan cemetery. Thanks to the indexers of this book, Peter Moore and Geraldine Mills, for diligent and thorough work.

My family, especially Eilish Pearce, and my wider Dominican family, have at all times given encouragement and support.

Dún Laoghaire, June 2017

LIST OF ILLUSTRATIONS

List of Abbreviations

A.F.M.	*Annals of the Four Masters*
AGOP	Archivum Generale Ordinis Praedicatorum, Santa Sabina, Rome
A.P.	Archives Propaganda Fide, Piazza di Spagna, Rome
Ambasciatore	Barozzi-Berchet, *Relazioni degli stati europei letter al Senato degli ambasciate veneti nel sec. 17.*
Archiv. Hib.	Archivium Hibernicum; Irish Historical Records
A.TdoT.	Archivo Nacional da Torre do Tombo, Lisbon
A.V.	Archivio Segreto Vaticano, Rome
Bibl. D'Ajuda	Bibliotheca da Ajuda, Lisbon
B.M.	British Museum, London
Bibl. Nat.	Bibliotheque Nationale, Paris
Brussels	Archives Generales du Royaume de Belgique, Brussels
Butler, *Gleanings*	W.F.T. Butler, *Gleanings from Irish History*
BV	Biblioteca Apostolica Vaticana, Rome
Cal. S.P. Ire.	Calendar of State Papers, Ireland
Clar. S. P.	Clarendon State Papers
Comment. Rinucc.	Commentarius Rinuccinianus
Costelloe	Costelloe transcripts from AGOP in Tallaght Dominican archives, Dublin
Corpo. Dipl. Port.	Corpo Diplomatico Portuguez
Fondo Santa Sede	Archivo de la Embajada de Espanga cerca de la Santa Sede in the archives of the Ministry of Foreign Affairs, Madrid
D.N.B.	*Dictionary of National Biography*
H.M.C. rep.	Historical Manuscripts Commission report

I.E.R.	*Irish Ecclesiastical Record*
I.H.S.	*Irish Historical Studies*
Moran, *Spicil. Ossor.*	P.F. Moran, *Spicilegium Ossoriense*
N.L.I.	National Library of Ireland
O'Daly, *Geraldines*	D. O'Daly, *History of the Geraldines*. Trans. C.P. Meehan (2nd ed. Dublin, 1878)
P.R.O.I.	Public Records Office of Ireland
Quadro Elementar	*Quadro Elementar des relações politicas e diplomáticas de Portugal*
Recueil	*Recueil des Instructions donnés aux Ambassadeurs et Ministres de France depuis les traits de Westphalie* (Paris, 1886)
Simancas	Archivo General de Simancas, Spain
R.I.A. proc.	*Proceedings of Royal Irish Academy*, Dublin

INTRODUCTION

It is difficult for young students of the early twenty-first century to understand the challenge, and thrill, of accessing information in those decades before electronic technology allowed inaccessible archival sources, the contents of rare books in out-of-reach libraries and archives, and the reading of theses and specialised studies to appear on a computer screen. In this century, it is now possible to research an historical subject without recourse to visiting archives and libraries, by going 'on line' and reading a document while sitting in front of a computer. The research for this study was conducted between 1956 and 1963 in archives in Ireland, Portugal, Italy, Spain, France and England, consulting original sources in Irish, Portuguese, Spanish, French, Italian, Latin and Tudor and Stuart English.

The publication of the career of an Irish diplomat, Daniel O'Daly (1595–1662), as a full-scale study in 2017 was made possible by the discovery in the University College, Dublin archives in Belfield of what appeared to be the only surviving copy of this author's Ph.D. thesis, examined in 1963, among the Dudley Edwards papers which had come into the archives some years previously. Among them, the O'Daly thesis had lain unnoticed until it was brought to the attention of Séamus Helferty, principal archivist. He, in turn, notified me and invited me to examine it in November 2013. I visited the Belfield archives to leaf through the neat, typed pages of the thesis, 'An Agent of the Irish Counter-Reformation, Dominic O'Daly' which looked like it had not been read.

I was puzzled. In those years of typed theses before photocopying machines made multiple copies available, it was quite a feat to produce four carbon copies, two of which went to the external examiners, one to my supervisor, Professor T.D. Williams, and one to the writer to produce when required. Over the decades since I completed the thesis I lost my own copy, and the Belfield archive possessed the only extant copy.

Professor Maureen Murphy of Hofstra University, New York, accompanied me on my inspection visit to the archives. She and Alan Hayes, the publisher and owner of Arlen House, urged me to publish the work. Since 1963, I had developed other interests. I had taken an active role in promoting the academic study of women's history, and the first essay I wrote after completing the thesis was on women's education and access to higher education. Occasionally, I had contributed essays and delivered talks on aspects of Daniel O'Daly's career, but I was reluctant to return to a subject which I considered I had outgrown. The manuscript had originally been recommended for publication, with some unspecified changes, and I was determined, if I were to publish, to find an Irish publisher. Unexpectedly, in the 1960s, Dan Nolan, editor of *The Kerryman* weekly newspaper and the co-owner and editor of Anvil Press, approached me with an offer to publish the text. I was happy to give the manuscript to him. When he returned it three years later, I had moved away from my seventeenth-century doctoral study and was immersed in editing and writing history textbooks, with the aim of making history more accessible to the general reader. The 1960s were pragmatic years for Irish publishing houses; textbooks sold while specialised studies of historical interest did not! As co-editor and contributor to an eleven-volume *Gill History of Ireland* which issued in quick succession between 1972–74, I was pleased that the series was acclaimed as a sensationally successful one, modestly priced and within the reading range of undergraduates and upper-school students. Prior to that, I had devised a second-level *A History of Ireland* series of three volumes, and co-wrote the last volume with Mark Tierney.

In 1978, I co-edited, with Donnchadh Ó Corráin, a series of lectures on women in Irish society. The producer of the RTÉ Sunday night programmes, Michael Littleton, expressed doubt about the willingness of an Irish publisher to undertake an edition of a book devoted to the history of Irish women! Arlen House, founded by Catherine Rose in 1975, took on the project, *Women in Irish Society: The Historical Dimension*, which sold out its first edition of 10,000 copies. It was subsequently published in the United States, and it is regarded as a landmark in the publishing history of Irish women.

Despite the urgings of Alan Hayes, who relaunched Arlen House in 2000, and Maureen Murphy, I was initially reluctant to re-engage with publishing the thesis. On re-reading the work, I see that Daniel O'Daly is an important character who deserves study in this new century. I am also intrigued to see early glimpses of my interest in women's history in the original thesis from 1963. I am aware that, with each generation, the interpretation of the past changes. Each generation writes the history of the past from a different perspective. Central to Irish academic historical research in the 1950s and 1960s was the Counter-Reformation period that stretched from the Council of Trent (1545–63) to the visit of Papal Nuncio Rinuccini to the Confederation of Kilkenny in 1845. Dr Tadhg Ó hAnnracháin's fine study, *Catholic Reformation in Ireland: The Mission of Rinuccini 1645–1649* (2002), signalled that interest in the Counter-Reformation as a dominant research interest waned in Irish universities after Ireland's entry into the European Common Market/European Union.

I thought if I were to publish my thesis, I would have to change its title to acknowledge Daniel O'Daly as King João of Portugal's accredited ambassador to the French court which was dominated, in 1656, by its powerful foreign minister Cardinal Mazarin. It proved unexpectedly easy to examine O'Daly's diplomatic career in the decade after the Peace of Westphalia (1648). It was a period of transition when secular diplomacy and career ambassadors superseded church agents employed as intermediaries between the Vatican and its system of papal nuncios attached to, but separate from, the various courts of Europe. The Peace of Westphalia and the Treaty of the Pyrenees (1659) ended the decades-long Hapsburg-Bourbon conflict and established peace between France and Spain. Portugal and Spain were to continue the conflict until 1668; however, the arranged marriage between the English King Charles II and the Portuguese Infanta, Catherine of Bragança, in 1662, strengthened the claim of Portugal to be a separate and medieval kingdom from that of Spain in the Iberian Peninsula.

The Restoration decades, better known as *A Restauração*, 1640–1668, were dominated historiographically by the studies of Edgar Prestage, an English scholar who defined the Restoration decades in a series of influential publications which have not been superseded. For readers of that period of Portuguese history, Prestage's *As Relações Diplomáticias de Portugal com a França, Inglaterra e Hollanda de 1640 a 1668* (1928), which established the framework for Portugal's foreign policy in the Restoration period was based on Prestage's earlier *The Diplomatic Relations of Portugal with France, England and Holland from 1640 to 1668* (1925). Prestage also considered the work of O'Daly. His monograph, *Frei Domingos do Rosario: Diplomata e Politico* (1926), clearly demonstrates O'Daly's influential role in the inner circle that gathered around the newly-crowned king and queen in the years between the Restoration, 1640, and O'Daly's death in 1662, as bishop-elect of the See of Coimbra. Yet another defining study by Prestage, *The Mode of Government in Portugal during the Restoration Period* (1949), was the English translation of the Portuguese version written in 1935.

An explosion of new research appeared in the closing decades of the twentieth century and into the twenty-first century which concentrated on fresh aspects of the Restoration period and are listed in an excellent bibliography in the two volume *Historia de Portugal* (2009), general co-ordinator, Rui Ramos. In keeping with my 1963 thesis, I have retained the original Foreword while changing the title for the purposes of this publication.

Dún Laoghaire, June 2017

FOREWORD

'The gentleman from Portugal', was the rather ambiguous title bestowed upon Father Daniel O'Daly, an Irish priest, by the papal nuncio to France in his dispatches for the year 1657. In a way, it emphasises a certain mysteriousness which the central character of this study possessed for his contemporaries.

The first concern of a biographer is the life-work of her/his hero, but historical biography may not be satisfied with the bare record of achievement; for in history, as in life, the hero does not always occupy the centre of the stage. He is the product of his age, the result of environment and heredity, the aggregate of personal qualities and interests. This biography then is an experiment in reconstruction; original documents and contemporary sources being used as the main medium of explanation.

Admittedly, it is a detective story, but to those who regard the study of an historical figure as light, pleasant, armchair reading, I issue a mild warning. The slow, inexorable piling up of evidence may tax the reader's patience. I beg her/his pardon. The tedium of dull reference may be the very detail needed to help grasp the cluster of associations. It may be the missing piece in the jigsaw that clarifies a series of relationships.

In presenting Daniel O'Daly to the general reader, I accept that many will be meeting him for the first time. He is singularly appropriate as a representative Irish ecclesiastic of the seventeenth century whose career involved him in political events in Europe at a time when the connection between Ireland and the continent was considerable and subtle. Born in the remote parish of Cillín Tiarna, County Kerry in 1595, his claim to history lies in a multiplicity of activities as diplomat, historian, founder of an Irish college abroad, and as a prime-mover in the Stuart Restoration of Charles II. He died in 1662 as bishop-elect of Coimbra, one of the most influential sees in Portugal.

Any research involves the patient accumulation of details, corroborative or conflicting as the case may be, from diverse sources. O'Daly's career brought him from Kerry to Spain, and from there to Louvain (Leuven). In the decade leading up to the peace of Westphalia (1648), he was in Portugal, rapidly assuming a position of political influence in that country. In the following decade, his diplomatic activities brought him into close proximity with Cardinal Mazarin, the papacy, and Charles Stuart. The retrieval of primary sources was a complicated process involving documents scattered in many archives and libraries in western Europe, and written in French, Italian, Spanish, Portuguese, English and Latin. For a relatively minor character of that period, O'Daly takes up considerable space in state papers.

In the academic thesis which is the nucleus of this biography, I made the observation that Father O'Daly was a fair example of the type of ecclesiastic whom the counter-reformation produced in Ireland. Accomplished, continental -trained, versatile, he was necessarily drawn into European affairs because of his Irish commitments. Subsequent research in the Vatican archives, in the Archivo General de Simancas and in Lisbon convinced me that the complex pattern of seventeenth-century diplomacy seemed to involve Irishmen such as O'Daly in a unique way. The analysis of his diplomatic negotiations on behalf of Portugal, struggling for recognition as a nation, affords a telescopic view of international relationships in post-Westphalian Europe. It is not only the career or reputation of one man that is being examined in this study, but the political existence of a nation.

During the several years in which I have been engaged in this work, the courtesy and helpfulness of many archivists and librarians have lightened the burden considerably. I acknowledge in a special way the generosity of those who made possible archival research in Rome, Spain, Portugal, Paris and London: namely, my religious superiors and University College, Dublin. My indebtedness to Professor R. Dudley Edwards and to his colleague Professor T.D. Williams in the History Department of University College, Dublin is great and, I think, beyond repayment.

Coimbra, April 1962

AMBASSADOR EXTRAORDINAIRE
Daniel O'Daly 1595–1662

Kilsarkan, County Kerry (c. 1960), where Daniel O'Daly was born
courtesy of Margaret Mac Curtain

I

ELIZABETHAN KERRY

A brilliant flare sped upwards for one brief instant, then a shower of descending sparks settled on the quiet waters of the evening Seine. There was a roar of raucous approval from the crowds clustered on the uneven quayside, which straggled haphazardly between the Port au Chance and the unfinished Louvre.

Passers-by, who paused to inquire, discovered that this was a display of fireworks given by the Portuguese minister to France to celebrate the coronation of the young Afonso VI, as the twenty-second king of Portugal. The time was May 1657. The occasion marked the determination of Portugal to abide by the Restoration of the monarchy achieved some seventeen years previously by Afonso's predecessor and father, João IV. The liveliest account of that bright scene comes from the enthusiastic pen of Vincent Baron, a popular Parisian preacher, who was obviously an ardent admirer of the Portuguese minister, Frei Domingos do Rosario, or, to give him the name by which he is best known, Father Daniel O'Daly.[1]

There were others, however, in Paris that summer of 1657 whose sentiments towards the friar diplomat were not quite as cordial as those of Vincent Baron. Sir Richard Browne, the English royalist resident in Paris, was thinking his sardonic thoughts about this man, whose arrival in the French capital some months previously had made Browne very curious indeed. He had straightway written to Sir Edward Nicholas, secretary of state to Charles Stuart in London, inquiring if it were true that Oliver Cromwell had provided an English ship to convey the Portuguese minister to Paris, via Havre le Grace. Why this sudden solicitude toward Portugal on the part of England?[2]

Similarly, the newly-appointed French ambassador to Portugal, Lieutenant General, the Comte de Cominges, was subjecting Frei Domingos to a very close scrutiny. A shrewd politician trained in Mazarin's school, Cominges had delayed his departure for Lisbon by several months in order to accompany the friar on his return journey to Lisbon and to observe him even more closely. Later, he was to confess, with a kind of reluctant admiration, that he was baffled by Frei Domingos' irritatingly amateurish method of diplomacy while, at the same time, the man himself held the confidence of the Portuguese queen regent Donna Luisa de Gusmão.[3]

The papal nuncio, too, Monsignor Piccolomini was forwarding to Rome very detailed reports on the diplomatic negotiations of the Portuguese minister, whom he carefully called, 'il gentilhuomo di Portugallo'. An interested party, Piccolomini was present at all the functions given by the diplomat. Why, then, did O'Daly withhold the fact that he was an Irish Dominican?[4]

Even Frei Domingos' former colleague, de Sousa Coutinho, whose blundering tactics in Paris had led to a peremptory request from Mazarin to have him relieved of his office, was kept well informed on all that went on in the French capital. From his new position in Rome, de Sousa became a critical, but understanding, spectator. He had written to the late king the previous year, words which had proved prophetic. 'The cardinal does not want peace, but he will never acknowledge this; he listens to all, and then does as he wishes himself'.[5]

Undoubtedly, tongues were wagging that summer of 1657. This Frei Domingos, accredited minister of Afonso VI of Portugal, owned no suite of apartments in the fashionable quarters which were growing up rapidly around the nearly-completed Palais-Cardinal. He lived simply with his French brethren in the Convent of the Annunciation off the rue Saint-Honoré.[6] People watched the friar as he moved among his guests that May evening, and they speculated. It was common knowledge that Donna Luisa de Gusmão consulted him on most points of home and foreign policy. Perhaps he was, as rumour had it, at home in the Portuguese court, a very wily diplomat, whose air of habitual withdrawal was a pose, behind which a quick, inventive mind was playing a subtle game with Cardinal Mazarin?

Frei Domingos de Rosario, the enigmatic Portuguese minister, was a Kerryman. A brief record of his earliest years has been preserved by his spiritual daughters at Bom Sucesso. This was a convent he founded for refugee Irish nuns at Belem, a quiet suburb of Lisbon. In an unpublished history of the convent, the following entry for 1639 occurs: 'Father Daniel O'Daly, known in the Order as Father Dominic of the Rosary, was born in Quilsarcon in the county Kerry in 1595'.[7] Thereafter, in a quaint Portuguese attempt to translate the Irish 'Kilsarkan', one meets the variations 'Hiltarsen' and 'Kilcarsen' while in another document, the name 'Kahvicon' is given as the original place of residence of the O'Dalys.[8]

Kilsarkan, in the present parish of Cillín Tiarna in County Kerry, is situated on a slight slope, overlooking the lovely valley of the Brown Flesk, and it commands a fine prospect of rolling hills, and small, winding, river creeks. The ruins of the Catholic church, unroofed by Elizabeth's soldiers in 1593, two years before the birth of Daniel O'Daly, may still be seen.

The Kerry countryside around Kilsarkan
courtesy of Maureen Murphy

When the young boy climbed the slopes that overlooked the winding valley of the Brown Flesk, and looked eastward, he saw, not just a pleasant prospect, but the wide acres that made up the O'Daly holding, the 'east fractions'. Around him were lands that had belonged to, or had been in the possession of, the family until recently; a broad strip of land, stretching from Noghoval-daly in east Kerry, through Ballydaly and Coolecarragh into Duhallow barony on the Cork border, his mother's country. Behind him were the grasslands of Cumacheo at the head of the Glenflesk valley, also a family possession. The O'Daly clan was a landed people, a family to be reckoned with, by local standards.[9]

Here in this remote district the young son of Conchubhar O'Daly grew up. Born in 1595, he was too young to understand what was happening to his country during the turbulent years of Elizabeth's reign. He was apparently the second son because mention is made of an older soldier brother, Denis, who later joined his brother in Portugal. There may have been other children in the family, for in 1662, a provision was made by the king of Portugal for seven of the O'Dalys of Kilsarkan, fugitives from the Cromwellian persecution in Ireland, and relatives of the bishop-elect of Coimbra.[10] His mother was an O'Keeffe from the neighbouring barony of Duhallow where her people were sub-chieftains of Mac Carthy Mór, powerful in their own right. She was not, as de Burgo, the Dominican historian, asserts, a Geraldine.[11]

His father, Conchubhar O'Daly, appears to have been a remarkable man. He was a soldier in the service of the earl of Desmond, and he shared hardships of the rebellion, even to the bitter end at Glanageenty. His son, Daniel, tends to give a somewhat idealised portrait of a devoted supporter of the Geraldine cause, and Daniel endows him with the qualities of physical courage and loyalty to a high degree. To dismiss Conchubhar merely as an intrepid soldier is to do him an injustice. A glance at the Desmond Survey, which was an inventory made of the Desmond estate in 1586, reveals in one half-concealed phrase another side of his personality, and evokes a whole tradition. There Conchubhar O'Daly appears under the title of 'the rimor of Kilsarkan'. To the modern ear, perhaps the title contains a hint of mockery, but for his contemporaries, it established him in a professional class, the bardic order.[12]

The bard, or *ollamh*, occupied a unique position in the Gaelic tradition and his office, both in its constitution and outlook, remained substantially the same throughout the middle ages. Through the bardic or literary families, the traditional Irish literature was developed and transmitted. As well as being poets, the bards also acted as lawyers and historians. Years later, when Daniel O'Daly was an ageing friar in Lisbon, conscious that he belonged to a great literary tradition and as one who bore the illustrious name of Ó Dála, he wrote a history of the Geraldines.

The O'Dalys (Uí Dalaigh) originally settled in Westmeath, in or near the barony of Corkaree. The real founder of the family was Cuchonnacht na Scoile, who died in 1139, and from him derived all the bardic offshoots of the O'Dalys. Gradually, they spread over Ireland and even into Scotland. They were driven by Hugh de Lacy, the Norman, from Westmeath, and a branch settled in Sligo. Another branch came south to Desmond and Raghnall O'Daly became chief *ollamh* to the Mac Carthy. This Raghnall seems to have been the ancestor of the O'Dalys of Muntervary in the Barony of West Carbery in County Cork, and as early as 1388 they were acting as bards to the Norman Carews. Eventually, many of the Norman families followed suit and adopted the Irish custom of keeping a bard, though it is not known for certain when the Geraldines became patrons of Gaelic literature. It could normally be assumed that the O'Dalys of Kilsarkan derived in some way from the Muntervary clan, but a scrutiny of Portuguese documents suggests more their affinity with the fifteenth century Corcomroe family in County Clare. These O'Dalys acted as bards to the O'Loughlins, but are more famous for the bardic school they maintained.[13] In the manuscript history of Bom Sucesso, the convent founded by Daniel O'Daly, the name 'Kahvicon' is given as the O'Daly's original home. The actual statement runs: 'The O'Dalys originated at Kahvicon, in the province of Munster, and had a house at Hiltareen'. Again in the Corpo Santo annals, the place names, Cahircon and Kahermacen, are both given as the original home of the O'Dalys of Kilsarkan. Cahermacan today is a townland two miles south of Ballyvaughan, County Clare.[14]

At what precise stage the Kerry family began to act as bards to the Geraldines is not definite, but a fairly complete picture of their functions and activities can be pieced together from an examination of Elizabethan documents dealing with the confiscation of land after the Geraldine rebellion. In a list of rents owing to the earl of Desmond, given both in the Desmond Survey and in the *Carew Papers*, some information is given about the poets attached to the earl Gerald:

> And the rhymer of Kylestercen, in the mountain of Slewlogher, used to give and deliver to the Constable of the Castle of the Island aforesaid, annually to the cost of the candles there expended.

This feudal service is reinforced by the statement:

> In the cantred of Ogonyll, lands held by the rimors of the earl in the mountains of Slewluacra, when the earl doth cross the mountains or take his journey betwixt Kerry and Conallacha, the aforesaid rimors are wont to bear the charge for a day and a night, coming and going.[15]

Apparently, there were two brothers living in Kilsarkan at the time of the Desmond rebellion, as the *Fiants* inform us. Conchubhar we know as the father of Daniel; Cuchonnacht is better known as a poet. Their father, Maoilseachlainn Óg O'Daly, was mocked in a contemporary satire. Both brothers forfeited their lands as a result of the rebellion. Cuchonnacht then went north to Hugh Ruadh O'Donnell with whom he remained for several years. In 1601, he was back in his native district where he conducted a school. His elegy describes his death in Folcha probably in the year 1642.[16]

Conchubhar, the father of Daniel, was also a poet. His son declared that 'he was a man of remarkable eloquence', and was sent on various missions by the earl to other chieftains of the south. An inquisition held in Dingle, in 1584, found that he had entered into rebellion with the late earl, and 'at the time of his entering into the said rebellion, he was seized in his lordship as of fee of Kilsarkan aforesaid with its appurtenances of land'. He too went north after the downfall of his patrons, and between the years 1584–9 he seems to have been in the Maguire country in the lordship of Fermanagh. He has been identified with Conchubhar Crón O'Daly who left Munster after the death of the earl and wrote a poem to that effect.[17] In 1592, Conchubhar was back in Kerry where he pleaded before a commission to be restored to his lands, to the amount of five ploughlands. He was unsuccessful; however, he lived on at Kilsarkan where he was associated with his brother in maintaining a school.

The Ireland of 1595, into which his son was born, was a country of changing values, immersed in the political upheaval known as the Nine Years War. With the passing of years came knowledge conveyed to Daniel, in many a firelight session, of the terrible happenings that had brought desolation in the time of his birth to the palatinate of Desmond. 'How could I, who am an Irishman', he was to write years afterwards in Lisbon:

> and the son of that Irishman, who leaving all he held dear even from his boyhood, sat by the hearth of those Desmonds, and when he grew up, was made the depository of their confidence , held command under them in their wars, and saw the slain Geraldines with his own eyes; how I repeat, could I, the son of such a father, commemorate them without sigh or groan?[18]

With that introductory passage, the son of Conchubhar O'Daly, 'rimor' and soldier of the Desmonds, opens his description of the tragic years that lay between the deaths of James FitzMaurice in 1579 and the assassination of his cousin, the earl Gerald in 1583. O'Daly's narrative is characterised by the vividness associated with childhood memories. He recalls details of the Munster countryside with the assurance of the familiar, and relates his father's account of the final disaster at Glenageenty, a story that was imprinted deeply in the boy's mind.

When Gerald FitzGerald succeeded to his patrimony in 1558 as the sixteenth earl of Desmond, he exercised almost sovereign sway over a territory of some half a million acres. In the decades that followed Elizabeth's accession to the English throne, she revived the Tudor policy of encouraging English adventurers at the expense of reducing Gaelic and feudal chieftains to the status of a subject people, loyal in church and state to England. Energetically she promoted the project of expanding the Protestant Church into all parts of Ireland, Munster being singled out for the experiment. The times called for Gerald to move with extreme caution.[19] By nature he was a caviller. Unless driven to it, he avoided taking a strong line of action. In the difficult situation created by the determination of the English authorities to suppress all local quasi-sovereign jurisdiction (whether Gaelic or Anglo-Irish), he managed to maintain his traditional palatine style until the advent of Sir William Drury to the presidency of Munster in 1576 brought matters to a head.

English law was enforced by means of sheriffs and justices. Castlemaine, the Desmond main castle in Kerry, was delivered up to Drury without active opposition. Then, in July 1579, James FitzMaurice FitzGerald, cousin of the earl Gerald, landed near Dingle at the head of an expedition which had received the approval of Pope Gregory XII. Forthwith, James proclaimed a religious crusade for the public Restoration of the Catholic faith in Ireland. The earl of Desmond found himself in an embarrassing position and held aloof. For two years, Munster had wilted under the iron discipline of Drury; now with the landing of FitzMaurice in Dingle, the expected invasion of Spanish troops seemed imminent.

The crown forces in Munster became more vigilant. Coercion hardened as the rising anxiety of Elizabeth's servants in Ireland drove them to extreme measures. 'If God give us bread', wrote the English commander to Elizabeth, 'we doubt not but to make as bare a country as ever Spaniard put his foot in'.

In an age when personal daring was at a premium, few figures emerge in such strong, uncompromising colours as James FitzMaurice FitzGerald, and few have received such scant attention from posterity. Less than a month after his landing, he was killed in battle with Sir John Burke of Castleconnell near the Shannon. His death forced Desmond from his cautious position of playing for time. He was compelled by ties of kinship and religion to enter the war, but he had little military capacity. By a curious irony, Gerald, a man cast in an unheroic mould, completely overshadows his more splendid cousin, mainly because of the melodramatic circumstances surrounding his death at Glenageenty.

Gerald was immediately proclaimed an outlaw in a document signed by Pelham, Malby, the mayor of Waterford and Waterhouse and seven of the Butlers, who, it was rumoured, were induced to do so in hopes of benefitting by the forfeiture of Gerald's vast estates. In England, the queen was displeased at the high-handed action of the lord justice in proclaiming the earl, but his answer mollified her. Gerald, 'in all his skirmishes and outrages since the proclamation, cried, "Papa," which is the Pope, above even you and your imperial crown'.[20]

From the point of view of the English authorities, the most disturbing element of the war was its religious aspect and its unifying result on the people. In fact, the pope had granted temporal jurisdiction over the city of Limerick and its surrounds to Gerald by a Brief dated 13 May 1580, and two weeks later, he granted 'a plenary indulgence as conceded to Crusaders to all who take up arms against

Elizabeth'.[21] Though Gerald was depending on substantial reinforcements from both Spain and the pope, he appealed also to his fellow countrymen 'to join in the defence of our Catholic faith against Englishmen which had overrun our country'. His call did not go unheeded. In Leinster, Lord Baltinglass and Fiach MacHugh O'Byrne rose in rebellion, and the victory of Glenmalure in 1580 filled Catholics with hope. The same year, a little force sent by the pope, under Colonel Sebastiano di San Joseppi, landed at Smerwick harbour and occupied Dunanóir (Fort del Oro), which was promptly besieged. That was in September. On 10 November San Joseppi surrendered. The massacre of over 500 of his soldiers followed. The full story still remains untold but it appears that San Joseppi was forced to surrender at discretion. His own reports to the pope as well as those of Dr Sanders, the English exile who had joined FitzMaurice's expedition, emphasise the helplessness of the besieged trapped in the fort.[22]

Most of the contemporary historians, O'Sullivan Beare, the Italian Muratori and O'Daly accuse San Joseppi of deliberate treachery and cowardice in yielding up the fort after forty days. 'But what is there so strong that treason and money may not overreach?' asks O'Daly, and answers his own question. 'The Spanish leader, called San Joseph, instead of animating his men to stern resistance, made terms with the English deputy, after stipulating the safety of his troops'.[23]

News of the disaster spread rapidly. In Leinster, Fiach MacHugh held out grimly until he received favourable terms. Lord Baltinglass fled to Spain. In Munster, John of Desmond was ambushed and killed by a spear – thrust at the hands of a former servant, Fleming, who had deserted to Zouch who had newly arrived to command the English forces in Munster. Previous to that, James, Gerald's younger and more capable brother, had been captured in a raid, and had been handed over to St. Leger. In Cork he had been hanged and quartered, and for months now, his head placed on a spike near one of the city gates was a grim reminder to all traitors.

Only Gerald now remained. He was an outlaw, not by choice, but by force of circumstances. To the young son of the 'rimor', who heard his father's eyewitness account, the last desperate year of Gerald's life became one of courage and pathos, and the poor-spirited Gerald took on a certain hallowed splendour. Keeping to the woods and bogs of north Kerry, he was deserted by all but a small bodyguard. 'Many a long and weary night did he spend, wandering through the bogs and mountains, deprived of the commonest necessaries for him and the few retainers who cling to him'.[24] In November 1583, near Tralee, Gerald was surprised in the night and murdered. The events surrounding his death were sordid and gloomy. A contemporary account tells how Gerald, for lack of food, had sent some twenty of his followers into the Castlegregory district. Conchubhar O'Daly was among them to 'take a prey' from the Moriartys. The cattle thus commandeered were followed by the owners and by some English soldiers who came upon Gerald alone and slew him in 'the ghastly wood of Derremore'.[25]

Unaware that the tragedy had occurred, Conchubuar O'Daly was close at hand 'watching the cattle that had been seized the day before'. So runs his son's version. Gerald's corpse was hurriedly conveyed through the byways of the hills to the little mountain graveyard of Kilnanonaimh, in the mountain range beyond Castleisland, the O'Daly country.

On Gerald's death, the 400-year-old inheritance to the Geraldines was declared forfeit to the queen. In the twenty-eighth year of Elizabeth's reign, an elaborate plan was drawn up for settling Munster 'with loving subjects of good behaviour and account', persons of Irish origin declared excluded. The decree ran, 'None of the meer Irish were to be maintained in any family'. It was not precisely demanded that the colonists should be Protestant, and in actual fact, some of the planters, like Sir Nicholas Browne, ancestor of the earls of Kenmare, were Catholic in their sympathy. Though the plantation succeeded in settling a number of English landlords among the Irish and Old English of Munster, the grantees did little to fulfil Elizabeth's expectation of either successful colonisation or steady revenue.

Elizabeth approved the final articles of the act which attainted 140 persons by name in June 1586. The lands of those who had actually perished during the rebellion were seized and distributed among some English 'undertakers', but the estates were restored to those, like the Knight of Kerry, who had submitted before Gerald's death. According to Bonn's statistical analysis, the final area planted was 202,099 acres out of the original 577,000 acres supposed to have fallen to the crown. In Kerry, the main lines for the settlement of the land were laid down by Elizabeth and then by James I and the policy of confiscating the lands of those who rebelled was pursued consistently. In most cases, the death-in-rebellion of a chieftain led to the forfeiture of all his lands to the crown. Most of the professional classes: bards, historians and gallowglasses were dispossessed. The 'literati' in particular suffered because they were found supporting a rebellious chieftain. This forfeiture of land was the lot of the O'Dalys.[26]

Besides the depletion of their lands, the unroofed church some small distance from their home was a constant reminder to the family at Kilsarkan of the Desmond collapse. The new plantation of the Welsh settler, Richard Meredith, close by, gave rise to talk, and with a touch of local satire, it became known as Dicksgrove. Though few of the settlers concerned themselves with the religious beliefs of those who lived on their lands, the O'Dalys must have heard with interest of the efforts of the new owner of the Geraldine castle at Castleisland, Sir William Herbert, to evangelise his tenants. He introduced the novel practice of preaching the divine service every Sunday in Irish to his Catholic tenants, a practice met with a blank disregard.

But neither the untimely death of Gerald nor the plantation which followed seemed to subdue the spirit of the Irish in Munster. Myler McGrath, queen's archbishop of Cashel, in a detailed report on the state of religion in 1592, wrote that the activities of popish prelates, priests, and other 'seminaries' had caused wholesale disaffection; an oath of allegiance to the pope was widely taken; not one marriage in twenty was celebrated in the established church; frequent pilgrimage to the abbey of Holy Cross near Thurles were held.[27]

The political outlook during the closing decade of the sixteenth century was one of growing optimism. Throughout the country the conviction grew that a foreign invasion was imminent, and the defeat of the Spanish armada in 1598 – by no means a decisive event to contemporaries – did not check the rising expectations of the Irish, or the increasing uneasiness of the English government in Dublin. With the escape of Red Hugh O'Donnell from Dublin Castle on the eve of the Epiphany, 1592, tension heightened in Ulster.[28] Around the Munster seaports rumours were flying of yet another Spanish expedition, and when the new primate Edmond MacGauran arrived in 1593 with a message from His Most Catholic Majesty, Philip II, that he was about to send help, a wave of optimism spread through the country. MacGauran's death, in an encounter between Hugh MacGuire's forces and those of Sir Richard Bingham, the English leader, near Tulsk later in the year, was the prelude to the Nine Years War.

In 1598, the battle of Yellow Ford occurred and, as a result, the Munster lords threw in their lot with the northern chieftains. Among them, James FitzThomas, a Geraldine and cousin of the heir-apparent, took a leading part and seemed destined to assume the hereditary title. He was recognised by O'Neill as the seventeenth earl of Desmond, and the Munster Irish were beginning to acclaim him as their leader. Elizabeth, with her usual political acumen, saw the danger and acted promptly. She nominated James FitzGerald, then in England, earl in succession to his father Gerald and bade him return to Ireland.

For the adherents of the Geraldine cause who had paid for their loyalty with the forfeiture of their lands, it was an humiliating experience to witness James's homecoming after more than twenty years. As a child in 1579, he had been delivered over to Sir William Drury as a hostage. He was duly transferred to England to be educated and indoctrinated by that *'homo non tem genere, quam scelere clarus'*, Myler McGrath. When James FitzGerald arrived in Youghal to assume his title, the report circulated throughout Munster that Gerald's son had returned. What happened next was full of dramatic irony. The account as told by the unknown author of *Pacata Hibernia* is the clearest, though it is substantiated in detail by O'Daly and the Four Masters.

The new earl James proceeded to Kilmallock in September, where:

> the confluence of people was so great, as in half an hour he could not make his passage through the crowd ... The next day being Sunday, the earl went to the Church of Ireland to hear divine service, and all the way his country people used loud and rude dehortations (?) to keep him from church. He was railed at and spat upon by those that before his going to church were so desirous to see and salute him; in so much that after the public expression of his religion, the town was cleared of strangers, and the earl from thence forward might walk as quietly and freely in the town, as little in effect followed or regarded as any other private gentleman.

The *Pacata* author goes on to observe that:

> from thence, none of his father's followers (except some few of the meaner sort of free-holders) resorted unto him, and the other lords of Munster, who had evermore been overshadowed by the greatness of Desmond, did rather fear than wish the advancement of the young lord; but the truth is, his religion being a protestant, was the only cause that had bred this coyness in them all; for if he had been a Roman Catholic, the hearts and the knees of all degrees in the province would have bowed until him.[29]

Possibly Conchubhar O'Daly was a spectator of the Kilmallock affair. The incident was discussed and analysed in the family circle. In his son Daniel's version, there is evidence of conflicting loyalty. On the one hand, Daniel takes a mild, even lenient, view of the affair and maintains a discreet silence concerning the Earl James's conversion from the Catholic religion. On the other hand, one senses a complex indignation in Daniel's account of those who defected from the cause of the usurper, James FitzThomas. Pervading his whole account is the realisation that the Geraldines had indeed passed away.

Life was still secure, however, in Kilsarkan, and the young sons of the 'rhymer' grew up in a comparatively untroubled atmosphere, and apparently in the traditional setting which lingers in the local name Noghovaldaly. Except for the brief excitement when Red Hugh O'Donnell, on his march to Kinsale, rested for a few weeks in the O'Daly country at Connelloes, passing over Slieve Luachra into Duhallow and thence to Kinsale, the two boys saw little to remind them of the changes taking place in their country. They may not have been conscious that around their small world in Kerry, the old Irish order, with its Brehon laws and clan system was disappearing. James, the luckless, sixteenth earl of Desmond, died a few months after the Kilmallock affairs, while his cousin, James FitzThomas, best known as the Súgán earl, ended his days miserably in the Tower where he died in 1608. Florence

MacCarthy, the strongest and most influenial Irish chieftain in the south was captured in June 1601, transported to England, and was imprisoned in the Tower. Ireland was shired, put under English common law, and in each county, the sheriff became the chief administrator of that law. Gradually, the important and privileged positions in the clans were falling into disuse, and a newer and sharper kind of class-distinction was evolving.[30]

It took less than a month to complete the process of transforming the Desmond palatinate into the English sub-division of shire. Writing to Robert Cecil in 1589, Sir William Herbert had stated, 'As Pembrokeshire was called "Little England beyond Wales", so do I hope to make "Kerry and Desmond" a little England beyond Ireland'. It was not until 1606 that plans were completed. The new 'shire' contained 1,154,036 acres of land. It was sixty miles wide and fifty-eight miles long. Most of its inhabitants, including the O'Dalys, remained ignorant of the fact that they now constituted a little England beyond Ireland.[31]

While still in his teens, Daniel made his decision to become a friar-preacher. He was unaware of the full complexities of the religious situation in Ireland, even though he realised the hardships facing a priest there. Years later he was able to give a minute account of the penal enactments in force during the first decade of James's reign. He was familiar too with the details of Bishop O'Hurley's brutal death, from the graphic descriptions that were in circulation during his youth. Undeterred by such obstacles, he accepted the challenge of the ministry in Ireland. When he selected the Dominicans and their rule of life, was he conversant with the full reality: that the friars were deprived by civil law of their monasteries, and by canon law, were termed 'excommunicated' for being *extra-domus*?

By the end of the sixteenth century in Ireland, most of the monasteries had been suppressed, but the friars and

Jesuits were active in every part of the realm, and indeed, they were the principal instruments for preserving the Catholic faith in the country. When, in 1603, James I succeeded Elizabeth, not only did he issue a proclamation commanding all priests to leave Ireland, but he enforced the recusancy laws by the double penalty of fine and imprisonment in 1605. These measures caused scarcely a ripple on the lay-mind of Munster. A few outwardly conformed, even while they continued to support and shelter the Catholic clergy. The position is summed up in a letter of the Protestant bishop of Cork, Cloyne and Ross, to Lord Deputy[32] Chichester, giving an account of the diocese – not without humour. 'An English minister must needs be beholden to the Irishry; his neighbours love him not, especially his profession and doctrine, they being compelled to hear him'. Not only that, went on the bishop wryly:

> but the conforming lords and gentlemen of Munster, such as Lord Barry of Buttevant, protect the priests and friars. These priests Sir John countenances openly at his own table ... were commending them to the world and applauding their profession and manner of life. They be sturdy fellows, well-fed and warm ... Besides these friars, every gentleman and lord of the country has his priests. Massing is everywhere. The ministers are not esteemed.

The Protestant bishop of Ossory, in 1604, gave the names of thirty priests in the diocese of Ossory alone, whom the people obeyed and followed. Justice Saxey reported that the Jesuits, seminarians, and priests swarmed like locusts throughout the whole kingdom, and added the interesting detail that they were harboured and maintained by the cities and walled towns. As the loyalty of the towns was essential to English policy, and the mainstay of its forces, 'special care had to be taken for preserving the good affection of the corporate towns'.[33] Consequently the penal laws were noticeably relaxed in the towns, and on the death of Lord President Brouncker,

Morrison his deputy, found the province 'swarming with priests and none of them could be caught', as he wrote bitterly to Salisbury. In fact, the counter-reformation was in full swing in Ireland. They country had become the object of intense focus for the Jesuits, while the older-established Franciscan and Dominican orders were reacting strongly after the first shock of spoliation had passed.

Possibly the O'Dalys were on familiar terms with the friars. There was a common bond of sympathy between them, for both friars and rhymers had enjoyed the patronage of the Geraldines. As on the continent, the friars were in the vanguard of the early renaissance, and congregated in the great medieval university centres, so in Ireland they attracted the classes that corresponded roughly with the professorial and student personnel abroad. Thus many bardic names occur in the annals of the various orders. A survey of the Dominican Regestum of Athenry reveals representatives of the great literary and Brehon families of Ireland.[34] Often they did not discard their secular professions on assuming the religious habit. The O'Dalys in the past had shown partiality towards the vocation of the friars, for two of its finest poets in the fourteenth century became friars, Tadhg Crookshank O'Daly, and Philip. In the next century, there was Angus O'Daly whose religious poetry earned for him the title of 'Angus na Diachta'.[35] Daniel was only following a well-defined tradition when he made choice of the friars' way of life as his career.

What does cause matter for conjecture is the phrase that occurs in all the Portuguese authorities, and in both O'Heyne and de Burgo. '*Caenobii Traliensis alumnus*' is how de Burgo describes him. The obvious explanation is that every Dominican novice was professed as the '*filius*' of a particular monastery, at that time, though he might never reside there. Strictly speaking, the young boy never

43

entered the abbey of Holy Cross, Tralee, much less received the habit there. In 1578, when Munster was seething with rumours of a Spanish invasion at Tralee castle, Sir Henry Davells, Justice Meade and Chartres were killed in their beds by Sir John of Desmond. It was tantamount to a declaration of war by the Geraldines, but the manner of its accomplishment was regarded as a 'deed of mysterious horror'. It was followed by the destruction of Tralee and the burning of the surrounding countryside. This act of defiance constituted, in effect, the outbreak of rebellion. A dispatch from Lord Justice Sir William Pelham forwarded to William Cecil on 10 April 1580 informed the latter that:

> all the country between the Earl's house of the island and Tralee [was] on fire, burnt by the rebels, and all the houses in Tralee burnt and the castle razed, saving the abbey, which they had not defaced, and there I rested a day. Finding the abbey a very convenient place for a garrison, I determined to leave one band of horsemen and 300 foot under Sir William Stanlie.[36]

Holy Cross Abbey, then, was not included in the general conflagration of 1579. It survived for a few years but ceased to operate as a priory. Tralee was re-burnt in 1583 by the English after the death of the earl Gerald, and there is no reason to believe that the abbey escaped the total destruction. Further information, chiefly on its material resources, is supplied in two contemporary documents, the so-called Desmond Inquisition of 1584 and the Survey of 1586.[37] It was evidently a well-endowed house:

> The site and House of the late friary of Tralee is situated in the borough of which river vessels may come to the wall of the said house at the spring tide. And the said house, which was large and ample before the rebellion, had a certain church adjoined it, in which the ancestors of the late earl were honourably buried. And now as well the aforesaid house and church are ruinous and in great decay.

So runs the Desmond Survey, and there follows s list of the various properties held by the friars outside the convent precincts, thirteen acres of land in the parish of Tralee, and two acres in Dingle.[38]

From the Survey, a complete picture emerges of a well-stocked monastery, possibly self-supporting, enjoying the patronage of the earls of Desmond and the liberality of the townsfolk. By 1587 the community was dispersed, the abbey apparently in shambles. Preserved among the Carew manuscript is a certificate of lands granted to Sir Francis Walsingham, Edward Denny and their associates dated 21 May 1587. 'The two castles with the priory and the town of Tralee and an hospital' are mentioned, but when Sir Edward Denny obtained possession of his seignory a short time after, he mentions that there was not a single habitable house in the town, and that he had to take up his residence outside it.[39]

If the friars were scattered, and their abbey in ruins, how then does one explain the genesis of young Daniel O'Daly's vocation to the Friar Preachers, and the apparent ease with which it was arranged and carried out? The Portuguese sources state that he was an alumnus of Tralee monastery, and then declare that when he had completed his secular studies at the Academy of Lugo, in the province of Galicia, he was received into the Dominican Order there. The obvious explanation is that after some twenty years, the community of Holy Cross was still regarded as a corporate monastery, and was receiving subjects, who carried out the work of the ministry in the Ardfert-Aghadoe diocese.

Within the Dominican order, each monastery was allotted a district known as its limitation (from the Latin, 'limes') or diet, within which the questors might exercise their activities, and preachers, the duties of their ministry. If the limitation embraced the entire diocese in a particular area, the custom arose of sub-dividing the territory into divisions known as '*termini*' (terms). To each term a special questor and preacher was appointed, known jointly as a '*terminarius*'. He possessed certain privileges as well as duties. He was still subject to the prior of his monastery, even when the term had a residence with a grange attached to it, and normally, not more than a six-month stay was allowed to the preacher who lived there during his missionary tour.[40]

The Kilsarkan house, with its well-known sympathy for the Geraldine cause, was a sure retreat for fugitive friars. It is far more likely that young Daniel encountered them at work in the countryside where they operated from the base of a terminer's residence close by. The document known as the Desmond Inquisition of 1584 does, in fact, locate such a term in the Manor of the Island.[41] When the young boy went to study at Lugo, he gave evidence of having been carefully tutored, and made rapid progress in his studies. Possibly Conchubhar, a gifted and cultured man, taught his young sons part of his own heritage, and the boys may have received some tuition, either at a terminer's residence, or from a fugitive friar-tutor.

About the same time that Daniel decided to become a friar, his brother, Denis, chose a military career. The brothers never lost touch with each other and were to pool common resources in several enterprises abroad. Of the two, Daniel was the more dominant personality, and Denis's career as a soldier was largely determined by his brother's resolute will. A tentative 1610 may be advanced as the date of Daniel's departure from Ireland on the grounds that he was ordained as a priest in 1618.[42] When Daniel left Kilsarkan and the pleasant valley of the Brown Flesk for Spain, he was beginning a career abroad which was to combine, in a curious pattern, the interests of his native country and those of his adopted one, Portugal. An Irishman, living in Europe in that century, had ample opportunities to use his talents in diverse activities.

In Remembrance Of
DOMINIC DE ROSARIO O'DALY O.P
BORN OF A BARDIC FAMILY
IN KILSARCON 1595
STUDIED IN BORDEAUX AND
ORDAINED A DOMINICAN
FOUNDED THE COLLEGE OF CORPO SANTO
AND THE CONVENT OF BOM SUCCESSO
IN LISBON 1639
SUCCESSFUL IN THE EMBASSIES OF KINGS
A MAN DISTINGUISHED FOR
"PRUDENCE, LEARNING AND PIETY."
WROTE THE HISTORY OF THE GERALDINES
IN 1655
BISHOP-ELECT OF COIMBRA, PORTUGAL
DIED 30TH JUNE 1662
BURIED IN LISBON

Daniel O'Daly's memorial stone at Kilsarkan
courtesy of Maureen Murphy

NOTES

1   V. Baron, *Liber Apologetic corum*, 11. 419.

2   Browne to Nicholas, 24 November 1656 (*The Nicholas Papers*, iii, 289–91).

3   B.M. Harl. MS 4547, f. 7.

4   A.V. Nunz. *Di Francia*, 110A, ff. 247–8.

5   de Sousa Coutinho to João IV, 1 April 1656 (*Corpo Dipl. Port.* XIII. 280–2).

6   T. de Burgo, *Hibernia Dominicana*, p. 492.

7   This history was compiled in 1936 from the annals of the different archivists of the convent of Bom Sucesso whose duty it was to record the more important events in the history of the convent. From the foundation the annals were written in Portuguese.

8   A.TdoT., Chanc. D'Afonso VI, vol. 24, f. 262.

9   Butler, *Gleanings*, pp 274–5.

10 A.TdoT., Chanc. D'Afonso VI, f. 262. Also Process of Inquisition of Daniel O'Daly, O.S.A., 22 October 1694 (Maço 50, no. 821 in same archives).

11 T. de Burgo, *Hibernia Dominicana*, p. 495.

12 Though the original Desmond Survey Papers were destroyed in the burning of the P.R.O.I. in 1922, several copies exist. (a) In the National Archives there is a calendar in English, part of the Desmond Survey Papers which were originally in Latin. It is a copy presented by S.M. Hussey in 1923, who had it privately printed. It deals with the Kerry section. P.R.O.I. M5037. (b) An English translation of the same portion of the Desmond Survey was published serially from August to October 1927 in *The Kerryman* with the editorial comment: 'the subjoined is a copy of a translation of the Desmond Survey, the original of which perished in the destruction of the P.R.O., Four Courts, Dublin. It was kindly forwarded to us for publication by Mr. M.J. Byrne, Solicitor, Listowel'.

13 A.F.M., pp 669, 671, 797. Hogan, *Onomastican*, p. 292.

14 The archives of Corpo Santo Lisbon were completely destroyed by the earthquake of 1755. The annals of the earliest years of the college, however, had been published in 1798 by a Portuguese Dominican Frei Lucas in the fourth part of his *Historia di S. Domingos*. In 1711, an Augustinian, Frei Agostinho, incorporated the annals of Corpo Santo into his *O Santuario Mariano*. Both these works are standard books of reference for Portuguese church history.

15 *Carew Papers*, i. 414–5.

16 Satire on Miler MacGrath by Eoghan O'Dubhthaigh in *R.I.A.*, 23N13, p. 192. See also T.F. O'Rahilly, 'Irish poets, historians, and judges in English documents, 1538–1615', in *R.I.A.* Proc, 70, XXXVI, 88–118 (1921–4).

17 The so-called vol. I, no. 4, pp 213–226 (April 1910): 'being a translation of a certified copy of a Record in the P.R.O.I. titled "Inquisition Exchequer Elizabeth: Kerry no.2"'.

18 D. O'Daly, *History of the Geraldines*, trans. C.P. Meehan (2nd ed., Dublin, 1878), p. 165. This source will henceforth be cited as O'Daly, *Geraldines*.

19 J. Begley, *The Diocese of Limerick in the 16th and 17th Centuries*, p. 13 *et Seq.* Though Begley places Gerald as the 15th earl, I have followed Lodge, *Complete Peerage* (ed.) G.E. Cockaine, i. 63.

20 Begley, *op. cit.*

21 A.V., Secretariat of Briefs, vol. 47, ff. 279, 312.

22 A.V., Nunz. D'Ingilterra I. f. 202 (for report of San Joseppi); f. 258 (for that of Dr Saunders). See also Henry Mangan, 'A vindication of Don Juan del Aquila', in *The Irish Sword*, ii, 350 (Winter, 1956).

23 O'Daly, *Geraldines*, pp 94–95.

24 *Ibid*, p. 121.

25 Examination of Owen Moriarty on 26 November 1589, reprinted in *Kerry Magazine* i. 98 (1854) from Thomas Churchyard, *A Scourge for Rebels* (London, 1584).

26 Pat. And Close Rolls reg. Eliz., p. 355.

27 R. Dudley Edwards, *Church and State in Tudor Ireland*, p. 263.

28 Paul Walsh, 'Historical Criticism of the life of Hugh Roe O'Donnell', in *I.H.S.*, i. 236–7.

29 *Pacata Hibernia* i. 163–4.

30 *Cal. S.P. Ire.*

31 For an account on the evolution of modern county Kerry, see J. King, *County Kerry: Past and Present*, p. 187 *et seq.*

32 Cloyne to Chichester, March ? (*Cal. S.P. Ire., 1606–08*, ii, 133).

33 Lords of Privy Council to Chichester, 21 February 1607 (*Loc. Cit.*, p. xcv).

34 A. Coleman, 'The Regestum of Athenry', in *Archiv. Hib.* i. 201–222 (1912).

35 R. Flower, *The Irish Tradition*, pp 116–17. Though Angus O'Daly wrote religious poetry, it is not known for certain that he was a friar, and many Irish scholars are of the opinion that he was not.

36 Pelham to Lords and Council of England, 29 March 1580 (*Cal. Carew MSS., 1575–88*, p. 233).

37 The coming of the friars in Kerry is inseparably linked with that of the Geraldines who received a 'charter of free chase and warren' in 1244. A year before, the Dominicans had established themselves in Tralee, at the invitation of Lord John FitzGerald. It was just twenty seven years after Dominic de Gusman had founded the order of Preachers. Tralee became the chief town of the Desmond Palatinate, and in the succeeding centuries, the link between the friars and earls became more intimate. Lord John FitzGerald had provided a monastery and endowed it, Holy Cross Abbey, and when both he and his son were killed at the battle of Callan, 1261, their bodies were interred in the priory grounds. Gradually, Holy Cross became the accustomed burial-place of the Desmonds, and even today a few broken slabs survive as a testimony.

38 Desmond Survey Papers, from files of *The Kerryman*, 15 October 1927, p. 11.

39 M. Hickson, *Selections from Old Kerry Records* (2nd Series), p. 104.

40 B. O'Sullivan, 'Mediaeval Irish Studies', in *Irish Rosary*, p. 47 *et seq.* (Jan.-Feb. 1952). Also consult R.P. Mortier, *Histoire des Maitres Généraux del'Ordre des Freres Precheurs*, iv. 124–27.

41 'Inquisition of 1584', in *Kerry Archael. Magazine*, vol. 1, no. 5, p. 274 (October, 1910): 'And in the Manor of the Island aforesaid with its appurtenances containing a carucates of land; belonged and appertained to the said late Religious House in Tralee, which late Religious House with its appurtenances (which he and his predecessors unjustly detained and concealed) is our lady, the queen's'. The version cited presents the information in a quite different way from the Desmond Survey.

42 Frei Lucas, *Historia de S. Domingos*, iv. 733.

II

STUDENT AND FOUNDER

Perhaps one of the most vital studies of the history of the seventeenth century in Ireland is a survey of the influences – religious, intellectual and cultural – which shaped young Irish youths abroad and which they carried back to Ireland. To set Daniel O'Daly against the background of his student days abroad is to trace the gradual development of a young continental-trained Irish priest of that century. Furthermore, it is reasonable to conclude that when the priest later came to found an ecclesiastical college, he would incorporate into such a foundation what he himself had found most valuable on the continent. His personality impressed itself in some measure on the college he established, and it, in turn, formed the students who passed through it, so that Daniel's career affords the reader a study in miniature of those influences at work.

Inevitably, the actual conditions among Catholicism in Ireland tended to be exaggerated on the continent. Distance lends enchantment even to religious persecution, and while the Regular Orders undeniably endured severe hardships during Elizabeth's reign, a certain amount of pious fabrication found credence abroad. Even within the Dominican order it was believed and quoted that of the 300 Irish Dominican friars who flourished when Elizabeth ascended the throne of England, only four survived into the next century. This mistaken idea of the paucity of friars in Ireland may have grown out of a letter written in 1593 which the acting vicar-provincial of the Irish province sent to his master-general, Mario Beccaria.[1]

It was a sombre letter, and it illuminates the agonising, and less spectacular, problems of internal government among the Regular Orders during the closing years of Elizabeth's reign. The letter, being a confidential report on the state of the province, understated or ignored those aspects of the vicar-provincial's problems of which the master-general was already fully aware. In that way, several false impressions appear to have arisen from a cursory reading of the letter, which after an urgent appeal to appoint a provincial, touched on the problems of the 'apostates of our order' and the 'non-reformati'. The four monasteries referred to at the beginning of the letter no doubt gave rise to the fable of the four Dominicans left in Ireland by 1603. The improbability of the figure is further demonstrated by the passage which deals with the separate jurisdiction exercised by the vicar of the 'non-reformati'.[2]

The Dominicans in Ireland were in a very depressed state between 1593–1603. Beccaria, master-general of the order at that time, in a visitation of Spain (1597) admitted that he did not know whether the provincial or vicar-provincial of the Irish province was still at large, because the persecution was so violent there that he had received no intelligence on the actual state of affairs for some time.[3]

By the end of the sixteenth century only one monastery, that of the Franciscans of Donegal, had weathered the storm of persecution, and even this last survival of a great

Irish tradition was dissolved in 1601. There was then no hope of educating boys for the priesthood, and the future for Catholicism in Ireland seemed precarious and unsettled. The saving factor was the marvellous system of seminaries abroad. These continental seminaries supplied a regular flow of both diocesan and regular clergies which never ceased and was at all times vigorous; at the same time they catered for many of the Catholic laity of Ireland. Universities on the continent offered a sincere welcome to the number of Irish students who sought in foreign lands the education that was denied to them at home.

For the secular clergy, the establishment of seminaries on the continent was a more complicated process than for the regular clergy. Usually, a number of Irish boys met together in a foreign city, and they lived in common under the unofficial supervision of some enterprising priest, commonly of the Irish secular clergy. Gradually such groups were organised into communities who agreed to live under a fixed rule in a college. Many of these groups or colleges were taken over by religious orders whose members were better equipped to guarantee the continuity of training. This was the way that the system of Irish seminaries for secular clergy developed on the continent.[4] While the Irish seminaries flourished on the continent, the episcopacy in Ireland was sustained.

For the regular clergy, the problem of education abroad was solved by the foundation of special houses on the continent to meet the requirements of their orders working in Ireland, and Phillip II constantly showed himself a most generous benefactor. So in Spain, in the Netherlands, and in Portugal, colleges were founded by vicars apostolic nominated by Rome and endowed to train young Irish students for the priesthood.

Bernard de Jonghe, the Belgian Dominican and chronicler of that province of the order, observed that in 1603, when MacDuany succeeded Crean as provincial in

Ireland, he left no means untried to provide for the education of young Irish aspirants to the priesthood in his order. An appeal made by them to the Spanish province met with a generous response, and a haphazard and insecure system evolved whereby groups of young Irish boys were trained in one or the other of the Spanish monasteries.[5] Only gradually with increasing numbers, did the necessity for some formal organisation become apparent.

Daniel O'Daly was sent to Lugo in the province of Galicia. At first, according to Frei Lucas, he attended the secular academy, where he made such rapid progress that he was shortly received and professed in the Dominican house at Lugo.[6] He took the name of Dominicus de Rosario (in Portuguese, Domingos do Rosario), and it is under this title that he most often appears in European politics. In English and Irish state papers, he is commonly referred to as Father Daniel O'Daly, which is the name he signs in a letter to James Butler, earl of Ormond.[7]

From Lugo, Daniel was sent to Burgos to complete his studies at St Paul's which was much frequented by Irish Dominicans during the decades following MacDuany's appeal. Spain, says O'Heyne, not only opened its monasteries and purse to these exiles, but it also gave them the principles of the religious life learnt in the country of St Dominic and St Teresa and a touch of the Spanish chivalric devotion to the cause of the Catholic faith which seemed to animate them with a bold and fearless spirit.[8]

As a student in Burgos, Daniel's life was a quiet round of study and prayer. Holidays were from mid-July until the feast of Holy Cross (14 September), as well as various weeks during the year.[9] The still-recent legislation on Study in the general chapter of the Dominican order held in 1580 was in use. Logic was to be taught as a foundation for philosophy, which was to lead on to theology. The whole period of studies lasted nine years, three of these being devoted to philosophy and four to theology. The first four years were novitiate ones. In the first year Peter of Spain, a great medieval commentator, was prescribed; in the second year, Aristotle was the course. Metaphysics followed. The theology course consisted of speculative and moral theology and comprised the whole of the *Summa* of St Thomas Aquinas. The students were directed to 'write the course', according to the method of Francis of Vittoria, a method much in vogue in Spain at the time.

A glance at the background of Daniel O'Daly's studies in the years preceding his ordination is valuable partly because of its influence on his character and chiefly because of his theological writing. Towards the end of the sixteenth century, a celebrated controversy occurred between the Jesuits and the Dominicans. The subject was a grave one: the doctrine of grace.

The Jesuits during the sixteenth century diverged from the traditional doctrine of grace as held by the Dominicans. The divergence, a reaction against Luther and Calvin, was hardly noticed at the Council of Trent. On 20 January 1582, however, a Jesuit Father at Salamanca University proposed a thesis on Christology. Domingo Banez, O.P., who held the chair of theology, refused to accept the Jesuit's ideas and a conflict began that raged for nearly twenty years. It was further complicated by the appearance of Luis de Molina's *De Concordia liberi arbitrii cum gratis donis,* and the controversy occupied the attention of scholastic Spain with public disputes at Alcala and Salamanca.[10]

Indeed, Spain was setting the pace in every field of theological activity just then, and again the Jesuits were the protagonists of the new Marian renaissance with its delicately-balanced question of the Immaculate Conception. The Dominicans in Spain, hampered by the profound difficulties of their official theology and by the opposition of authorities as weighty as Thomas Aquinas and Bernard of Clairvaux, were placed in the position of re-assessing the traditional doctrine. Consequently, a most salutary 'family' argument arose, which was helpful to young students like O'Daly who were being trained in the 1610–20 period. Side by side with this theological interest in Mariology, the more popular devotion of the Rosary received new impetus from the *Bulla Sanctissima Rosaria Julius* (1612), and Paul V gave special faculties for this devotion in Ireland. Such debates created an intense intellectual life within the Dominican order in Spain. When the Dominican master-general Secchi went on his visitation to the Iberian peninsula between 29 October 1617 and the end of November 1619, he found religious vitality at a high pitch, and, for the most part, studies were pursued so earnestly that he pronounced the Spanish province to be in the foremost rank of the order.[11]

In Burgos, with its narrow streets, numerous fountains and historic cathedral where El Cid and Don Fernando had been laid to rest, Daniel O'Daly was duly ordained. The exact date is unknown as no records are known to have survived.[12] Daniel was evidently proficient at both theology and philosophy; based on his performance in the disputation at Coimbra University in later life, he was also a good rhetorician. Frei Lucas recorded that Daniel held the chairs of philosophy and theology successively at Burgos.[13] This was unusual. The Dominican order in Spain was enjoying a theological revival and the appointment of one so young in religious life is puzzling. There is the further complication that de Burgo clearly states that O'Daly passed from St Paul's at Burgos to read philosophy and theology at Bordeaux. For lack of precise documentation, the disparity between the two accounts cannot be reconciled.[14]

By 1623, Father Daniel O'Daly was back in Ireland attached to the Emly diocese. From the nature of his activities, it is clear that even as a young priest he realised the urgent need to provide native seminaries for Irish clerical students. The religious outlook seemed favourable. In the years that intervened between his departure from Ireland and his return as a priest, the country had experienced a resurgence of Catholic life. The counter-reformation movement was working along organised lines. There were in Ireland over two hundred Friars Minor scattered among the ordinary people; the Jesuits were setting up schools; the Capuchins, a little later, concentrated their missionary activities on the Anglo-Irish aristocracy. In a speech delivered to the Irish delegates who went to London in 1614 to discuss matters dealing with civil and religious liberty, James I inveighed against the activity of the Irish secular clergy, particularly those of Salamanca College, and denounced them as traitors.

Everywhere in Ireland a vigorous attempt was being made to restore Church autonomy by the appointment of bishops, and when the newly-established congregation of the Propaganda Fide in Rome came to consider Ireland's position as a missionary country in 1629 it was found that it belonged to a special class: a country which had a vigorous episcopacy even as it endured severe persecution. This created a problem. The regular clergy, and some of the secular clergy, coming over from the continent to Ireland complained to the Propaganda Fide that they were not accorded the latitude granted to their brethren in mission countries or in 'persecuted' countries which were the divisions made by Rome after 1622. The Irish bishops, with the approval of the Holy See, maintained that their sole aim was to restore and organise the dioceses on a regular basis in conformity with the decrees of Trent; therefore, all clergy must conform to normal jurisdiction. This attitude caused a certain amount of tension between the regular and secular clergy in Ireland for a considerable number of years.

From 1613 on, the Dominicans were slipping back quietly to Ireland. At first, according to an unsigned report from Louvain in 1626, they assembled in the two or three remaining convents, or in solitary units, until gradually they held twelve houses again.[15] According to Archbishop Matthews of Dublin, there were twenty Dominicans in the country in 1623; three years later, there were fifty.[16] Eight of the monasteries were in towns; four were in the countryside. Where the old priories could not be rebuilt, the Dominicans lived among the people, occupying a dwelling-house which contained an oratory, a dormitory and a refectory. The scarcity of Dominicans made the recruitment of new members imperative. It was a task to which Daniel O'Daly applied himself diligently, first in the Emly diocese and then from the revived priory of Tralee. At this period, he worked closely with his fellow Dominican Fabian Mulrian who remained a life-long friend. Their aim was the revival of the Cashel priory, then in ruins. It had been the seat of a medieval *studium generale*, and Mulrian, in particular, conceived the rather ambitious project of establishing a university in Cashel.[17] In 1623, however, housing accommodation in Cashel was meagre, and O'Daly and Mulrian led fugitive lives in the hills and valleys of west Tipperary and east Limerick. Possibly, since both men had received a good education, they were sent to run one of the hedge schools which were common even then.

Of the twelve houses operating in 1626, Tralee was one of the earliest, but the Dominicans there did not re-occupy the former site of Holy Cross Priory. Instead, they lived in a house held in the name of some lay-person in the vicinity of the old priory.[18] At some time between 1620–24, O'Daly returned to Kerry. During his brief sojourn in Kerry, a number of Kerrymen joined the Dominican order. They were associated with him in Lisbon and later distinguished themselves in their ministries in Ireland. Among these were the Moriarty brothers and Thomas Quirke. Meanwhile it had become increasingly obvious during

Viscount Falkland's tenure as Lord Deputy of Ireland (1622–1629) that the founding of a *studium generale* in Ireland was not feasible. As early as 1608, negotiations to establish a Dominican college for the Irish nation somewhere in Europe were initiated by Father Daniel Crean. In 1613, Dr Lombard, archbishop of Armagh, petitioned the king of Spain on their behalf, and two years later, Paul V issued a brief granting the Irish Dominican permission to found a house. It was only in 1624 that the Irish Dominicans succeeded in opening a house of studies with hospice attached in the St Niklaashof on Mont-Cesar, overlooking the university town of Louvain.[19] Simultaneously, Father Daniel O'Daly was recalled from Munster to take the chair of theology in the new house of studies in Louvain. The same year he was appointed rector of the '*domus*' there.[20]

It was the beginning of a most unusual career. Daniel was then twenty-nine years of age. In a sense, he was at the peak of his intellectual vigour, though he was later to play a more distinguished part. At twenty-nine, however, his gifts were considerable, and his faults, which years of administration were to emphasise, were not apparent. He was, according to some of his contemporaries, a personality of unusual persuasiveness and charm. All through his life he had the gift of retaining the affections of such diverse characters as João IV of Portugal; Luisa, his wife, shrewd and full of commonsense; Terence Albert O'Brien, O.P.; and Vincent Baron, the French Dominican who met him under circumstances unfavourable to O'Daly in 1640 and remained his enthusiastic admirer until death separated them.

Besides that attractiveness, Daniel had the most necessary qualifications for one who was to move in European circles: the gift of languages, a ready turn of speech and a distinguished bearing. He spoke several languages fluently, a rare enough accomplishment in that century.[21] He spoke Spanish; Latin, the medium of teaching in a Dominican house of studies, he wrote with a terse clarity that characterises his *Geraldines*. His letters written in Portuguese were direct and to the point. On the other hand, his style of English, as far as one can judge from a letter to Ormond, was written in the typical, rather inflated, Caroline prose, and leaves an impression of obsequiousness and flattery. French he must have spoken well, because he was engaged twice in embassies to Paris, and he lived for over two years with his French brethren there. We know, too, that he acted as interpreter between the French ambassador to Portugal, the Comte de Cominges, and Queen Luisa during the years 1657–1659.

We know something about Daniel's appearance; however, no portrait of him is known to have survived. In 1639, Sir Arthur Hopton, English ambassador to Madrid, wrote to Secretary Windebank complaining of the treasonable activities of the friar whom he called Daniel Hodal. Windebank described O'Daly as '… a very tall, black man and speaks very big'; he followed with a guess at O'Daly's age and attire.[22] Daniel's handwriting, of which several specimens are extant, is interesting. In Portuguese documents, it is large and forceful with a rather flamboyant signature, Frei Domingos do Rosario; in English, he wrote in a small, neat hand. His manner was grave. According to Vincent Baron, Daniel's mode of life in Paris when he served as Portuguese ambassador was 'austere and pure'. At the same time, a reading of the *Geraldines* would suggest that he inherited the fiery temperament of the *file* as well as the poet's tendency to exaggerate or to overdramatise an issue. An active, energetic man, he walked long distances till he suffered from gout later in life.

Daniel O'Daly was, then, a fair representative of the continental-trained Irish priest of that period. He had the added qualifications of a studious disposition and a reputation for learning. At this point in his career, it is worth speculating as to why Daniel was neither appointed bishop of Ardfert-Aghadoe nor of Ross, both of which were vacant for sixty years. The diocese of Ardfert-Aghadoe, which had eighty parishes, had not been visited for twenty-eight years, according to an attestation made by O'Sullivan More on 29 February 1629, and it had only fifty-two secular clergy.[23]

In a letter of recommendation 'to all persons whomsoever he shall meet', Maurice O'Hurley, bishop of Emly, described Father O'Daly as possessing apostolic zeal, integrity, prudence in faith and doctrine and the gift of counsel. It was a glowing tribute from the bishop under whom O'Daly had worked. '*Apud nos vivendi, integritate, ministrandi, sedulitate, hortandi, monendique assiduidate ...*'[24] The impression O'Daly left in Munster of his being a vigorous and energetic administrator was still strong in 1631. On 3 May of that year, a petition was forwarded to Rome requesting that the see of Ardfert be filled by Daniel O'Daly alias Dominicus de Rosario, a Dominican friar. The petition was signed by the leading Kerry families of the district, and it throws an interesting light on the fusion of Irish and Anglo-Irish families in pre-confederate Ireland: Maurice FitzGerald of Lixnaw, Edmund FitzMaurice, Donal Mac Carthy More and Eugene, son and heir of O'Sullivan More. Patrick Raleigh, warden of Youghal and pronotary apostolic, signed the petition and affixed a handsome seal.[25] Another petition, signed by fourteen priests of the diocese, was forwarded to Rome about the same time. The document stressed the fact that, from their point of view, O'Daly was the most acceptable, '*ex mero charitatis et justitiae motu f'ri Dominico aliisque anteferendu approbamus*'.[26]

Nevertheless, O'Daly was not appointed because, as Malachy O'Queely, archbishop of Tuam, pointed out in a letter of 20 June 1633, 'although Daniel O'Daly was pious and learned, Richard O'Connell had twenty-four years' experience of the diocese, and being vicar-general, had a far better claim to the bishopric'.[27] There was the further consideration that O'Connell's brother solicited Wadding's influence on his behalf. 'But the same appointment depends on Father Luke ... my brother, Richard, should obtain it, if Father Luke should be on his side'.[28]

In 1624, Daniel O'Daly took up his residence in the great university centre of Louvain. The Spanish Netherlands were again undergoing one of their periodic military upheavals. Governed by the archduchess Isabella, in the name of her cousin, Philip IV, the real ruler of the Spanish possessions was Don Gaspar de Gusmão, Count-duke of Olivares, better known to posterity by the sobriquet, 'Conde-Duque'.

There is a famous painting in the Prado Museum of Madrid of Philip IV being crowned by the hands of Conde-Duque. It is a picture worth studying because it sums up an era, and its significance lies in the reversal of the functions and destinies of those two men. There is Philip IV, with his long, boneless face and its vacuous expression. The Don Juan of his age, his greatest malaise was his inertia of will. Above Philip stands the figure of Olivares, dark, brooding and masterful with a massive head and powerful shoulders, the figure of a dictator. He is smiling his usual faintly-crooked smile, and his black, sunken eyes show a sly, ironic amusement in their depths. With the death of Philip III in 1621, power passed into the hands of this thirty-four-year-old noble who had gained complete ascendancy over the mind of the young heir to the throne, and the peace, so happily maintained in the Spanish possessions, crumbled. Hostilities were renewed with Holland, and under the guise of ideals and glorious deeds, Spain had to suffer wars undertaken by Conde-Duque almost without interruption for the next quarter-century.

In that same year as O'Daly modestly took up his new post, Armand Jean du Plessis, Cardinal Richelieu, became prime-minister of France and found that Spanish troops held the line of the Rhone from Strasburg to Rees. The Rhenish palatinate was in the hands of the Bavarian allies; the Dutch were being hard-pressed from the Spanish Netherlands. It was part of Richelieu's political genius to be concerned always with the balance of forces. Immediately, he promised aid and money to the Dutch. An annual grant was pledged to Christian IV of Denmark on his invasion of Germany. Spain and England had quarrelled – one of Conde-Duque's greatest mistakes – and with the marriage of Henrietta Maria and Charles I, England became the ally of France instead. The Thirty Years War was spreading beyond the borders of the empire, and the way was opening for ceaseless foreign intervention. For the two men who led France and Spain, it was a struggle that decided, not only whether France or Spain should prevail on the continent, but whether Spanish or French influence should predominate in the fields of literature, art and diplomacy.[29]

It was, too, a question of personal rivalry between Richelieu and Olivares. Much has been written on this aspect of their relationship, but the similarity of their work and methods has escaped general notice.[30] Both showed a predilection for employing obscure priests and friars as their secret agents and kept in view any likely candidate who crossed their paths. Significantly, the Irishman, Daniel O'Daly was to be scrutinised and marked down by both ministers. All that was still in the future; just now, as rector of an impoverished 'domus', Daniel O'Daly was a very harassed young man.

The small house which the Irish Dominicans had rented on Mont-César was rich in historical associations if nothing else. It had belonged successively to the Knights of Malta and the English Jesuits. Blessed Thomas Garnet, who was martyred at Tyburn, was one of its inmates. In 1624, a dozen Irish Dominicans were living there but permission to live as a community was only granted them two years later on condition that there would be no questing in any form. The material supplies were to come from Ireland or England. The following year the numbers had increased to seventeen. Ideally the Irish Dominicans hoped for a community of twenty-four, with a prior, sub-prior, eight philosophy and eight theology students, some priest-professors, and some lay-brothers, but the cost of maintaining such a community would be one hundred florins per man per annum, as well as the annual rent.[31] O'Daly spent, at the most, four years in Louvain. He taught theology to the three student-priests there while a certain Father Michael of the Holy Ghost taught philosophy. By April 1627, the material resources of the small community had broken down completely. No food or help of any kind came from Ireland. The appeals they launched to the governor of Flanders and to Rome make pathetic reading. On 20 September 1626, Father Ross Mac Geoghegan, O.P., the Irish provincial, requested from the archduchess a share of certain taxes on the rich abbey-lands that were in her hands to bestow, seeing that the 'charta' of the king of Spain, which had been presented to the Flanders' financial council on behalf of the Irish Dominicans, had not prevailed. On 3 February 1627, Isabella appealed to her nephew, Philip IV, for the Irish Dominicans who for two and a half years had been maintained by the Irish people until estranged relations between Spain and England had caused supplies to cease. In his reply, Philip reminded his aunt that there was a clause in the original permission which forbade them to seek alms in Louvain, and he suggested that the matter be referred to Louvain university and to other grave bodies in the city.[32]

In April, Isabella was again writing to her nephew concerning the Irish Dominicans. She had consulted the archbishop of Malines and the university authorities, and they had agreed that the Irish friars were in need of subsidies. A few months later, the Dominicans presented a petition to the archduchess in which they stated they were destitute, possessing neither altar-linen nor a library. Considering the vast resources of the king in his campaign against heresy, they asked only that a subsidy sufficient to maintain twenty-four friars be given them. A further appeal from them on 31 July and another less than a fortnight later indicates how serious was their financial embarrassment.[33]

Meanwhile, O'Daly and his community were besieging Rome with their desperate persistence. On 16 April 1627, the provincial again launched the first appeal to Propaganda Fide, and six more petitions followed during the year: to the archbishop of Cologne, to the nuncio at Brussels, to the archbishop of Malines, to the university of Louvain, to the Benedictine abbots, and finally to the archbishop of Cologne again.[34] All were dead letters. Clearly a decision to move from Louvain was indicated and two possibilities were tentatively explored. Ferdinand II wished to restore Catholicism in Bohemia and on 31 July 1627, the edict of Cardinal Harrach proclaimed that all nobles leave the country within six months or embrace Catholicism. At first, the older orders undertook the mission of bringing Bohemia back to the faith, and the Irish Dominicans applied without success to Rome for permission to make a foundation somewhere in Bohemia. Subsequently, Propaganda Fide entrusted the entire mission to the Jesuits.[35]

There seemed equally little chance of success for the alternative proposition. In an undated memorial of 1628, presented by the Irish provincial to Propaganda Fide, it was dated that:

a certain devout person, [male sex], a native of Lisbon, led by a pious desire to have the faith propagated in the northern parts of Europe where heresy abounds desires to found a college for the Irish Dominicans at Lisbon at his own expense, and to endow it with 'congruous and perpetual' revenues so that it should not be a burden to the inhabitants of that city. Since by royal decree new communities are forbidden to beg – unless with the express leave of his Catholic majesty – I, the provincial of Ireland, [no name appended], ask that a special Brief be expedited to him for that purpose.[36]

As early as October 1625, Father O'Daly had been granted permission by his master-general to go to Madrid for a year on provincial business and to procure aid from the king for the Irish house in Louvain.[37] There is no evidence that he went then, but towards the end of 1628, he left for Madrid to represent matters there. This business, according to de Burgo, Father O'Daly dispatched with considerable success, and the Dominicans remained on at Louvain. It was not until 1648 that Propaganda Fide gave them an annual pension of 320 Roman crowns on condition that four missioners be sent every six years to Ireland from the Louvain house. De Burgo estimated that the average number of students became twenty, and this, he adds, was to become the standard number in Rome and in Lisbon. In 1658, the community moved to a new house, and the following year, the college was incorporated into the university of Louvain. Finally, in 1666, the friars had the satisfaction of seeing their new church completed and consecrated by Nicholas French, bishop of Ferns.[38]

When Daniel O'Daly left the Netherlands for Madrid was he under the impression that a Dominican college in Louvain for his countrymen was problematic?[39] The financial crisis was to pass, and the money became, if not plentiful, at least available to the Irishmen there, but O'Daly did not resume his post nor apparently did he ever return to Louvain. He remained in Madrid for a few months, long enough to get the necessary permission from

Philip IV for a foundation of a college in Lisbon. What impressions he formed of that monarch and his fastidious court, he never disclosed, nor did he ever mention his association with Olivares, as later he identified himself with the duke of Bragança, and later still, with Charles Stuart.

The visible façade of Spain was that of a great nation, with a splendid court at Madrid, full of genius and adorned with famous men like de Lope, Calderón, Velázquez and Quevedo. Inwardly there was an atrophy of the national spirit which revealed a general lack of interest with the world outside the peninsula. Frivolity, cruelty, lack of idealism and perversion of all kinds were to be found in the court of Philip IV as well as a piety which expressed itself in many exaggerated forms. Philip IV was a curious mixture of the extremes of immorality and religious fervour. Without strong ethical or intellectual principles, he loved to endow monasteries and convents, and to promote schemes for apostolic missions in his colonies. Timid and superstitious, he sought counsel of the mystic Sister Maria de Agreda and neglected the advice of his confessor, the theologian John of St Thomas. Indeed, Philip spent his life moving between the subdued flattery of nuns and the more demonstrative appeals of the courtesans. It was a period marked by sensuality and licentiousness; yet, pulpits were erected, confessionals thronged and the voices of preachers heard with respect. It was the great age of Spanish letters, drama, art and music. Theology was vigorous. It was also the cycle of Spain's greatest decline. Over this inert and decadent court, the imperious figure of Conde-Duque with his positive qualities of ambition, energy, rectitude and loyalty, loomed like a colossus.

It was not difficult for Daniel O'Daly to extract permission for a Lisbon foundation from the king. As early as 1615, a papal brief had been given for the foundation which at that time was sponsored by no less a person than Hugh O'Neill, the earl of Tyrone.[40] Now in June 1629, O'Daly, accompanied by two Irish friars, arrived in Lisbon. Close to Ireland, Lisbon has a mild climate. There are no extreme periods of heat and cold that make the Castilian plateau unpleasant for an Irishman during the greater part of the year. Already, in 1629, Lisbon was supporting a very fine secular college, St Patrick's, for Irish clergy, and a decade later, the city was to provide a convent, that of Bom Sucesso, for Irish-born nuns of the Dominican order.

The Irish friars had brought letters of introduction from the court of Madrid. O'Daly's methods were systematic. He first won over the Portuguese Dominican provincial, Father João de Vasconcellos, who belonged to one of the most influential families in the city. Then he presented himself to the archbishop of Lisbon, Dr Rodrigo da Cunha, and by 6 November he had obtained a licence to establish a hospice for Irish Dominicans in the city. The licence was signed by Dr Framello, bishop of Hieracense, and it declared that the religious who lived in the hospice might exercise the ministry of visitation and confession until opportunity occurred to preach the Catholic faith in their own country.[41]

The foundation began modestly. Three small houses were acquired in the Cotovia district outside the city. There the Irish friars lived for a short time; later, they exchanged their property for a more convenient site near the convent of Our Lady of Loreto where they were allowed to say Mass. Their new dwelling-house was small – so cramped that the oratory became their dormitory by night. In mid-September 1633, two Portuguese nobles, impressed by the Irishmen's mode of life, gave them a patio near their own houses. Here the friars erected a cloister, and as there was room for a chapel, they began to build. On 21 November 1633, the first Mass was said in the new building, but the chapel was not completed until 1636 when permission was given to reserve the Blessed Sacrament. Meanwhile, in 1634, the Dominican master-general raised the status of the house to that of a college, constituting O'Daly its first rector. He was to govern with the title of vicar of the hospice. Gradually, the young college began to assert itself. Two years later permission was granted to the friars to live as a community with the observances according to the constitutions of their order.

Velázquez's portrait of Philip IV, King of Spain
copyright: The Frick Museum

In the beginning, the college was maintained privately by the munificence of certain wealthy citizens, notable Margaret, duchess of Mantua and governor of Portugal. She took a personal interest in the project and paid a weekly visit to the friars. On 16 April 1639, the series of licences began granting Frei Domingos do Rosario an annuity of five thousand cruzados settled in real estate and in bonds. The reasons for giving the annuity were set forth in the licences: the extreme poverty of the Irish friars and their inability to support themselves.[42] At intervals extending over a period of twenty years, the Irish friars received increases of their annuity which synchronised with the founder's absences from the college on matters of state business. In the years 1649–50, two petitions for financial aid were received and granted by João IV of Portugal. In 1655, 'four measures of wheat each, (to sell or to use), were to be distributed to the friars for a period of five years'. The license does not state whether the distribution was made annually or monthly.[43]

In December 1640, the Restoration of the Portuguese monarchy was effected by a coup d'état. With it came O'Daly's rise to a position of influence in the new king's household. Following close on the Restoration, O'Daly was appointed confessor to the queen, Luisa de Gusmão, who was related to Don Gaspar, Conde-Duque of Olivare, but she preferred to remember that she came from the same stock as Dominic de Gusmão, founder of the Friars-Preachers. Consequently, she took an active interest in the affairs of the Dominican order in Portugal, and proved a generous benefactor to them during her reign.[44]

How did a foreign friar, and one who apparently enjoyed the patronage of the Spanish government, become so acceptable to the Bragança household? A letter dated 16 February 1647 from the new king, João IV to Frei Domingos do Rosario begs him to interest himself in the welfare of the Compton family, and states that he, the king, is prepared to pay the dowry to the convent Frances Compton wished to join, namely that of Bom Sucesso. Her father, Sir Henry Compton, was the English ambassador to Portugal for Charles I during the years 1646–48. This letter is the first official one extant from the king to the friar, and it asks a favour.

During the reigns of Philip III and Philip IV, the Portuguese clergy had become increasingly worldly and relaxed. The Dominican province there was in a chaotic condition because of political divisions among the brethren. So disturbed was the province in 1640 that a French commissary-general, the Dominican Vincent Baron, was sent to Lisbon. The Irish friars, being foreigners and distinguished for their rectitude and observance, were not involved in the political difference that divided their Portuguese brethren. Furthermore, they were preparing for a perilous mission to Ireland. It was their reputation that persuaded Luis de Castro and Antonio do Covilho to present them with the patio which was the real beginning of the college. Luisa de Gusmão was a pious woman, and it is likely that she chose her confessor based on the general esteem that the Irish friars enjoyed. O'Daly's personality, too, helped to augment his ascendancy over the queen's mind. Another slight factor was the king's personal desire to employ Irishmen in his service. Thus the tutor of his eldest son was a certain Peter Power, a layman who had fled the religious persecution in Ireland, 'a man of great wisdom and solid virtue'. His son was to succeed O'Daly as queen's confessor in 1661.

In 1644, Father O'Daly was in Rome at the general chapter of his order. He requested that the college in Lisbon be recognised as a *studium generale* for the Irish province and that the convent of Bom Sucesso, established on 12 November 1639, be placed under the care of the Irish province. Both his requests were granted and in recognition of his services, he was promoted to the grade of Master in Sacred Theology, the coveted S.T.M., the greatest honour the order can bestow. With him at that general chapter was Father Terence Albert O'Brien, the Irish provincial, who was also honoured by the S.T.M. O'Brien had not abandoned the project of establishing a *studium generale* in Cashel, but, in the meantime, he was anxious to see both foundations in Lisbon, and he carried out a visitation there before returning to Ireland. While at Lisbon, news reached him of his appointment as bishop of Emly. In a letter dated 29 December 1648, the master-general, Thomas de Turco, nominated O'Daly vicar-general with full powers over both foundations. A letter to the newly-elected Irish provincial, William Burke, dated the same day, endorsed the appointment.[45]

In the twenty years that had elapsed since the first venture in the Cotovia district, its founder had become an international figure in his order who enjoyed the confidence of the master-general, not only in affairs concerning the foundation in Lisbon, but also in matters that were of a semi-confidential nature. In 1650, for instance, he was instructed by the master-general, John Baptist de Marinis, to escort Brother Thomas Howard, the young grandson of Thomas, earl of Arundel, from Rome to the priory of Rennes in Brittany, and to bring letters from de Marinis to the exiled Henrietta Maria of England. Early in the new year, the master-general wrote thanking him for the safe arrival of his young charge whose dramatic entry into the order had already caused his superiors some moments of uneasiness.[46]

Shortly after the Restoration of the monarchy in Portugal, Luisa de Gusmão had offered to defray the cost of a new site for the college on an estate which lay opposite the royal palace. The proposed site contained the hermitage of St Peter Gonzales, patron of fishermen and known locally as Corpo Santo. To obtain the plot, three persons had to be approached, two of whom did not wish to sell. It was not until 1659 that the whole property passed into the hands of the Irish Dominicans, the queen paying over eight thousand cruzados in all. In the intervening years, O'Daly had to overcome difficulties that would have intimidated a less forceful character. At the outset of the negotiations for the sale, he received three injunctions from the city council of Lisbon. The first demanded that the work be postponed indefinitely; the second stated that since the hermitage of Corpo Santo was an appurtenance of the royal family, it was inalienable; the third injunction made it known that the clergy of the parish of St Paul had no desire to admit a convent of foreign friars into the parish. Lawsuits followed and finally in 1659, the city council granted freedom of terrain to the Irish friars, and the clergy of St Paul's lost their case to Father O'Daly in the ecclesiastical court. On 4 May of that year, the foundation stone of the new college was laid with the chief members of court and church in Portugal being present.

The original church of Corpo Santo, which was destroyed by the earthquake of 1755, was large. There were nine chapels, a main altar and two side ones. It possessed a magnificent baroque doorway of the Nativity. The ecclesiastical authorities in Lisbon transferred the relics of St Peter Gonzales to the church of the Irish Dominicans because the old hermitage had stood on the site of the new college which then became known as Corpo Santo.[47] Gradually, the friars won a recognised place for themselves in the religious life of the city. A government decree of 3 November 1660 ordered that the new college be paid the same amount as the seminary of St Patrick for the Irish secular clergy, and permission was given to the Irish Dominicans to receive Mass-stipends and alms.[48] A request to Rome from the Friars to have Corpo Santo raised to the status of a vicariate exercising pastoral work was granted about the same time.[49]

The Church of Corpo Santo, Lisbon
courtesy of Maureen Murphy

For O'Daly it was no light task to choose and discipline young men for the hazardous mission in Ireland. By 1663, it is estimated that more than forty alumni and lecturers of the Lisbon foundation had set out for Ireland. The first to meet his death was Father Arthur Geohegan who had joined O'Daly and his two companions in the small house at Fangas da Farinha in 1631 as O'Daly mentions in his *Geraldines*.[50] Father Geohegan was censor of books at the port of Lisbon, and in the spring of 1633, he set out for Ireland via London to select students for the college. Arrested in London on a false charge of treason, he was executed in November of the same year:

> The death of the Irish Dominican has done more good rather than harm to the Catholic cause, seeing that almost everybody judged that he died innocent of the crime of which he was accused. A number of priests have been liberated from prison by order of the king, with however, the obligation of returning when sent for.[51]

Father Tadhg (Thaddeus) Moriarty, who had lectured in the college in its early days, met a similar death in 1653, though in a different manner. While the Cromwellian persecution was raging, an opportunity was offered to Moriarty of escaping to a safer place, but he courageously refused to use it because of Catholics in need of his priestly ministrations. He was taken prisoner and carried to Killarney where he was put to death.

O'Daly lists nine friars who died in a heroic manner in Ireland, and these he claims for the Lisbon foundation. As his *Geraldines* was completed by 1653, the men he mentions in his book were in a very real sense the founders of a tradition which gave to Corpo Santo the title in Portugal of the 'seminary of martyrs'.

The formative years of Corpo Santo reveal the founder's character. O'Daly was a practical man with an eye for the opportune. His patient negotiation of a suitable site, and of the train of lawsuits which followed, reveal a certain tenacity. His method of putting the college on a firm economic basis by means of a state grant indicates an orderly and realistic mind. In 1648, representation in his favour to the master-general requesting that he be appointed vicar general of the Lisbon foundations demonstrates that he possessed an important quality in any administrator, that of arousing loyalty in his subjects.

His tenure in office was by no means smooth. To financial worry and lawsuits were added internal troubles resulting from a clash of personalities. The Irish exiles dispersed over the continent by persecution could not lay aside the old feuds and jealousies which had kept province at variance with province. Ulstermen looked askance at men of the south and the west, and fierce envy raged between Connachtmen and Munstermen. De Marinis, the master-general, writing to the Louvain foundation in a letter dated 6 June 1654, reminded a Cork Dominican of this unhappy state of affairs:

> We are also aware, to our intense annoyance, that in this small Irish nation, even in its present state of disastrous exile, men's minds are sundered by the divisions of the country, and discordant factions burn with implacable animosity toward each other.

Besides this factious spirit of provincialism, there was another cause of unrest. Father William Burke, Senior, had been elected provincial towards the end of 1648, and for some obscure reason, proved extremely unpopular with many of the Irish Dominicans, though he was a learned man, an able and energetic administrator and not ambitious of office or preferment.[52]

While the discord was more obvious in the Louvain house, the Lisbon foundation, too, was chafing under the discipline of the new provincial. In a confidential letter of the master-general, Thomas de Turco, to the provincial, dated 29 December 1648, the main cause of the tension was outlined. The provincial was accused of being unduly influenced by unreliable gossip received through correspondence from a subject in one of the Lisbon houses, and consequently his administration of those foundations was prejudiced. Moreover, complaints had been received from both houses that the provincial was sending more subjects from Ireland than either house could hold. The provincial was then informed that Father Dominicus de Rosario had direct control of the Lisbon foundations henceforth as vicar of the master-general.[53] O'Daly immediately adopted the custom of appointing friars from each of the provinces in turn to the different offices in the college because of the strong tendency among the brethren to retain regional loyalty to one or other of the four provinces of Ireland. Eventually the college personnel consisted of six permanent officials: the regent of studies, *lector, primarius, lector vespertinus*, lecturer in Sacred Scripture, master of students, and *lector atrium*.[54]

In this survey of the career of Daniel O'Daly as student and founder, the name of Bom Sucesso has occurred frequently. Around the labours of Father O'Daly on behalf of this foundation, the legend of 'Dominic of the Rosary' has grown. His promise to erect a monastery for Irish-born nuns, undertaken lightly enough, was to involve him in a series of adventures which brough him face to face with the leading figures of Europe. The college of Corpo Santo grew from a small, respectable beginning which had received the sanction of a pope, two kings, and the great Hugh O'Neill. In striving to get the permission to staff a convent, already acquired and financially guaranteed, O'Daly, through one of the unpredictable turns of history, walked right into the spider's web of contemporary diplomacy.

NOTES

1   MacDuany to Master-general, 1 August 1593 (AGOP, IV. 48, vol. ii, f. 87).

2   The phrases *'non-reformati'* and *'omnes apostates nostrae religionis'* are misleading. In the first place *'religionis'* does not mean 'religion' but 'order'. When the communities of monastic houses, suppressed by law, went to live with their families or with lay-folk, they were technically excommunicated for living outside their monasteries, and yet they had no monasteries in which to live. Probably from the context, MacDuany simply wished to have their position regularised. In a document among the Fondo Borghese in the Vatican archives, a certain Marchese de Vimioz asked permission to found a convent near Lisbon for Irish 'reformed Dominicans' (A.V., Fondo Borghese, I, 939, ff. 434v–435).

3   AGOP, Reg. Beccaria, IV. 64, f. 192⁰.

4   R. Corboy, 'The Irish College at Salamanaca', in *I.E.R.*, series 5, lxiii. 247–52 (June 1944). See also *Proc. I.C.H. Comm. 1957* for papers read on 'The Cura Animarum in the seventeenth century'.

5   B. de Jonghe, *Belgiana Dominicana*, p. 417.

6   Frei Lucas, *Historia de S. Domingos*, iv. 733.

7   O'Daly to Ormond, recd. 28 August 1650 (*Carte Papers*, xxix. 506).

8   J. O'Heyne, *Epilogus Chronologicus* (ed.), A. Coleman (1902), p. xvii.

9   R.P. Mortier, *Histoire des Maitres Généraus O.P.*, v. 265–69.

10 P.M. Canal, 'El P. Luis Aliaga y las controversias teologicas de su tiempo', in *Archiv. FF Praed.*, i. 107–57 (1932).

11 AGOP, Reg. IV. 58–60, 62, 64.

12 During the Napoleonic wars and on at least two other occasions, the records and manuscripts of many Spanish monasteries suffered ireparable harm. The existing records are now housed in the Archivo Historico Nacional in Madrid. For the most complete and up-to-date account of the sources of Dominican history in Spain cf. P. Hoyos, *Registro Documental*, vols. i, ii (Madrid, 1961).

13 Frei Lucas, *Historia de S. Domingos*, iv., 361.

14 T. de Burgos, *Hibernia Dominicana*, p. 419. O'Daly's name does not appear in the list of Irish priests at Bordeaux drawn up by Tobin for Carew on 27 February 1621. Viz. T.J. Walsh, 'Some records of the Irish college at Bordeaux', in *Archiv. Hib.*, xv. 92–141. At the general chapter of the Dominican order held at Bologna in 1615, it was decreed that one priory in the province of Toulouse should accept the reform. Bordeaux priory was

designated as the priory of exact observance *'ad unguem'*, and a *studium generale* was set up there. The history of the reform of Bordeaux priory is long and intriguing. On 15 April 1617, the master-general ordered the expulsion of rebellious religious there, and these were replaced by religious from other houses. According to one document in the archives of the master-general there is a slight but definite link between the Irish O.P.s and Bordeaux college for the Irish secular clergy (AGOP, IV. 60, f. 267). *'Die 7 Jun. 1616. Pater Frater Vincentius Hoganus, et Pater frater Joannes Foxius ex Conventu Pampelonensi Provincinae Hyspaniae et Pater frater Thomas Byheus ex Conventu Tholosae Congregationis occitanae reformatae sacerdotes hybernie pro gentis illius spirituali profectu, Hereticorum conversione, Catholicorum confirmare etc. dumodo prius accedat approbatio et consensus Reverndorum P. Patrum Prassedentium dictorum conventum de consilio Patrum-qui secundum Deum et conscientiam suam de mature discussa, et sufficientia praeictorum perpensa ut quod conveniens indicaverint decernant, Instavit ut dicti Patres mitterentur Dominus Dermitius Catheus nobilis Hybernus, prraefectus Seminario Hibernorum Burdegale et Vicarius Apostolicus in diocesibus Vatterfordens, i et Lismorenti in Hybernia, cui bene noti erant, et ipse testatur eosdem Patres auriculum Actium S. Theologiae partim in Congregatione exulum Clericorum nostri ordinis praefecisse hoc testator literaras Reverendissimo Magistro ordinis directas dataus Burdegale, die 24 februari 1616'.*

15 P.P. Moran, *Spicil. Ossor.* i. 161. (Report of Ross MacGeohegan, O.P., Louvain 1626, may be found in A.P., Lettere Antiche 294, f. 11).

16 P.P. Moran, *History of the Catholic Archbishops of Dublin*, ii. 169.

17 Cf. J. Leonard, 'St. Vincent de Paul and M.G. Tomasso Turco, O.P.', in *I.E.R.*, series 5, p. 129 (February, 1936).

18 'Kerry history and antiquities', in *Kerry Archaeol. Journal*, no. 2, p. 145 (October, 1913).

19 S.L. Forete, 'I Domenicani nel carteggio de Card. Scipio Borghese, Protettore dell'ordine (1606–1633)', in *Archiv. FF Praed.*, xxx.

20 A.P., Letters Antiche 294, f. 114.

21 G. Mattingly, *Renaissance Diplomacy*, p. 214, *et. Seq.*

22 Hopton to Windebank, September 1639 (*Clar.S.P.*, ii. 69).

23 M. Brady, *Episcopal Succession*, ii. 57–8.

24 Moran, *Spicil. Ossor.*, i. 132.

25 *Op.cit.*, pp 54–7.

26 A.P., Lettere Antiche 14, f. 40.

27 Moran, *Spicil. Ossor.*, i. 186.

28 O'Connell to Pore (alias Bishop Comerford), 1 November 1630 (*H.M.C. rep.* of Franciscan MSS 1906, pp 30–32.

29 G. Marañón, *El Conde-Duque de Olivares* (9th ed., Madrid 1959), p. 310.

30 Cf. A. Leman, *Richelieu et Olivares* (University of Lille, 1938).

31 C. Reusens-Barbier, *Analectes pour sesrvir a l'histoire ecclesiastique de la Belgique*, pp 149–59. A.P. Lettere i. 158 (for report on Dominican College of Louvain).

32 Brussels, Carton 1168 (Archives generals du Royaume de Belgique).

33 *Loc. cit.*, Carton 2017.

34 A.P., Scritture 387, ff. 146, 313. Lettere I, ff. 140, 158, 160, 174.

35 *Ibid*, Scritture 387, ff. 321, 403. viz. L. Von Pastor, *History of the Popes xxviii. 126–32* (ed. Roma, 1942–53).

36 A.P., Scritture 389, f. 337.

37 AGOP, IV. 64, f. 148.

38 T. de Burgo, *Hibernia Dominicana*, p. 419.

39 In 1630, a third attempt was made by the Irish friars to make a foundation at Beavais-sur-mer in Vendée which was in Hugenot country. Nothing came of the projected foundation.

40 A.V. Fondo Borghese, series I, no. 943, f. 418 (Notice of desire of Count of Tiron to have a house and college built for Irish Dominicans near Lisbon). *Ibid.* ff. 434v–435v.

41 National Library Lisbon (Reservados), Fundo Antigo 145, ff. 300–03v.

42 A Tdo T, Liv. De consultas a repostas du Gov. de. Castello (1639), f. 97v.

43 *Loc. Cit.*, Chanc. De João IV, Livro XXI, ff. 151,208.

44 H. Raposa, *Dona Luisa de Gusmão* (Lisboa, 1946), p. 217.

45 T. de Turco to O'Daly, 29 December 1648 (Transcript Lisbon 8 in Tallaght archives, Dublin).

46 G. Anstruther, *A Hundred Homeless Years* (Blackfriars, 1958), p. 224.

47 National Library Lisbon (Reservados), Fundo Antigo 145, ff, 304, 309–310.

48 A.TdoT. Chanc. D'Afonso VI, Livro XXIV, 309.

49 B.V. Chigiani R.I.4, ff. 150–51.

50 O'Daly, *Geraldines*, p. 364.

51 B.V., Barb. Latin Ms 8105, f. 61.

52 An interesting comment is supplied by the nuncio in A.V. Inghilterra 7, f. 279. '*Il Dominicano Burgo d'Hibernia mandato Commissario dal sou Generale comincia un pucca a farsi sentire, e Dio faccio, che dalla suz pucca prudenza non nasca qualche inconveniente. Io gli ho parlato, e parlaró in buona forma, perche ha bisogno di Freno*'.

53 De Turco to Burke, 29 December 1648 (*Costelloe* ii. I in Tallaght).

54 De Burgo, *Hibernia Dominicana*, p. 424.

III

THE LITTLE CLOISTER

'My little cloister', Catherine of Bragança used to call it when, as an old woman, ex-queen of England and regent of Portugal, she used to visit the convent so favoured by her parents. Certainly when one emerges from dimness into the sudden greenness of the cloister with its delicate spray of water from the central fountain, it is not difficult to understand the affection of the Braganças for this convent so intimately connected with their own lives.

For Catherine, it was one of the quiet pleasures of her old age to spend some hours in Bom Sucesso.[1] Perhaps she recalled her sun-filled, untroubled childhood when her mother, Dona Luisa, took her to visit the monastery to play gravely in the gardens near the river. Perhaps she napped in the sun, remembering without the pain, her loneliness as a young, unwanted bride in the strange English court when the thought of a familiar place like this cloister was an unbearable reminder of her mother and her dear 'Pedro'. One can envisage her there by the fountain sitting and dozing, a small, tired, dumpy woman, drooping a little now that the fire of her life had been extinguished, but still capable of an occasional flash in the expressive dark eyes which were her one claim to beauty.

The Bom Sucesso Cloister
courtesy of Maureen Murphy

The convent of Bom Sucesso is situated between the busy Rua Bartolomeu Dias and the river docks. It is in an industrial area where tall factories crowd the skyline and skirt the enclosure wall, and yet the convent remains aloof from the traffic that roars ceaselessly past the cobbled archway of the entrance. In structure, it is almost unchanged from the convent that grew out of the villa of the countess Atalya in the decades following its official foundation, 21 November 1639.

The building does not suffer from the defects one associates with transformed residences. The refectory, the chapter room and the choir form an harmonious unity on the ground floor, and a wide stone staircase with shallow steps leads into the dim and spacious corridors of the upper storeys. The original doorway and barred windows, a feature of Lisbon architecture, remain intact. The refectory is a fair representative of the tile-work for which Portugal is justly renowned, and it preserves the original colour scheme of blue and gold with a freshness remarkable after three hundred years. The reading pulpit of dark wood is built halfway up the wall facing the superior's table, and a fine seventeenth century canvas of the Last Supper commands the attention when one first enters the room. The pattern of tiles, repeated along the sides of the atrium and staircase, unexpectedly lightens the little oratory that dates back to the foundation. The original statue of Our Lady of Bom Sucesso, from which the convent received its name, is still venerated by the people of Lisbon in the church adjoining the convent.

A certain flavour of romance and mystery surrounds the movements of the friar in the decade preceding the foundation of Bom Sucesso, partly through the appellation the convent got of being 'purchased with Irish blood', and partly because of the difficulty of tracing its founder's movements in that decade. The story of Bom Sucesso is told briefly in the manuscript history of the convent.

In 1624, a Portuguese noblewoman, the countess of Atalya, converted her country villa at Belem into a convent, and between that date and 1630, she made several attempts to staff it, first with members of the Jeronomite order, then with nuns of St Paula, and finally with Franciscan hermits. Though the countess was willing to endow the foundation, and in one case had signed the legal documents, each time the official licence from the government had been refused. O'Daly, with his customary talent for business, offered to use the vacant building for Irish nuns, and he promised to secure the official licence from Philip IV. His offer was accepted by the countess but negotiations were further delayed by a legal difficulty she had not anticipated; she had signed over the property in 1630 to the Jeronomite nuns.

Accompanied by a certain Peter Jannes, O.P., a Spanish friar, O'Daly set out from Lisbon on foot and, on arrival in Madrid on an unspecified date, he presented his petition to Philip IV. The council of state rejected the petition. The matter was not ended, however, for the king was anxious to raise troops in Ireland and to carry on the war Spain was then waging against the Netherlands. O'Daly was recalled and a bargain was struck. If the friar succeeded in raising troops in Ireland for Philip, on the accomplishment of his mission the charter for the new foundation would be granted. In due time, O'Daly returned to Madrid having successfully carried out his task and, though fresh disputes arose, he eventually obtained the royal license which was dated 21 March 1639.[2]

This is the version presented in the convent annals. While monastery records possess a certain guarantee of credibility and a higher motive for care may be inferred than that which inspires the average compiler of state papers, a certain eclecticism makes them suspect as historical documents. In state papers, the secret network of government negotiations is laid bare with a kind of artlessness that appears genuine. Monastery annals, on the other hand, set out to edify, and their use as scientific documents is severely curtailed by the selectivity of the annalist. In general, the value of convent archives is limited to an examination of profession books, registers, state and legal documents, dates and the facts of recorded events.[3]

There is sufficient evidence in state papers, in contemporary printed histories, and in the registers preserved in the archives of the Dominican master-general, to enable us to conclude that the foundation of a convent for Irish-born nuns was accomplished under unique circumstances. An examination of English state papers and of reports of papal nuncios of that period would seem to prove that the account of the origin of Bom Sucesso is not merely credible but authentic.

In 1633, probably before October, a report from Spain mentions a certain:

> captain and Donnell Daly making all the means to raise sedition in Ireland, in so much that they have gotten O'Neale to go for Spain to parley for them ... there is one John O'Daly who now, since the death of the earl of Desmond, as they term him in Spain, calls himself a brother to the said earl, being before but an ordinary seaman.[4]

The report goes on to state that there were rumours about plotting with priests and friars in Spain to put heart into the Irish, 'that before long they will ease them of their griefs'. These men, so ran the report, knew all the harbours and creeks of Ireland. Daniel had a brother who became a captain in the army and took part in the '41 rebellion. Several members of Cuchonnacht O'Daly's family found their way to the Iberian Peninsula. In a further report dated 12 October 1633, the location of the O'Daly faction was placed at San Sebastian near Biscay, 'and therefore subject to the king of Spain'. This report mentions rather significantly that a ship belonging to one of the faction, a

Captain Prinyville of Tralee, was captured at Kinsale, but it was released when it was found that its owner was protected by the Spanish Resident in London.[5]

A much more concrete incident was recorded by the English secretary of state, Sir Francis Windebank, in a letter of 29 December 1637 to Lord Aston, English ambassador at Madrid:

> There was here last summer one Daly, an Irish friar, disguised and in the habit of a captain, who came from Spain and never presented himself to the superior of his order here, as your lordship will perceive by the enclosed. It seems he is a very dangerous person and did practice much among the Irish here to make a party for Spain in case of rupture between the two crowns. From hence he went to Ireland and there did the like. Which coming to my knowledge, I called his superior (whose name is Dade) to account for it, and he assured me that he knew nothing of his being here till he was gone. And in detestation of such an incendiary, he brought me of himself this enclosed letter to his superior in Spain which is left open purposely for your lordship to peruse. You may please to cause the letter to be delivered and to join in demanding justice and in procuring punishment to be inflicted on the delinquent according to the letter; and withal to carry a watchful eye over the Irish in those parts, who certainly have some design in hand, in case of an ill-intelligence between us and Spain.[6]

Thomas Middleton, better known in English state papers as Dade, was the harassed Dominican vicar-provincial in England at the time. Though he had only seven subjects to care for, his path was beset with difficulties. On the one hand, he became involved in trying to keep the peace between the seculars and regulars while steering a middle course himself; on the other hand, he was accused of identifying strongly with the Jesuits. Officially a prisoner in the Clink, he was given permission of egress from time to time. It was quite likely that he did not hear of the Irish friar's mysterious activities and O'Daly evidently did not call upon his fellow Dominicans.

The reason becomes obvious from two reports of George Conn, the papal agent in England: O'Daly was on a recruiting expedition to raise soldiers for the king of Spain.

As early as 4 December 1637, Windebank had spoken to Conn 'of a certain Irish Dominican having procured in England subscriptions to a blank document from divers of that nation to carry into Spain', and he left the matter at that.[7] O'Daly, as he testifies himself, was in Munster in 1636, 'on a mission from Castile', and a full report of Conn's on 23 July 1638 makes his errand almost certainly a recruiting expedition:

Father Dominic of the Rosary, alias Daly, an Irish Dominican, having both in England and many times in Ireland moved a practice in favour of the Spaniards, is now back in Spain protected by the Conde-Duque, being unwilling to render obedience to the superior of his order. The provincial (Dade), has told me that he had the approval of the nuncio, but I asked him, (the provincial), to keep quiet until we are certain of the truth. The provincial told me that Daly brought certain blank sheets with him from Spain, and that he boasted that he wished to hand over Ireland to the Spaniards without any risk. The master-general of the Dominicans will speak with your eminence, and it would be well not to show too much concern, seeing that the Spaniards seize every occasion to stir up trouble.[8]

The odd thing about the whole affair was that neither Windebank, who brought the matter to the notice of the papal agent, nor George Conn realised clearly what was afoot.

Though there seems to be no truth in the statement that O'Daly refused to obey his superiors, two small entries in the Registers of the master-general have some relevancy here. On 24 June 1639, permission was given to Frei Domingos do Rosario to transfer his affiliation from his convent and original province of Ireland to the Portuguese province and to a convent there designated by the Portuguese provincial. No hint is given for the Irishman's decision, but another short entry throws light on O'Daly's machinations at this period. 'On 12 June a precept was given to Pater frater Dominicus del Rosario that he might implement the negotiations of the king of Spain, laid upon him'.[9]

In 1640, the friar was again in England. The previous September, Sir Arthur Hopton, who had replaced Aston in Madrid, had written a long account of O'Daly's treasonable activities to Secretary Windebank:

> I am to acquaint Your Honour that I am come to the knowledge of a conspiracy between the fugitive Irish, that are here, and some Romish bishops that are in Ireland, for the rebelling of the kingdom against His majesty. Certain bishops, whose names are as followeth, the Archbishop of Castellaccia and Toamens, Bishop of Limerick, Oimolacephi, whose name is Hurley, (and) of Waterford, have written to the Irish lords here, inviting them to go to Ireland; saying, they are not the sons of good Catholics, unless they take this time to relieve their Country and Religion, assuring them that the country is in a fit disposition for it. Whereupon divers meetings have been held here. The names of them that have met are, Tyrone, who is here, Tyrconnell, by his letters, who is with the army in Catalonia, the Earls of May and Berhaven (as they call them) Don Gulielmo Burgh, and some Churchmen, the chief whereof are two friars of the Order of St. Dominick. The name of one is William Gerardin, or Gerard, Son to the Knight of Query; the name of the other is Daniel Hodal; here he is called Fray Domingo do Rosario. After many meetings, it is resolved that these two friars shall pass presently into Ireland, Gerard by Bilboa, and Hodal by Lisbon, where he is already, and hath been this month, if he be not passed. Gerard is a man of forty and five years old; he wears a tawny cloth suit and a coat of the same, laced with silver and gold lace; his hair, which is brown, long, the sleeves of his coat faced with satin.
>
> Hodal is a very tall black man, and speaks very big, and is about the same age that the other (is) and his clothes near the same colour. These carry letters of credence, and nothing else, all being referred to their relation. The letters are to the Earls of Antrim and Westmeath, the Viscounts Barry and Roche, (and) to another Earl, whom my correspondent could not

name, but he said he had been a prisoner in England, to the Barons of Exchequer and Britas, to M'Morris, to the Knight of Query, to Salivan More, and a general letter to all the Gentlemen of note. There is in Ireland one called Cornelius Quilin, an abbot, who is to be employed herein; and after these are going, Don Dermian O'Brien.

I believe some of these names may be mistaken, for he that gave me the relation could not speak them but in Spanish. The end of these men's going to Ireland is to discharge, and prepare, and if matters fall out well, then the lords are to go thither.

I cannot inform Your Honour what encouragement they have from hence; but I am told that Hodal had given him by the Conde-Duque, when he went away, two thousand double pistoles. And Tyrone is kept here from his regiment, with pretence of want of money; but he is every day with the Conde-Duque, morning and evening. And I am told that in these meetings there were two Spaniards. I will not affirm anything without being certain; yet, I do mainly suspects they have some encouragement from the Conde-Duque; though methinks the plot hath no 'capriche' enough to be his.

I believe these men may stay their journey expecting ... Irish ships with fish. It will therefore import that the Lord Deputy of Ireland should have timely notice thereof. I desire to know, whether I shall give my reward, or what, to the discoverer, who is a man of quality; for Your Honour knows how I am restrained in this matter of my extraordinaries.[10]

The new papal agent in England, Carlo Rossetti, continued the story. In his report of 13 January 1640, he wrote:

the Father Provincial of the Dominicans was with me on Wednesday last to inform me that they had imprisoned Father Dominicus del Rosario of the same order, who came from Spain and carried letters to Don Alonso de Cardenas, ambassador of his Catholic Majesty at this court. The letters were concerned with the erection of a monastery of nuns in Flanders and immediately on his incarceration the letters were taken from him, read by the ministers, and then handed on to Don Alonso ... this friar had been sent to prison because he had been accused of treason against His Majesty (Charles), and for that reason it was useless to say more until he had heard the result of his examination which had already been carried out. When this appears to concern a point of religion I will not neglect to do all in my power for his release, but I will hold my hand in waiting for the opinion of those ministers of state.[11]

'The convent of nuns in Flanders' was Bom Sucesso, Lisbon. It is not certain where O'Daly was imprisoned nor how he was released from there. The extract quoted suggests that he had powerful friends, and possibly, like Captain Prinnyville some years earlier, his release was effected through the good offices of the Spanish ambassador, Don Alonso de Cardenas. An entry, dated April 1640, in the registers of the master-general that mentions the friar in connection with a permission for the new monastery gives the impression that O'Daly was back in Lisbon. The annals record that O'Daly brought two young postulants with him from Ireland sometime before 21 November 1640.[12] At this time, O'Daly had powerful advocates in high places. Since 1638, he had been one of the active intermediaries between those who were conspiring to place the duke of Bragança on the Portuguese throne and the duke himself. There is the further mystifying complication that even as early as 15 August 1638 he had been marked by Cardinal Richelieu as favouring the French influence in Portugal.[13] About O'Daly's connection with Conde-Duque Olivares, Spanish state papers remain silent.[14]

It had been an uneasy decade in Lisbon. There was, primarily, the growing discontent with the Conde-Duque's domineering methods of government which flared into open resentment against his subordinate, Miguel de Vasconçellos, in 1640, and plunged Portugal into war with Spain for eighteen years. Even more serious than the political unrest were the violent and unseemly clashes between church and state authorities in Lisbon which culminated in a general interdict in September 1639.

Though the opposition was centered on the person of Monsignor Castracani, bishop of Nicastre and apostolic collector for Portugal, the situation had arisen out of the religious policy of the Spanish monarchs. It is only necessary to read the repeated, and at times violent, briefs of popes Paul V and Urban VIII to comprehend the underlying bitterness of the relations between Spain and the Holy See. Philip IV had tried to adopt a domineering tone toward the papacy which his government was incapable of sustaining. The secular authority, though vested in the person of Philip IV, was realised in Olivares as an absolute, despotic, wholly personal power, even while he exercised it as a minister in the name of the king. Philip IV and Olivares would have liked to have adopted a strong line with the papacy, but ironically neither of them was in a position that Borges has termed a policy of 'Cesaropapismo'.[15] This theory of absolutism found vigorous opposition in an unexpected quarter, namely, in the apostolic collectors in Lisbon who were appointed by the popes and fulfilled the function of the papal nuncio in Portugal.

The relationship between the Portuguese church and the Holy See was also an unhappy one. As early as 27 June 1617, the collectors claimed that 'the goods of unfrocked religious who had abandoned the cloister' went to the Holy See. This claim was immediately repudiated by the reigning monarch, Phillip III, and a heated exchange followed on the question of benefices in general. In a letter of 25 March 1618, the king gave the collector the choice of leaving the kingdom within eight days or of submitting to the royal tributes. The collector capitulated and shortly after was recalled to Rome; Vincent Landinelli, bishop of Alberga, was appointed in his place.[16] An uneasy truce prevailed until 1633 when the whole question of benefices erupted.

In that year, the collector, Laurence Tramelli, launched an interdict for eight days on the whole city of Lisbon and censured the royal ministers. With the appointment of Monsignor Alesandro Castracani, bishop of Nicastre, to the post of collection in 1635, the tension between Rome and Madrid was strained to the breaking point. On this occasion, the Spanish government interfered directly in appropriating the goods of certain chapels throughout Portugal. The clearest account of the following six years is to be found in the reports of Castracani, and in the version of Nuncio Jachinetti in Madrid, an interested spectator, and in the stream of letters that came from Cardinal Barberini and Urban VIII in Rome to their representatives in the Iberian peninsula. One gets the impression that Castracani, a determined character who saw clearly the issue at stake, was at times too headlong and imprudent. Reading the reports of Nuncio Jachinetti on what he laconically dubbed '*questo negotio delle capelle*', one senses his regret as the mismanagement of the affair, though he was prepared to support his colleague.[17]

Undoubtedly, the powers which the papal representatives exercised over the Catholic peasantry of the peninsula were deeply resented by King Philip, and a process was immediately set afoot against the collector to compel him to retract his edict on 16 March 1636. Like the court procedure of eighteen years earlier, the collector was again given the choice of leaving the kingdom or of retracting his censure in a pastoral. Castracani submitted. The pastoral duly appeared 5 April 1637. Tranquillity was restored. Once again the crown had won.[18]

In the reports of the following fifteen months, Castracani is lucid and interesting. He comments on the growing political significance of the duke of Bragança and the duke's reluctance to accept any post under the government of Margaret of Mantua. Castracani speaks of the power of Miguel de Vasconçellos, secretary of state in Margaret's government, and he reports on the simoniacal appointment of the bishop of Algarve in 1638. 'Miguel de Vasconçellos is the real bishop of Algarve', he complains acidly. There was unrest in Evora and two factions were noticeable; the Marchese de Pueblo against Conde-Duque, and Miguel de Vasconçellos representing the interests of the Spanish crown.[19]

On 5 June 1638, the pope, aware at last of the critical plight of the Lusitanian church, launched a bull condemning the court sentence of 16 March 1638 against the papal collector and threatening to excommunicate the ministers responsible. The government defended itself by prohibiting the publication of apostolic letters. Castracani not only promulgated these, but he also renewed again, 25 June 1639, the excommunications of two years previously. A royal mandate ordered that the collector was to be expelled from Portugal unless he amended his decrees. The collector resisted, and his temporalities, even his breviary, were seized, and he was kept closely guarded in his room. He made his escape through the window and found refuge in a Franciscan monastery. The justices pursued him, broke into the cloisters, and carried him by force to Madrid.[20]

This coup caused a general outcry against the unnecessary violence of the deed, and a report of 19 December 1639 from the nuncio in Madrid mentions that the bull placing Lisbon under interdict had been released but had not yet reached the governor, Margaret of Mantua.[21] For more than a year the city languished under the interdict, 'in a desolation of temples and a fear of divine retribution', while the tension between Rome and Madrid was so great that Urban VIII is reported as saying to the Spanish ambassador that 'he would not cede (his right) either to the menace of prejudice, or to the promise of advantage for his House'.[22] In Nuncio Jachinetti's report dated 30 April 1640, we learn that Castracani had received a new appointment, and a few months later, the nuncio observed that the Consulta's decision in Lisbon was unfavourable to Castracani.[23]

Portugal suffered as a result of the diplomatic juggling between Madrid and Rome. On the one hand, Urban VIII, as far as possible, maintained good relations with Philip IV as a means of conserving the interests of the Holy See in Spain. On the other hand, Olivares increased the punishment inflicted on the apostolic collector and aggravated the resentment. According to Nuncio Jachinetti, the situation could have been eased by 'a mature viewing on each side'. The Castracani affair was to prejudice the Holy See against the December revolution of 1640, and to suspend diplomatic relations between Portugal and Rome for over two decades.

Its effects on the religious and moral life of Lisbon were lamentable. A dangerous kind of spiritual isolation set in which was furthered by a hostile Spain, and by an unsympathetic Rome. Laxity among the secular clergy was almost universal, and under Philip IV's reign was tolerated as normal. Among the regular clergy the situation, though much healthier morally, was complicated by internal factions arising out of political partisanship after 1640. That Portugal survived as a vigorous Catholic nation was due, in large measure, to the energy and piety of the new monarch and his wife.

This troubled atmosphere was the background that led up to the patient founding of the convent of Bom Sucesso. The royal license is dated 21 March 1639. It granted:

> Frei Domingos do Rosario permission to found a convent for the Irish in the city of Lisbon or its vicinity, for fifty religious, and to have revenues to the amount of 5000 cruzados in annuities, or at least half that sum in landed property.

This charter was followed by the formal approbation of the Portuguese provincial, Frei João de Vasconçellos, 15 June 1639. Final permission for the foundation was given by the archbishop of Lisbon, 29 August 1639, and two months later the formal opening took place on 21 November 1639.[24]

The earliest printed records of the convent described the details of the ceremonies inaugurating the convent of Bom Sucesso.[25] The formal opening was a very splendid affair. Even after four centuries, the account of that November day still glows with the pageantry that filled the temporary chapel of the foundation. The governor of Portugal, Margaret of Mantua, was there surrounded by her courtiers. Elegant and fastidious as always, a contemporary portrait reveals clearly that she had grown gaunt with the worry of recent events. Music for the high mass was supplied by her own royal choir and the guest preacher was her favourite, a certain Frei Domingos de São Thoma who was attached to the chapel-royal. The Portuguese provincial, Frei João de Vasconçellos was present as were the communities of the Portuguese and Irish Dominican friars. The little chapel overflowed with spectators and friends of the community.

The Dominican convent of Setubal had supplied two nuns to train in the young community, and the habit was given to five postulants on that inaugural day. For spectators, there is a poignant emotional appeal in the ceremony of Reception, and there was an added interest for the many who watched that particular ceremony. Donna Magdalena de Silva Menezes had waited nearly a decade for this day. Her entrance into an obscure new foundation caused some excitement in the aristocratic circle of Lisbon in which she moved. Her wealthy family opposed her decision. They claimed her decision had been made under the influence of her confessor Frei Domingos do Rosario. During her long life in Bom Sucesso, she held most of the important offices at one time or another, and she was responsible for planning and carrying out the building schemes which were not completed until 1670. A strong character, she was evidently gifted with great intelligence, and seemed to possess a deep and solid spirituality and a sweetness of character that fascinated her contemporaries. It was mainly her personality that founded the tradition of Bom Sucesso.

Luiza de Mello, the second postulant, was also a penitent of Father O'Daly. Younger and less forceful than Magdalena de Silva Menezes, she was a member of one of Portugal's oldest families, and she met with the same relentless opposition from relatives. The following spring, she was also accused of influencing her young step-sister to enter the new foundation as a novice. Of a vivacious disposition, she was subject to occasional flashes of rebellion which she strove constantly to overcome. She died on 28 March 1651.

Leonor Kavanagh, the third postulant, arouses interest in even a casual reader of the annals. Her varied and colourful career reflects the hurly-burly of seventeenth century Ireland, and the tremendous zest for living which characterised Irish people of all classes then. A widow in her late fifties, she had met Father O'Daly in Castile where she was living quietly in retirement after the death of her husband, Donal an Spainneach, in 1631. She was a Kavanagh of Polmonty and Borris, and her father, Brian, had arranged a marriage between her cousin Donal and herself. She was the mother of five daughters and one son, Morgan, who was killed near New Ross in 1642. The widow Kavanagh was a great-souled woman. She lived another forty years in Bom Sucesso, and she carried out the offices of prioress and mistress of novices at different times. One suspects that it was due to her energetic, if not dominating, personality that the convent preserved its national characteristics in the first precarious years of the new foundation. One gathers, too, that she was a plain-spoken woman.[26] The remaining postulants were Leonor de Calvario, a relative of Countess Atalya, and Jacintha, whose family name has not survived. All that is known about her is that she was over fifty years of age and she was a penitent of Father O'Daly.

The convent was dedicated by Frei Domingos to Our Lady of Good Success because of the mysterious little statue that had been given to the countess by a stranger in 1623.[27] For some months the countess owned apartments in the convent outside the enclosure; however, she reserved the right granted to foundresses to enter within the enclosure as she desired. She herself administered the temporalities of the convent: a mill, a farm, and a spring of water which supplied the surrounding district. These were the chief means of support as young Irish girls without dowries were accepted. The Countess Atalya died in January 1640, her mission accomplished. It had taken sixteen years to bring the foundation into being. When she began the project in 1624, after the death of her second husband, she had no thought of founding a convent for dowerless Irish girls. Did she have misgivings about the tall Irish friar who had so persuasively offered to staff her empty convent? Yet there was a liberality about all she did. In her own right, she was one of the richest and most propertied women in Lisbon, and she administered that property herself. Because she was accustomed to rule, one would be inclined to think of her as imperious and assertive. On reading her last will and testament, one is left with a prevailing sense of her magnanimity. She left all she had to Bom Sucesso. Later, in his confidential report to the master-general, O'Daly described her estate as a vast fortune.[28] 'That she may be able to offer as a token of love to Our Lady, this monastery for noble ladies of the most Christian kingdom of Ireland', so runs O'Daly's comments. For centuries, the office of the dead was said once a month for the repose of her soul, and the small, tiled oratory that she decorated for her personal use is still preserved intact.

Though Frei Domingos had been granted permission to transfer to the Portuguese province of the order in July 1639, he did not avail of the permission. Nevertheless, he maintained harmonious relations with the provincial, Frei João de Vasconçellos. Though related to the notorious Miguel de Vasconçellos, Frei João is remembered in Portugal as a zealous reformer who was nominated visitator of Coimbra university by pope Urban VIII. He had befriended the Irish friars when they were poor and unknown, and he would have liked to have incorporated them into the Portuguese province of the order. It says much for the growing prestige of O'Daly in Lisbon that the master-general ordered him to preside over the elections for provincial of the Portuguese province at the 1645 chapter, and employed him frequently as visitator in the following years.[29]

Humanly speaking, the establishment of Bom Sucesso represented a personal triumph for O'Daly. He had been through many hazards for his cherished project. In fact, the whole personality of the friar undergoes a subtle change when he is viewed in the light of his transactions for this convent. His striving to achieve this objective brought out a nobility of purpose which was not always present in his other activities. The tall figure, dressed as a sea captain, raised sedition in the English seaports and vexed the crown officials to the point of exasperation. He won women over to his cause and retained their loyalty. It was his gifts as confessor which first attracted the notice of Luisa de Gusmão, and through her, that of her husband, King João IV. Later in his career, O'Daly encountered Queen Henrietta Maria and played a significant part in forming an Anglo-Portuguese alliance. Catherine of Bragança, daughter of Luisa, wished to bring him with her to England as royal chaplain in 1661. In the troubled years of the new foundation of Bom Sucesso, O'Daly was the final arbitrator of the minor vexations and clashes that occurred in the life of the community. In 1648, a remarkable tribute was paid him when he was appointed vicar in perpetuity of the convent.

What was the nature of O'Daly's power? His career suggests that of Richelieu's famous understudy, the Capuchin friar, Leclerc du Tremblai known in history as 'L'Eminence Grise'. As there was a hidden gentleness concealed in the rather repellant character of the Capuchin which appeared in his letters to his foundation of nuns in Paris, so also in this period of O'Daly's life there was a sincerity of purpose which rescues him from the role of mere diplomatic intrigue.

O'Daly's constitutions for the convent of Bom Sucesso indicate his own spiritual values while serving as a measure of seventeenth century convent life. O'Daly received his own religious formation in Castile and would be inclined to incorporate those features of Spanish piety which he found most helpful to himself and successful for souls. In general, the constitutions of the nuns of the second order of St Dominic followed the same pattern laid down at the reform of 1378. In 1690, the Cloche-printed edition more or less standardised the constitutions of the various second order convents.[30] It may be assumed that O'Daly drew on the prevailing constitutions of other Dominican convents in Lisbon, particularly those of Setubal and the Blessed Sacrament monastery whose tradition and spirit of observance he both admired and desired for Bom Sucesso.[31]

According to the formal approbation of the provincial, Frei João de Vasonçellos, dated June 1639, the convent was to be cloistered and of strict observance. Full faculties were given Frei Domingos do Rosario to establish there 'whatever statues or laws he might judge necessary for the enforcement of the above'. The following rules were to be observed by the nuns of Bom Sucesso: midnight rising for matins, reciting the rosary and the litany of Our Lady in common after prime, receiving Holy Communion twice a week, fasting and taking the discipline. Silence was to be observed ordinarily in the course of work and to be unbroken during the whole of Lent except when visiting the sick. Work was to be done in common, all taking their turn in the kitchen. Poverty was to be strict and the furniture allowed in the nuns' cells was, in fact, bare to the point of asceticism. The provincial added to these rules several others. Papal enclosure was to be adopted with the corresponding restrictions on the visits of relatives. Choral recitation of the divine office was to be obligatory, and the use of linen and meat was limited to those who were gravely ill.[32]

This somber picture of conventual life in the seventeenth century invites comparison with the rule of life followed by the English Dominican nuns of Vilvorde. Their constitutions were drawn up by Father Thomas Howard, later to become cardinal, whom O'Daly had escorted as a novice to Rennes in 1649. Though the horarium in both convents is similar, in the Howard constitutions, less emphasis is placed on corporal mortification, and there was greater freedom allowed.[33] There is evident in the Irishman's constitution an asceticism and a stress on penance that may have been due to the prevailing custom in Lisbon. It may have been attributed to the love of exterior mortification for which the friar was eulogised in contemporary sketches.[34]

The early years of Bom Sucesso were full of the tensions which are the lot of new foundations. There were buildings in progress, adjustments to be made, and the gradual tempering of ascetical life by the mystical. In the royal charter of foundation, Philip IV declared explicitly that he had granted permission to Frei Domingos do Rosario 'to found a convent for the Irish in the city of Lisbon or in its vicinity, for fifty religious'. Applications for entry were not scarce though numbers averaged about thirty normally. The first community was a mixture of Portuguese and Irish and the annals succeed in giving a sense of personality, and a passing hint as to the nature of the crises that passed unrecorded for the most part. The monastery of Setubal, on which Bom Sucesso was modelled to some extent, had supplied two experienced nuns to train the young community. Mother Antonio de Gesu, whose surname has not survived, was a remarkable woman. Aged thirty-four, austere in the Setubal tradition, she was the first prioress and she also instructed the first novices. There is evidence in the annals that she would have preferred that the new community affiliate with the existing Portuguese province. In this project she apparently received opposition from among the members of her own community at Bom Sucesso. Though no names are mentioned, one recalls the strong-minded widow of Donal an Spainneach. Only two events are recorded of her term as prioress. Four young Irish girls sent by the Irish provincial, William Burke senior, arrived unexpectedly in Lisbon seeking permission to enter the monastery. Mother Antonia delayed their entrance without disclosing the reason and representation was made to the master-general who acted decisively. Father Burke was removed as vicar of Bom Sucesso and, in his stead, Father O'Daly was appointed vicar in perpetuity.[35] The four young ladies were admitted to the monastery and in due time were professed. Only one name has survived, Agnes Shanley. The other event recorded of Mother Antonio's time as prioress was her request to be relieved of office when Father O'Daly was appointed vicar at the end of 1649. He refused. She died during the year, in October 1649.

Among the half-forgotten names of those early nuns of Bom Sucesso, that of Eleanor, daughter of John Burke of Brittas, shines out. The posthumous child of a soldier, whose heroic death canonised him in popular veneration as a martyr, she became the sole heiress of her house when her brother died in Castile while he was still a student. Her mother naturally wished her daughter to marry and she was displeased when Eleanor refused and indicated that she wished to join the foundation in Lisbon. Her career in the convent is told briefly and impersonally in a document drawn up by O'Daly after her death in 1651:

> Frei Domingos O'Daly met Eleanor Burke and her cousin Ursula in the city of Limerick when O'Daly was on a mission from Castile. In the interview, he promised that he would receive them in the new monastery as soon as the king granted permission for the foundation. He placed them under the direction of the Dominican provincial of Ireland, James O'Hurley, who was a relative of theirs. Eleanor and Ursula became tertiaries (in Limerick) and led most penitential lives. Eleanor was severely tried by a temptation that she would not be saved no matter how much she mortified herself. In 1639, the new monastery was opened, and Frei Domingos sent for Eleanor and Ursula, who arrived the following year. They received the Habit in November 1640 and were professed thirteen months later. Henceforth, the life of Eleanor was one of great austerity, and she seemed always absorbed in prayer. On being asked her method of mental prayer, she replied that she knew nothing of methods, and that all she did was to say the rosary, one mystery alone, being sufficient for a lifetime. She held the office of procuratrix (steward) for some time, and she was also portress. In 1651, she fell ill and suffered much with great tranquility, dying on March 25.[36]

O'Daly was not present at her death bed, but he landed from an English ship some days later. At the general chapter of the Dominican Order held in 1656 at Rome, Eleanor Burke's sanctity was recorded in a brief, but touching statement.[37]

Meanwhile the task of completing the plan of the monastery was carried out by the various prioresses working in consultation with O'Daly. In 1645, the foundation stone of the church was laid and the bishop of Targas, unable to attend, authorised Frei Domingos to officiate in his stead. The church was formally opened in

1670 as the date over the massive door still reminds the visitor. The design follows Portuguese baroque style which superseded the beautiful and characteristic Manueline style of architecture exemplified in the nearby Jeronomite monastery.

The church is typically Lisbonese in its mixture of Gothic and classical. In the following centuries a flamboyant ornamentation indicates Arabic influence. One is struck by the contradictory elements in the church. On the main altar there is a massive silver tabernacle, the work of the famous Evano of Lisbon. Its exquisite enamel work was produced by the equally famous Bento Coelho da Silveira. The exuberant gilt-work of the side altars, which were additions of the following century, challenges the quiet beauty of the centrepiece.

The small statue of Our Lady of Bom Sucesso is a perfect example of Portuguese church art. It stands less than a foot high and is made of wood. There is an expression of great sweetness and majesty in the Virgin's face. The statue is dressed in the period costume of the time which is associated with Catherine of Bragança. All through the church there were distinct Irish influences. A side chapel is dedicated to St Bridget; another is dedicated to St Patrick. The Rosary altar arrests the attention of the Irish visitor who recognises in the seventeenth century statue of the Virgin the well-known representation known to Shannon-siders as 'Our Lady of Limerick'. Was it designed or brought to Lisbon by Eleanor Burke? There is no record in the annals.

At the time of its foundation, the convent of Bom Sucesso was ideally situated on the banks of the Tagus in the middle of a fertile 'quinta' or estate which possessed a much coveted spring of water. Gradually the Lisbon Camera, the most powerful civic body in the city, seized much of the land, including the water supply so that today a network of quays and factories stretch between the convent and the smooth waters of the Tagus. Yet early in the morning or late at night, one may still visualise the beauty of the original site chosen by the Countess Atalya. Until the convent school of Bom Sucesso expanded, the enclosure walls defined an area of modest dimensions where pumpkin vines and exotic ferns grew in profusion and the small-tiled shrines, where lizards flashed in the hot sun, reminded the visitor of the villa and the owner who so generously gave the convent to the Irish.

In determining the value of O'Daly's work as founder of two monasteries, it would hardly be an exaggeration to claim that Corpo Santo, Lisbon, Holy Cross, Louvain and San Clemente, Rome (1667), were responsible for preserving the Irish province, but it can be remarked with some justice that Corpo Santo was the principal novitiate house for the province during the greater part of the eighteenth century. Finally, it was the sale of Corpo Santo property that financed the purchase of the Tallaght estate outside Dublin which became the Dominican novitiate in 1856.

Both Corpo Santo and Bom Sucesso occupy a unique place in the history of Portugal. They became, in a very real sense, neutral territory in times of war. For the half-century following the year 1834, the community of Corpo Santo was the only one which had full liberty to work in Portugal; all religious orders were proscribed by the Masonic government in those years. Similarly, in 1910, when a republic was established in Portugal, all religious were expelled from the country except the communities of Corpo Santo and Bom Sucesso who, by a curious twist of history, were protected by the English government. Between 1910–1917, the school attached to the convent was the only Catholic school permitted to remain open by the republican government.[38]

The Bom Sucesso High Altar
courtesy of Maureen Murphy

Both foundations were due to the energy of one man. In reviewing the origins of Corpo Santo and Bom Sucesso, we see the Kerryman at his best. These were his contributions to his country and his order, and we may expect to find in these undertakings a rectitude which was questioned in other spheres by many of his political acquaintances. It would seem from this survey of his two foundations that Father O'Daly was by nature a practical administrator. He displayed a tactful efficiency in overcoming legal and financial obstacles. He possessed the gift of interesting people of influence and affluence in his projects, and he could call forth loyalty from those subject to him. He was tenacious, almost ruthless, in seeking to further his aims. For most men, it would have been a life's work to found and endow a college and a convent. For O'Daly, it was one of the several occupations that filled his busy and eventful life. We have seen him as a Dominican working for and in his order: an Irish priest apparently absorbed in his ministry. It is then with a sense of surprise that we discover yet another facet of his personality which placed him in the wider setting of European diplomacy.

NOTES

1   Augusto Casimiro, *Dona Catarina de Bragança* (Fundacão de Casa de Bragança, 1956), p. 512. In a letter to her brother Pedro II, she wrote, 'Here I am near the Dominican convent, very quiet like a desert, where I can perform all my devotions'. Egerton, letter 156.
2   Archives Bom Sucesso, Lisbon. Manuscript history of the convent, pp 1–12.
3   T.P. O'Neill, *Sources of Irish local history*, pp 12–13.
4   Report to Secretary Windebank, Before 1633 (*Cal..S.P. Ire.* 1647–60, addend. 1625–60, p. 180.
5   *Ibid.*
6   Windebank to Aston, 29 December 1637 (*Clar. S.P.* ii.3).
7   A.V. Nunz. D'Inghilterra 7, f. 7.
8   *Loc. Cit.*, f. 105. The Spanish nuncio remained silent on the activities of the friar. O'Daly, as he testifies himself, was in

Munster in 1636 'on a mission from Castile'. (Testimony of Frei Domingos do Rosario concerning Sister Catherine Burke, among manuscripts in Archives of Bom Sucesso). The master-general, Ridolfi, was at this time immersed in diplomatic negotiations for Urban VIII. While in Paris the French prime-minister, Richelieu, had in his service the Dominican, Père Carré. In fact, during the whole of Ridolfi's master-generalship, Dominicans were being constantly employed on secret missions for the heads of states. Mortier VI. 388.

9   AGOP, IV, 74, ff. 110,150.

10 Hopton to Windebank, September 1639 (*Clar.S.P.* ii. 69). A document in Fondo Santa Sede in the Ministry of Foreign Affairs, Madrid, throws an interesting sidelight on the activities of the earls of Tyrone and Tyrconnell. As early as 13 March 1626 they were mustering their friends, vassals, and the ecclesiastical dignitaries of Ireland with a view to insurrection. (Fonda Santa Sede, Leg. 58, f. 397).

11 B.V. Barb. Latin MS646, f. 346.

12 Archives Bom Sucesso, Documents relating to Eleanor and Ursula Burke, 1640.

13 Rodrigues Cavalheiro, *1640. Richelieu e O Duque de Bragança*, pp 38–9.

14 Conde-Duque was noted for employing obscure foreigners, and ecclesiastics for his missions. It was quite common for secretaries of state, prime ministers and ambassadors to carry away documents with them when they left office.

15 F.A. Antunes Borges, 'Provisão dos Bispados e concilio nacional no reinado de João IV', in *Lusitania Sacra*, vol. ii. 111–291 (1957).

16 Rebello da Silva, *Historia de Portugal nos seclos XVII e XVIII*, iii. 257 *et seq.*

17 A.V. Nunz. Di Portugallo 22, 23, 153, 155; Nunz. Di Spagna 83.

18 A.V. Nunz. Di Portugallo 23, ff. 89–90.

19 *Ibid*, ff. 93–128.

20 A.TdoT, *Corpo Chron.*, pt. ii, maço 371, doc. 177 for edict *A. divinis;maço 372, doc. 39 for royal mandate of expulsion; ibid*, pt. iii, maço_32. Dpc. 44 for Consultas.

21 A.V. Nunz. Di Spagna 83, f. 115v.

22 Nicoletti, *Vita de Urbano VIII*, vol. 7, f. 704 in B.V.

23 A.V. Nunz. Di Spagna 83, ff. 229–85.

24 Archives Bom Sucesso, Documents relating to foundation.

25 A. Carvalho, *Corografia Portugueza* iii. 660–62 (1708). G. Cardosa. *Agiologio Dominico* i–iii (1657) finished by Joseph de Natividade

17121, vol. vi. 618–620. National Library Lisbon (reservados), Fundo Antigo 145.

26 *P.R.O. Inqusitions*, Postmortem and Attainder (Leinster, Charles I) no. 2.3.12, the Kavanagh family.

27 Archives Bom Sucesso, Manuscript history, p. 6. 'A pilgrim called one day to the Quinta of the countess, and asked the porter if the countess would like to have it (the little statue). On beholding the little image, she was enchanted and sent her servant to ask the price. When the servant went out to the patio, the pilgrim had disappeared, and no one knew where he had gone or in what direction'. It was several years later that the Statue was invoked under the Spanish title of Good Success which eventually became the name of the convent.

28 AGOP, IV, 74, f. 3.

29 AGOP, IV, 112, ff. 310, 324, 475, 479.

30 R. Bracey, 'Records of Nuns of Second Order O.P.', in *Catholic Record Society*, no. 25, pp 176–241 (1925).

31 The monastery of the Blessed Sacrament was founded by a certain Count Vimicosa in 1607 for his wife who became a nun there. The count was received into the Dominican order and received the name of Frei Domingos do Rosario. In 1615, he was active in getting the earl of Tyrone to intercede on his behalf with the pope and Philip III for the foundation of monastery for the Irish Dominicans in Lisbon. He died at the age of 82 on 30 July 1637.

32 Archives Bom Sucesso, Documents concerning the foundation.

33 R. Bracey, *loc. Cit.*

34 Joseph de Natividade, *Agiologio Dominico* vi. 620.

35 AGOP, IV. 87, f. 52v.

36 Archives Bom Sucesso, Testimony of Frei Domingos do Rosario concerning Sister Catherine Eleanor Burke (undated).

37 Extract from Acts of General Chapter O.P. held in Rome 1656. *Eleanora de Burgo. Hanc vitae rationem pia virgo prosequntur in Hibernia interim dulcique Patria relictis laeta migravit, ubi Sacro velo suscepto ac Solemni Professione menta Rosariam aliaque pauperrima supellex pro pretiosos jam thesauris asserventur in publicam Testimonium Probitatis* (Romae, 1656).

38 D.J. O'Doherty, 'The Irish Nuns of Lisbon', in *I.E.R.*, series 5, xix. 222–33 (March, 1922).

IV

PORTUGUESE AMBASSADOR AT PARIS

In the margin of an original document now in the ministry of Foreign Affairs in Paris there is a small, innocuous-looking gloss, the significance of which has been lost on many of its readers. The document is Richelieu's celebrated *Instructions* to the Sieur de Saint-Pé, his secret envoy bound for Lisbon in the autumn of 1638. Though short, the document is rich in content. The envoy was instructed to contact a certain Captain George d'Azevedos in Lisbon, and through him, to arrange a meeting with the 'chancellor'. He was to lay Richelieu's offer before the 'chancellor'.

The document reads:

> first of all, the envoy will find out from the chancellor and the Captain d'Azevedos if the Portuguese wish to rebel openly, so that the French may go with a naval army and capture all the forts which lie between the mouth of the river at Lisbon and the Belem tower, and deliver them into their [Portuguese] hands. Equally, France would leave them to act purely and simply of their own accord without doing anything else except

to give them this initial help; or if the aforementioned chancellor, d'Azevedos, and others to whom he will make this proposal, show him that they desire greater help, he will ask what assurance the country of Portugal wishes to save the French and the Dutch – or the French only – whatever appears best to them to organise themselves in their own country. If they were helped by an army of 12,000 men with saddles, firearms, pistols and a naval fleet of fifty ships, in this case it would only be just that the aforementioned helpers should have some port and place of disembarkation and the assurance that they will not be ill-treated.

The envoy was further instructed to negotiate a suitable port and to declare France's sincerity in wishing the Portuguese to be delivered from Spanish subjugation:

France desires nothing else but the glory of helping them and is sure with their help to be able to do this. She will give them annual and perpetual succour, on this condition: that they withdraw themselves from obedience to the king of Spain forever, the envoy is to add that if they wish to banish the Spanish from their territory, France very willingly will not desire to share in the conquests, and agrees that all should belong to the man they will elect as king. If this is the duke of Bragança and he assents, France will approve; if not he, and then one of the heirs of the last kings will be sent to them.[1]

Finally, the envoy was to obtain a determined and precise response to these propositions, and if the Portuguese wished, they might send an envoy of their own choosing to Paris to give more certainty and information on what was necessary.

Few documents of the Portuguese Restorations have caused such controversy as the *Instructions* to Saint-Pé. What Richelieu envisaged as 'annual and perpetual help' was never translated into concrete terms. The 'chancellor' referred to in the document remains a mystery. Recent historians have suggested various personages, and the most likely candidate would seem to be Dr João Pinto Ribeiro, prime-mover in the conspiracy to overthrow the Spanish government in Lisbon.[2] As early as 1632, this influential political writer had put forward his views on patriotism in a famous pamphlet and had urged all loyal Portuguese to resist Castilian absorption.[3] It was he who personally offered the crown of Portugal to the duke of Bragança on 12 October 1640. Through his hands passed the subsequent correspondence between the duke and the conspirators; Ribeiro dispatched the courier to Villa Viciosa, the home of the duke, on the night on 1 December 1640, announcing the success of the revolution and summoning the duke to Lisbon for his coronation.

Then there is the unsolved problem of the extent to which the conspirators committed themselves to Richelieu, and whether they sent a special agent back to France with the French envoy as had been suggested in the concluding lines of the *Instructions*.[4] Finally there is the marginal gloss, small enough to escape notice: 'Du cabinet du R.P. Dominique du Rosaire, Envoye du Portugal'. In actual fact, O'Daly only became accredited minister to Paris in 1655. This was August 1638. Was he, then, a party to the French interest even before the Restoration took place? Was he, as one writer has suggested, the secret envoy Richelieu had in mind when he dictated his *Instructions* to Saint-Pé?[5]

To understand the political ethos of Richelieu's diplomatic activities, it is necessary to read and re-read the original documents concerned. Only then can one grasp something of the minute complexities of his diplomacy. At all times objective and method are essentials in diplomatic actions. Always at the heart of the diplomatic problem is the question of war and peace, security or uncertainty but with succeeding centuries, methods of achieving objectives changed. For Portugal, in the Restoration period, the diplomatic objective was laid down at the first meeting of the *Cortes* early in 1641; however, that objective was unclear. For, Richelieu, on the other hand, method had been brought to such a pitch of perfection that it effectively screened the end he had in view. The diplomatic agents of

Richelieu were chosen chiefly from a class of men likely to prove personally loyal to the king, and rarely from the ranks of ecclesiastics whose relations made them less trustworthy. They were followed and directed with incessant vigilance by Richelieu. Richelieu's diplomats were meant to suggest rather than to realise, to observe, to criticise, to reflect but not to act on their own initiative.

The confidential nature of the negotiations made all the difference between diplomacy as it was practised in Richelieu's era and as it is understood in modern times. It was customary then for heads of state to employ special accredited envoys whose interventions were indispensable to the march of negotiations. If the business were successful, the credit went to the master; if failed, blame was heaped on the envoy. Diplomacy indeed meant peace for the Portuguese, but in the prevailing atmosphere it was actually a war of insidious half-promises and artifices waged ceaselessly by pen, by word and even by silence.

Eduardo Brazão remarked, 'It is impossible to study the political history of Portugal without the framework of its diplomatic history' and he has pointed out the close communication between France and Portugal from 1634 onwards.[6] Thus one does not take a phrase out of a document and magnify it disproportionately. O'Daly's diplomatic activities must be set within the framework of a larger canvas. While he had apparently been pre-occupied with the affairs of his order, and in particular with the needs of the Irish Dominican province, Portugal had undergone a change of government in 1640. O'Daly was appointed confessor to the queen shortly after, a position he retained until his death. With the years he acquired influence with both the queen and her husband, King João IV, at first in religious matters only but, eventually, in political and diplomatic issues as well. It is now generally conceded that he was the unofficial Portuguese ambassador to England in 1650. By 1655, he was transacting official government matters for João IV in Paris, and in 1656, he was appointed Portuguese ambassador to France. In that year, he was also sent as envoy to pope Alexander VIII on a mission from king João IV during the years of the Portuguese Restoration.

From the union of Spain and Portugal in 1580, divergence of interests had made it obvious that a united Iberian Peninsula would not be permanent. For the Portuguese, political survival as a nation was manifest in an articulated desire for freedom from Castilian domination; whereas, the Spaniards deplored what they termed 'the disease of separation' on the part of Portugal. The reign of Philip IV tended to be wracked with violence and excesses scarcely unequalled in the history of Spain. Conde-Duque Olivares, the prime-minister and real ruler of Spain, adopted rigid measures to regularise the finances of both countries by means of heavy taxation on Portugal. This announcement in January 1629 caused widespread discontent, and the imposition of a further tax two years later fanned the smouldering fires of resentment. The adoption of this harsh policy towards the smaller country coincided with the appointment of a cousin of Philip IV, Margaret, widow of the duke of Mantua, to the regency there. Miguel de Vasconçoncellos, who was sent from Madrid as secretary of state to assist her, had been associated with Conde-Duque Olivares and had aroused the hostility of the Portuguese.

During the quarter century, Olivares had become absolute master of imperial Spain. If he had assumed dominion, it was because his will to rule, his rectitude and his energy were superior to the inert and disorganised social forces which surrendered passively, but sullenly, to his dictatorship. In 1640, the stage was set for his inexorable and inevitable fall. Many factors contributed. Physically and mentally, Olivares was exhausted and had become increasingly subject to fits of depression and melancholia until his mind gave way completely some months before his death in 1645.

Marañón, in his analysis of Olivares' downfall, has pointed out that a dictator possesses an intense feeling of aggrandisement and material grandeur, but he lacks a deep sense of responsibility. For the Spaniards, Olivares' most unpardonable offence was his *'antipatico'* attitude towards the regions he governed, and the patriotism of the Spaniard is, above all, regional. Unpardonable, therefore, was his treatment of Catalonia, a Spanish region possessing its own language and racial characteristics. Apart from Olivares' initial error of imposing a central authority on people who had a minimum cordiality and sympathy for Castile, he added the arbitrary levying of taxes and soldiery for wars which were neither national, nor religious. In 1640, Catalonians rose in rebellion against him.[7]

Then Olivares committed a fatal mistake. He tried to levy an army in Portugal to fight the Catalonians, and he demanded new taxation from that country. The previous year, he had appointed the wealthy duke of Bragança as Governor of the Arms of Portugal, a position for which the duke had little relish and in which as a servant of Philip IV, he would appear less eligible for the Portuguese throne. It was a shrewd and pre-meditated appointment on the part of Olivares, and it deserved better fortune. The duke's objections to the appointment were overruled, and he began reluctantly to raise troops, still refusing to commit himself to any of the advances made by rapidly-growing groups of conspiring nobles. To Conde-Duque's chagrin, it was the ambition and influence of Olivares' own cousin Luisa de Gusmão with whom he arranged her marriage to the duke of Bragança who convinced the duke to take the throne of Portugal in October 1640. In a public speech at Madrid, Olivares accused Luisa as being the true instigator of the Portuguese insurrection.[8]

Peter Paul Rubens' portrait of John, Duke of Bragança,
later João IV King of Portugal (c. 1628)
public domain

Late in the evening of 1 December, the conspirators, joined by a crowd of citizens, swarmed up the palace steps in Lisbon. With a few stray shots, the Spanish garrison was dispersed, de Vasconçellos was killed and Margaret of Mantua was put under arrest. She was taken from the palace in Lisbon and placed in a convent outside the city. From there, she was sent to Spain with much respect and consideration, the archbishop of Braga escorting her and many of the city governors and local nobility coming out to greet her as she passed along the way.[9] Meanwhile, the duke of Bragança arrived in Lisbon on 6 December, and nine days later, he was solemnly crowned in the great square, the Terreiro de Paço, in Lisbon. A glimpse of the new king as he appeared to his subjects in those early days is given us in a contemporary letter. 'The new king', wrote Vincente Mobili, papal representative in Lisbon:

> is aged thirty-five with a straight bearing and well-formed. He is fair with a full face, of a fresh complexion but marked with pox. He has a good nose, a large forehead and a lively pair of eyes. He speaks little but what he says is concise and relevant. He is a large eater, not caring much for delicacies and he usually drinks water. In matter of dress, he is scrupulously neat but simple in his mode of attire. He is a great hunter and a tireless worker. He has some austere customs, fasting every Wednesday and Saturday, but he is very affable and easy of manner when giving an audience. He is also just.[10]

The palace revolution that led to the crowning of João de Bragança as King João IV of Portugal had succeeded more through Spanish weakness than through Portuguese strength. For years, the new dynasty was to live under the shadow of a possible reconquest, all the more real as Spain's debility might be only temporary, and Portugal might unexpectedly be assaulted by Spain's overwhelming forces. In January 1641, João IV summoned his parliament or *cortes* to which all three estates sent representatives in the time-honoured Portuguese manner. The immediate challenges were the strengthening of national fortifications and training a weak army for war. Over and above these needs, the king and his parliament had a three-fold task to perform: they were to conserve the Portuguese empire such as it was; they were to reintegrate the small mother country with her immense overseas colonies, and they were to reconquer the territories that had been pirated by the Dutch trading companies overseas.

Luisa de Gusmão
public domain

Another problem demanding immediate attention was that of gaining foreign recognition. The Thirty Years War was still in progress. On one side were Spain and the Empire; on the other side were France and her allies, the chief of which were Holland and Sweden. England, torn by internal strife and soon to develop into civil war, could take no part in European politics for ten years. João IV and his counsellors now recalled that Richelieu, on two occasions, had promised the Portuguese the support of France. João IV was quick to realise that although French recognition and assistance were all-important, they would not suffice if a general peace were made, and Portugal was left to fight alone against the whole strength of the Spanish army. Nothing less than an alliance which would be both offensive and defensive would protect Portugal. This diplomatic process, known as the 'league' became the cornerstone of Portuguese policy in the Restoration period.

Perhaps the Portuguese definition of what João IV and his first parliament understood by the 'league' is best summed up in the *Instructions* given to the first ambassadors appointed 21 January 1641. It was an alliance 'from which none of the contracting parties might depart without the consent of the other, the allies France, especially the Netherlands, and its object was to carry on war against Spain and her possessions in Italy and Flanders. The first ambassadors were instructed to ask that a French fleet be sent to join that of Portugal and attack Spanish ports. They were also to try and raise a regiment of cavalry in France and to obtain officers, arms and ammunition. All these aims seem to have fallen within the scope of the 'league', and even in 1657, when O'Daly was acting Portuguese ambassador in Paris, none of these demands had been relaxed.[11]

Catherine of Bragança
courtesy of the National Portrait Gallery

The recruitment of diplomats is, in a sense, empirical; at moments of intense political activity it is not always easy for a small state to produce the fully-equipped diplomat. The most difficult task of all is to select the man best suited to the post. It is to the credit of João IV that a magnificent school of diplomacy was built up in a period when, politically, his newly-acquired throne seemed without foundation. He was by nature cautious to the point of being incapable of committing himself absolutely to offensive tactics of war. He preferred rather to negotiate patiently recognised diplomacy channels while retaining the right to make the final decision himself. The diplomatic missions he envisaged were of a delicate nature. Although he had been acclaimed as national king in all the Lusitanian colonies except Terceira, Ceuta and Tangier, the situation in the colonies was grave. There was clearly only one course to follow: to benefit from the revolt of Catalonia, and to procure the protection of the adversaries of Spain. In her overseas colonies, Portugal had three enemies who, paradoxically, were vitally important to her as European allies: England, Spain and the Netherlands.[12]

João IV of Portugal was inclined to look back towards the monarchial ideal expressed in the figure of Don Afonso Henrique, first king of Portugal, so his selection of ambassadors may have been influenced by his wish to keep alive the political concept of Portugal as a nation totally constituted in the middle age. During the sixteenth century, diplomatic missions were mainly carried out for the Catholic courts of Europe by religious of that Church. Members of religious orders were selected because they were thought to possess certain advantages over secular diplomats. As priests, they had easy access to royal courts; as confessors, they knew how to guard secrets; as religious, subject to an immediate superior, they were ruled by obedience. Furthermore, when travelling, they did not demand either exorbitant salaries or excessive expenses;

their handling of business showed a tact and shrewdness which they had acquired in their dealings with human nature in the course of their ministries.

During the fifty years that Portugal remained united to Spain, theories of statecraft had changed and by 1640, most governmental negotiations were passing into the hands of secular diplomats. The shift of opinion had been brought about by the counter-reformation papacy with its highly-organised nunciatures. It was felt that priests were divided in their loyalty. Quite early in the seventeenth century, diplomatic theory lost any overtones of religiosity and developed a species of diplomatic mercenary who was ready to be hired by any power or to compute skillfully any interest.[13] It was into this milieu that João IV sent his first envoys. With one major exception, they were all priests, and it was to be their particular achievement that, side by side with the Portuguese secular diplomats, they won for Portugal the independence which from the beginning they seemed powerless to achieve. Two of these religious envoys were native-born Portuguese, Frei Diniz de Lencastre, O.P., nephew of the king, and Padre Antonio Vieira, S.J. Preacher-Protector of Brazil. The other two were comparative strangers to Lisbon. Dr Richard Russell of the English college in Lisbon had an active share in the dynastic alliance between Portugal and England. Frei Domingos O'Daly, the Irish Dominican, served as official ambassador to France and to Charles Stuart. In many respects his career parallels that of the Jesuit Antonio Vieira, with whom he is sometimes compared.[14]

The parliament of January 1641, which João IV had summoned immediately after his coronation, ratified the king's selection of ambassadors. Promptly, he sent envoys to the pope, and to the governments of France, the Netherlands, England, Denmark and Sweden. As far back as 1373, the English had made a solemn declaration of alliance with Portugal. In London, in 1642, the Portuguese emissaries signed a treaty with Charles I by which they gained English recognition. No real help could be counted on from England for years to come because its civil war intervened. In 1654, Oliver Cromwell renewed the old alliance by another treaty, and in 1661, with the wedding of Charles and Catherine of Bragança, a new treaty was signed.[15]

The Young Charles II
courtesy of the Collection of the North Carolina Museum of History

Charles II arriving at Dover
public domain

Portuguese negotiations at The Hague began also in 1641. The Dutch, at this time, had a double game to play. On the one hand, in their wish to weaken Spain, they recognised Portugal as an independent state. On the other hand, the Dutch wanted to continue conquering the Portuguese empire. They promised to consent to a ten-year truce with João IV, but they took their time about ratifying it. In the interval, the Dutch rushed instructions to their overseas officials to seize as much Portuguese territory as possible before the truce went into effect. They wanted particularly to gain a foothold in Angola and to ensure their new Brazilian possessions of a slave supply. The most formidable enemies of the Portuguese colonies were the Dutch companies of the East and West Indies. Although initially a private enterprise, they enjoyed a certain official status guaranteed by the Dutch government. Over the years they had acquired predominance in the administration of the United Provinces which made diplomatic negotiations between the two countries difficult and complicated. Briefly, it meant that the ambassadors of João IV had to gain the goodwill of the two trading companies to get even a hearing in the estates-general.

Thus an uneasy situation was created between the Dutch and Portuguese as early as 1641; at war in the colonies, they both desired peace in European waters.[16] Saint-Fé, the French consul at Lisbon, was instructed to declare to the new king that France would agree to make no treaty with Spain unless Portugal were included in it.[17] The separation of Portugal and her extensive colonies from Spain was of great value to France. From Richelieu's point of view, the December revolution of 1640 occurred at a convenient juncture of the Thirty Years War. It compelled Spain to divert her army in the Pyrenees into Catalonia against Portugal. Richelieu gauged correctly that Portugal would fight to the last, seeing that her political existence was at stake; hence, he realised that he need not give her the subsidies that he granted the other allies who, but for them, would not have continued the war. The aspect which galled the Portuguese particularly was that France poured out subsidies on Sweden and Holland lavishly, but it refused every demand made by the ambassadors of João IV in the years following the Restoration.

The ambassador whom the Portuguese *cortes* selected for France in 1641 was the nephew of the king, a priest and friar, Frei Diniz de Lancastre, O.P. His mission proved unsuccessful as did the later ones of the Jesuit, Antonio Vieira in 1646 and 1647. The French, however, signed a treaty with the Portuguese representatives at Paris on 1 June 1641, contenting themselves with a secret article promising to do their best when making peace with Spain to reserve the right to help Portugal if their allies would enter into a like agreement.[18] They gave as excuse for not entering into formal alliance with João IV that Louis XIII could do nothing without the participation of his previous allies, Sweden and Holland.

The death of Louis XIII in 1642 following close on that of Richelieu later in the same year placed the astute Giulio Raimondo Mazarin at the head of the government of France. Mazarin's sincerity in the cause of Portugal was doubtful; his avarice was legendary. After the Fronde, Mazarin bore a private grudge against Portugal because it had not helped him financially in his war with the French nobles. The position of the Portuguese ambassadors in Paris became increasingly embarrassing after 1648. The Thirty Years War had ended, and though France and Spain continued to be at war for another eleven years, there was no longer the urgent need of Portugal's help. Yet, Mazarin continued to toy with Portugal because it was his practice to negotiate continually either in public or in secret, even when he did not expect immediate results. As Richelieu remarked in his *Spiritual Testament*, 'it helps one to understand what is going on in the world'.

At the beginning of 1651, Francisco de Sousa Coutinho was transferred to Paris from The Hague as Portuguese ambassador to France. He had acquitted himself with distinction at The Hague, and it was mainly through his diplomatic efforts there that Portugal recovered her most important colony, Brazil. Now, at this critical time, João IV placed him in Paris. It was the most difficult post for a Portuguese ambassador. Coutinho was one of the few professional diplomats in the government, and he had represented João IV when João was the duke of Bragança at the court of Philip IV of Spain. Brusque of speech, impetuous and fearless, he was also wily. Coutinho took liberties of speech with his old master, now his king, using the familiarity of an old retainer, writing to and abusing him with a rough frankness. In his letters to the king, he frequently censured the policy of other Portuguese ambassadors. Thus he vigorously opposed Vieira's negotiations in Paris because they interfered with his own transactions at The Hague. He judged rightly that if Portugal had concluded the treaty Vieira was negotiating, the whole country would have passed into French hands.[19] Later, Coutinho made O'Daly the subject of two important letters to his king.

Shortly after his arrival in Paris, Mazarin, in dire need of money, resolved to bargain with Portugal. In return for entering into a formal alliance with Portugal, France would receive three million ecus. Coutinho agreed, and he went to Lisbon to lay the proposal before the government; however, it excited such opposition that he returned to Paris without a definite answer. He had promised Mazarin that Portugal would assist an expedition against Naples undertaken by the French in 1654. Acting in the interests of his country, it would appear that Coutinho deceived Mazarin completely because neither money nor ships came from Portugal and the French fleet lost time waiting for the Portuguese in Toulon. On reaching Naples, the French found that any hope of initiating a rising was too late, and Mazarin attributed the failure of the enterprise to Portuguese inaction. He complained bitterly about Coutinho who was recalled from Paris in deference to Mazarin's resentment.[20]

At the same time Mazarin resolved to send a special envoy to Lisbon with the double object of recovering part of the expenses of the Naples expedition and of persuading João IV to take the offensive in the war against Spain. For this mission, Mazarin chose a man of a middle-class family, the Chevalier de Jant. The detail that is part of the historical process often obscures the personalities which vitalise a period. Behind the familiar figure of Mazarin, lesser characters tend, in the eyes of posterity, to become cyphers who carry out the bidding of their master automatically. Jant, however, who may be described as one of Mazarin's useful tools, was a bibliophile and an experienced traveller.[21] The Comte de Brienne, secretary of the department of foreign affairs in Paris during Mazarin's regime, loses his anonymity on closer examination and emerges as a humane, prudent and gifted administrator who spent his declining days alternately delighting and boring his grandchildren with his *memoires* which were later published in three volumes after his death.[22]

Among the secret *Instructions* given by Mazarin to Jant, two clauses refer indirectly to O'Daly. Jant was to assess the dispositions towards France of the ministers in the government of João IV. He was to indicate to Mazarin which of the ministers were partisans of Spain and which were loyal to the new king. He was also to discover the most influential of them, and he was to endeavour to win him over to the French interest by offering him the annual pension of a thousand ecus.[23]

When Jant started for Lisbon on 11 April 1655, he had in his possession a recommendation from the French secretary of state de Brienne that he should make the acquaintance of Frei Domingos do Rosario, a friar in Lisbon. He was also instructed to familiarise himself quietly about the revenue of Portugal, and about the sum of money the Portuguese king actually had in his treasury. Jant was to appeal to the maternal ambition of Queen Luisa by making an alliance between her eldest surviving daughter, Catherine, and Louis XIV. He was to assure the queen privately that Mazarin would use his best endeavours to induce Louis to consider the advantage of such an alliance when he had arrived at the age of marrying on the condition that Luisa would direct João IV to continue the Portuguese war with Spain with energy.[24]

Jant's *Public Instructions* are dated 23 February 1655. Wordy and repetitive, the document embodies the usual French formulae which João IV had heard so often since Frei Diniz de Lencastre had first gone to Paris. The two main points of the *Instructions* were a demand for money, and an annual offensive campaign against Spain at the frontiers or else a supply of warships, all expenses being defrayed by Portugal.[25]

The formal defensive war, adopted initially by necessity by João IV in 1641, was decided by the mildly spectacular victory of Montiza early in 1644 and was won by 1648. From then on, the war in the peninsula demanded an offensive policy which João and his ministers were reluctant to pursue because it was the poverty-stricken inhabitants of the eastern frontier who would suffer. Also, since the Spanish wing had been defeated decisively first at Montizo, and later in the Alentejo district, from which they were completely ejected, the Portuguese felt themselves in an unshakeable position. An offensive policy at this stage would be an error, and the king was quick to see that Mazarin's suggestion would immediately transport the theatre of war into Castile. The most considerable number of Philip's troops would converge upon the Portuguese army. From Mazarin's point of view, Spain would be considerably weakened at the defence of the Pyrenees, and the French army there would gain a series of brilliant, rapid and inexpensive victories. This fact João IV duly noted as being inimical to the interests of Portugal.

It was April when the Chevalier de Jant arrived in Lisbon. Three days later, on 14 April, he had his first audience with King João IV. Claiming the right to speak frankly, Jant addressed him in a harsh and aggressive manner in the presence of the court accusing him of timidity and indecision. The king listened quietly, flushing a little, and then answered briefly and with dignity. He refuted Jant's accusations and appointed commissioners to treat with the French envoy. Jant had followed his *Instructions* to the letter, but he had merely irritated his listeners. The audience finished, the chevalier was presented to the queen. He summed up his impressions of

Luisa de Gusmão for de Brienne in a much-quoted phrase, *'cette grande princesse, qui peut passer pour une des plus parfaites, des plus eclaires, et des plus accomplies de tout le terre'.*[26]

Jant delivered three more memorials to which the secretary of state Vieira da Silva replied on behalf of his majesty of Portugal. The king was prepared to enter into a formal alliance with France and to make such money payments as his finances allowed. He would not grant subsidies to France to carry out hostilities elsewhere rather than at the frontiers.

This created an impasse. The Chevalier resolved to leave Lisbon. The appearance of the Barbary pirates at the mouth of the Tagus made Jant less enthusiastic to embark. A fortunate attack of light fever kept him in bed for the greater part of June, though he heard all that went on in Lisbon through his colleague, Roquement, in Lisbon. On 24 June, he learned with alarm that the Spaniards were negotiating a truce with Portugal, and he revived sufficiently to send a lengthy memorial to the king from whom he received a firm and uncompromising reply. To resolve any misunderstanding between the two countries, João IV was sending the queen's confessor to Paris with Jant. The king wrote a rather long letter to Mazarin and a brief letter to Louis XIV. In his letter to Mazarin, João IV stated that his policy would remain defensive, but:

> in the interests of France and the preservation of the kingdom,
> I am resolved to demand help in the form which Frei
> Domingos will ask, to whom I have referred Your Eminence.

Terminating all negotiations with Spain, João IV concluded with a few general observations to show his keen awareness of the political value of Portugal to both France and England.[27]

Jant, hearing of the friar's appointment, changed his own plans in order to travel with O'Daly and both embarked on a ship bound for St Malo. For three days, the ship lay becalmed in the hot, sticky heat which afflicts Lisbon in July. On the third day, the king sent a peremptory message to O'Daly to return immediately to the city. In his report of 24 July to Mazarin, Jant observed that envious people had discredited the friar with the king by saying that he was a foreigner and a pensioner of France.[28] This is an interesting remark. It was during these same years that the Irish priest was finding the city council of Lisbon and the clergy of St Paul's so slow to yield up the site of Corpo Santo. There may have been some personal spleen against the foreign friar for whom the queen was financing a new college.

Although the criticism was not sufficient to ruin the friar's mission completely, it so far influenced the king that Jant reported O'Daly as saying he would rather go to Algiers than be obliged to carry only words to France.[29] Behind the petulance of the friar's remark may be sensed the wider policy of his master João IV. A shrewd man, the king was indefatigable in pursuing a patient series of negotiations which may have compensated for a certain lack of valour and irresolution in the tactical decisions of war. In the matter of Portugal's relations with France, he exhibited a restraint which admirably foiled Mazarin's own tactics. João IV had reflected well during the three days when the ship carrying his envoy to Paris became becalmed in the estuary which his palace on the Ajuda hill overlooked.

From his accession, João IV had always been deeply influenced by religious advisors, especially the idealist, the Jesuit Antonio Vieira. In a letter to the king, now a classic, Vieira had reasoned philosophically that to change the defensive character of the war to an offensive one involved too great a risk.[30] Until the king died in 1656, Portugal held firmly to its defensive policy. João IV had no illusions about the political opportunism of France, but he realised that the three legal documents signed with France,

England and the Netherlands in the early days of the Restoration constituted the greatest support of national independence with the defence of the frontiers and with the desperate resistance of Brazil and Angola to the Dutch overseas. João IV temporised with Mazarin and sent the queen's confessor to Paris. Meanwhile, in the three days' interval, he had again received a concrete proposal from Spain for a truce. He countermanded the mission of the friar immediately, bidding him to return to Lisbon.

Jant resumes the narrative. The perceptive Roquement, always *au courant* with the latest news in Lisbon, wrote him an urgent letter begging him to disembark and take immediate action 'in his own name and that of the cardinal'. The Chevalier returned promptly and demanded an audience of their majesties. As he said himself, he represented all imaginable ills for Portugal which he could summon up, *ex tempore,* to prevent them from accepting the terms of the truce. The king replied calmly with an ultimatum. The formal alliance between France and Portugal must be concluded by Jant there and then. The Chevalier capitulated, still protesting that he might fail to constitute a league proper as his powers were only verbal instructions to do all that would benefit his country. In his confidential report to Mazarin, Jant declared that he consented to negotiate, being influenced by the queen, O'Daly, and the Marquis de Niza, all three 'zealous for the interests of France'.[31]

The '*pour parlers*' began. Jant found the financial terms offered by the Portuguese unsatisfactory and re-embarked. On board once more he received a message from O'Daly. In his opinion, Jant's stubbornness was the cause of the failure to effect an alliance between the two countries. The messenger, a friar from O'Daly's own monastery, also delivered a note from the queen. It was then, 23 July, less than a week since O'Daly and the Chevalier had first embarked for St Malo. Jant's account of what happened next is best given in his own version which was always written in the third person:

> The chevalier made some strange reflections on this matter and considered that the person who had been recommended to him by Monsieur le Comte de Brienne to serve as his guide was le Pere Dominique, and that the other great hope of His Eminence was the queen of Portugal who had given many signs of her affection for France. Taking all things into consideration, he resolved to remain with the intention nevertheless of deferring the conclusion of the league as long as possible, until he got news from France.[32]

Jant demanded five days to reconsider. In the interval, the tragedy of Salvaterra took place. The Spanish troops had tried to bribe the governor of a Portuguese frontier town to open the gates if a small force of Spaniards were sent to occupy the town. Accordingly, thirty-seven officers, disguised as peasants, were dispatched to take the fortress and were massacred by the entire Portuguese garrison. João IV is believed to have sanctioned the act, and to have boasted that 'it was a holocaust offered for the unity of Portugal and France'.[33]

It was the end of July. The document was ready for Jant's signature. Realising the diplomatic repercussions of the Salvaterra affair, he hesitated. At this point, O'Daly intervened decisively in an unusual and half-medieval role. He summoned the Chevalier to his bedside, where he was laid up with gout. There, according to Jant, he improvised a situation. Having sent for the Blessed Sacrament, he swore on the salvation of his soul that France would lose the Portuguese alliance if Jant abandoned it at that juncture. In a document embodied in his *Negotiations*, the Chevalier sets forth his reasons for signing the treaty after certain modifications were made by O'Daly. For one who professed the *'politique'* of Machiavelli, Jant's arguments are remarkably theological. One suspects the influence of Frei Domingos do Rosario, master of theology. Indeed, though Jant does not mention the friar by name, he says significantly that 'he was obliged to serve this expedient (of signing the treaty) by a person of great experience and of extraordinary zeal for France': which may equally have been the queen, for whom he expressed great admiration, or O'Daly.[34]

Jant signed the *'liga formal'*, as it is known in Portuguese history, on 7 September 1655. He signed it with the mental reservation that since the treaty had to be ratified by Louis XIV, failing its ratification, the treaty would become invalid. The details of the treaty are embodied in *Tratados* which, while signed formally on both sides, was repudiated cynically by Mazarin. Early in October, the articles of the treaty were submitted to the French secretary, de Brienne, by Coutinho, then on the verge of quitting Paris under the cloud of Mazarin's displeasure. For five years, Coutinho had worked for the realisation of the *'liga formal'* and now, when it was almost an accomplished fact, Mazarin rejected it. Jant was recalled, though his biographer, Tessier, states that the cardinal was not displeased with his conduct in this affair. He was satisfied that Jant had done good work in Lisbon by securing a pensionary of France in the person of O'Daly, and in winning Luisa de Gusmão, the queen, to the French interest. Unfortunately, Tessier does not mention his source for the statement.[35] Jant's observation, though unsubstantiated, is the basis for the allegation that O'Daly was in the pay of the French.

The Chevalier lingered, an unwanted guest, in Lisbon. Coutinho had taken up residence in Rome, his new post, having left many secret sympathisers in Paris, including the papal nuncio, Monsignor Guido di Bagno. The latter reports the departure of Coutinho for Rome where 'he fears the opposition of the Spaniards in that city'. In the same week, that of 17 October 1655, the return of Jant is noted by the ever-watchful nuncio who doubts that a treaty between France and Portugal will be ratified.[36] It was imperative to send a special envoy to Paris from Lisbon and the choice fell on O'Daly largely because of the esteem he enjoyed with their majesties and partly on account of his part in the recent signing of the treaty.

Once before, in 1646, João IV had sent another religious to Paris for that purpose and under similar circumstances. Passionately interested in politics and fearless in the face of the opposition, Antonio Vieira had almost signed Portugal away but for the timely, if brusque, intervention of Coutinho from The Hague. O'Daly's career has been contrasted with that of the Jesuit, but whereas Vieira was a celebrated pamphleteer and political writer, Daniel O'Daly left no political writings and our opinion of him as a diplomat rests on the evidence of his own dispatches to the king and to the council of state, in the testimony of contemporaries, especially those remarks in the minutes of the council of state and in the confidential reports of men like Jant and Monsignor Guido di Bagno.

At this time, Daniel O'Daly was a man of sixty years of age who possessed a wide experience of people and of ecclesiastical and political affairs; yet, his appointment was not agreeable to all the Portuguese ministers. A memorandum was presented to the king by Don Diogo de Lima, Visconde of Villa Nova, who represented the discontented faction. The long document called the king's attention to the following points. Jant had been introduced to the friar through de Brienne, the French secretary of state, whence it might be assumed that there was a person in Portugal with whom the French government was on terms of understanding. Even if such were not the case, the friar was lacking in those qualities which the visconde deemed necessary for the projected negotiations. Even if he possessed those qualities, Don Diogo continued inexorably, it was not fitting that he should treat because he was Irish and had been educated in Spain. He was personally acquainted with Philip IV and had served as his agent in Ireland. But the most damning fact about O'Daly in Don Diogo's eyes was O'Daly was partial to the French interest; since he had to treat on behalf of the Portuguese, was it not dangerous to select one whom the French had already chosen to further their interest.[37]

Evidently Jant's *Secret Instructions* were known in Lisbon and the fact that de Brienne recommended O'Daly to Jant as a useful acquaintance seemed to be common gossip among courtiers. Don Diogo's document shows signs of irrationality. O'Daly is accused of being partial to Spain because he had served it in pre-Restoration days. So had João IV, king of Portugal. Simultaneously, the friar is charged with serving French interests, though France and Spain were at war at this time. Don Diogo states that O'Daly had informed the French envoy, Jant, about the great wealth of Portugal, but this was incorrect on two scores. Portugal was impoverished as Jant made clear in his own confidential report to Mazarin, and O'Daly was later to write a curt letter to the cardinal in 1658 reminding him of Portugal's insolvency.[38]

There is finally the consideration that O'Daly was a foreigner and an Irishman. He left no political writings as such, but he wrote a *History of the Geraldines*. From that work, it would seem that Daniel O'Daly had not forgotten his native country and the persecutions it was even then suffering under Cromwell's regime. What may have seemed O'Daly's partiality towards France may well have been determined by political events in his own country where there were two factions: the Anglo-Irish party led by Ormond and the Old Irish party which the O'Neills united around them. The former party in the troubled months of 1649–50 had claimed dependence on the Stuart kings and looked to France for help; the other party relied on Spain. It was with the Stuart cause that O'Daly identified himself as an Irishman, and because he acted as a go-between for Charles Stuart at various times between

1649–61 he found himself drawn into the impulsive missions that Henrietta Maria was perpetually initiating from her retreat in Saint-Germain.

Don Diogo's protest cannot be dismissed as being motivated merely by personal animosity. It was the first public expression of disapproval on the part of the faction that wished for O'Daly's overthrow in the Portuguese government. The Irishman found the French court hostile. In his dispatches to Lisbon, the friar states that the French did not wish to admit any envoy of João IV because it was said in Paris that the Portuguese promised much and then found it impossible to keep their word. This they gave as the reason why a foreign friar had been chosen for the diplomatic mission instead of a Portuguese nobleman. It was only towards the close of the year that O'Daly reported his first audience with Mazarin which he said had been obtained through the good offices of Jant.[39]

In fact, the frigid atmosphere of the French court was due to de Sousa Coutinho who had just departed. The strength of the cardinal's dislike for Coutinho may be inferred from a remark by Jant:

Nothing but the waters of the Rio de la Plata or the pastilles of Peru could wash and perfume the evil odours of his (Coutinho's) person will leave behind, when he departs from France.[40]

After a further delay, O'Daly had an audience with Louis XIV, who was then eighteen years of age, with the silent, grave and confident reticence which even then characterised his personality. The question of a marriage with Catherine, eldest surviving daughter of João IV, was introduced and, according to O'Daly, was considered very favourably.

That was in February 1656, but the situation, as it was understood by the council of state in Lisbon, was summed up by the secretary of state in the March session of the council's meeting. Frei Domingos, da Silva reported, had persisted in his efforts to engage Mazarin who had made it obvious that Jant's league would not be ratified. Mazarin had consented to draw up a new treaty. The Portuguese word here given in the text is 'tratado', which can equally mean 'league' or 'treaty'. In view of the emphasis placed by João IV on the terms determined by the first parliament of 1641, it may be assumed that O'Daly was bent on getting terms along the traditional lines from France. At the same audience, the question of the marriage alliance had been introduced. The secretary of state then gave his opinion: 'although Frei Domingos was a very good subject, he himself proposed that the king immediately nominate an ambassador who would be a person of service, rank and merit'.[41]

João IV ignored the suggestion of the secretary. Instead, he dictated a letter to Frei Domingos, through the secretary, ordering him to continue the negotiations 'with all possible zeal, insofar as the king would nominate no other ambassador'. How deep the understanding between the king and the friar was at this time may be inferred from João IV's letter of 6 May 1656 to O'Daly in Paris. Written in code, it expresses concern for the future of Portugal and the hope that the king's younger son, Don Pedro will be able to carry on the work of the government. 'A matter I write of with little relish', the king remarked, and he discussed with a fine objectivity the qualities and deficiencies of his son Pedro. He did not even consider Afonso who, in fact, did succeed him. It would seem as if already, in May 1656, the king had a premonition of his approaching death and of the difficulties that might follow, so he spoke his mind to the friar.[42]

In Paris, O'Daly was in an invidious position. The papal nuncio notes in a letter, dated 2 April 1656, that:

the Portuguese resident was being called, more often than usual, to audience with Mazarin who, it is commonly said, feared his patron (João IV), was treating with the crown of Spain.[43]

Technically Mazarin had never refused to enter into formal alliance with Portugal, and yet when the friar asked repeatedly for a written official reply for his master, it was not forthcoming. Finally, on 20 May, the answer was delivered. An unsigned copy of the letter exists in the archives of the Ministry of Foreign Affairs in Paris, but the letter was written by de Brienne at Mazarin's dictation, and it was this copy that went to João IV.[44]

The letter states that Jant had exceeded his powers and that Louis XIV did not find it convenient to make a new treaty with the king of Portugal, seeing how negligent the latter had been in the observance of the earlier alliance. João IV had not proceeded against the Spaniards as he could have, while the French on their side had attacked consistently. The best manner of forcing Philip IV to abandon his aggressive policy towards Portugal was to invade the part of Spain nearest to the Portuguese border; then, Philip would be only too willing to accede to the demands of João IV and his people. On the same date, Louis XIV wrote to the king of Portugal expressing similar sentiments.[45]

So the matter rested. In June, O'Daly received a sharp reminder from Mazarin telling him that his presence at the French court was superfluous. 'The cardinal has no time to give an audience, as the summer campaign occupies him completely', reported the friar to the council of state.[46] In July, O'Daly was back in Lisbon. From the minutes of the July sessions of the council of state, it would seem that O'Daly gave a most optimistic – and misleading – impression of affairs between the two countries. He had, according to his report, successfully brought the two objects of his mission to their concluding stages. The French had accepted the terms of the formal alliance, which Jant had proposed, but it is not at all clear whether

O'Daly meant the earlier form of the previous year, or the newer version which Mazarin had given permission to Jant to draw up some months previously. O'Daly reported that the French were favourable to the projected marriage alliance, but since Portugal could not afford to pay the sum demanded, it had been suggested that Tangier in north Africa be ceded. O'Daly added that the best means of concluding these negotiations was to bribe the cardinal with a present of 600,000 cruzados. The council was pleased to consider the friar's proposals, though surprised at the declarations so opposite to the sentiments of the letters received from Louis and Mazarin. On the other hand, it was well known that the cardinal was habitually short of money. Then too, the tentative negotiations between France and Spain seemed to be coming to nought once more, so that an alliance such as Frei Dominos offered, seemed plausible. However, João IV reserved his decision and with his customary caution resolved to await events.[47]

Later that month, news reached Lisbon that France and Spain had again broken off relations. João IV determined to send O'Daly back to Paris with new powers. The minutes of the council of state for 26 July give details of the appointment. He was to treat of the marriage alliance, and he was to resume formal negotiations for the league. As dowry for Catherine, he was to offer a maritime city in Africa with a harbour suitable for maintaining French fleets and with fortifications. Tangier in north Africa was suggested or Mazagoa, further south. The rest of the dowry, amounting to a million cruzados, was to be divided among persons who carried the matter through. Mazarin's share was to be 600,000 cruzados.[48]

In August, the king wrote to Louis XIV and to the cardinal informing them of his decision to send Frei Dominigos back to Paris. The copy of the king's letter to Louis is the usual letter of credence, short and courteous in form. His letter to Mazarin is a spirited defence of his own policy, setting forth the reasons why, from his point of view, an aggressive campaign against the Spanish army was not viable. O'Daly had full powers to transact all business and to conclude the league.[49]

It must have been in August of that year, too, that the Portuguese secretary of state, da Silva, wrote to the former Portuguese ambassador to France, de Sousa Coutinho, then in Rome, to hand over all papers and particulars relating to the Portuguese embassy in France to Frei Domingos de Rosario who was succeeding him in the post of the ambassador to that court.[50] Coutinho had previously written to King João IV in April concerning the friar's activities in Paris and though usually harsh in his denunciation of bad policy, he took a mild view of O'Daly's difficulties in that capital. Coutinho's time there had given him a better understanding of the cardinal's cat and mouse tactics with Portugal. He wrote:

> I had in the post a letter from Frei Domingos do Rosario with news which would upset me as it had upset him if I did not know France better and if I were not in Rome. He spoke to me of a Castilian friar who had arrived in the court and had several audiences with Cardinal Mazarin. The Castilian complained that our efforts had interfered with his plans already advanced – the arrogance of him! The cardinal does not want peace, but he will not acknowledge this. He listens to all and every proposal, and then does as he wishes.[51]

Both João IV and Coutinho were aware of the complex and untrustworthy character of Mazarin. They realised, too, that he had every ambassador watched; everything affecting the political, military and commercial interests of France was reported. The cardinal was familiar with all the parties and factions of every country. Court intrigues, however trivial, were brought to his notice. The characters, the weaknesses and the dispositions of sovereigns and their ministers were of interest to him. Mazarin considered them all useful in suggesting means to his desired ends. He was the best informed person in Europe.

'News which would have upset me if I did not know France better – and if I were not in Rome', Coutinho had written to the king. Behind that slight remark lay Portugal's most vexing problem, her relationship with the Holy See. It was not merely a question of recognition by the Vatican but of the Restoration of the monarchy. It involved the more serious question of the appointment of bishops to Portuguese sees and of the danger of a national church. Around the perimeter of what was essentially an internal dispute ranged the attitudes of France and Spain towards the papacy. To embarrass the Portuguese diplomats still further, there was the accomplished alliance with Cromwell and the mooted association with Sweden, both of which made João IV less acceptable to the Holy See. During O'Daly's stay in Paris, a series of letters concerning his activities passed between the nuncio in Paris, the papal secretary of state in Rome and the Spanish nuncio in Madrid. At the same time, Philip IV was writing to his ambassador in Rome about the Dominican. It is no wonder that João IV and his ambassador in Rome were disposed to take a lenient view of the friar's failure to elicit a favourable reply from the cardinal at Paris. It was part of a greater issue.

The *Instructions* for O'Daly's second mission bear no date, but they were probably written in September, as the king's letter of credence was dated late August. His directions were those drawn up in the minutes of the council of state. The document began with a flattering eulogy about the qualities of the new ambassador and he refers to his skill in treating in accordance with his *Instructions*, and to the satisfaction and prudence with which he had conducted his previous negotiations.[52]

O'Daly's return to the French court was duly noted by the nuncio on 24 October 1656, and his brief notice indicates that rumours were circulating around the person of the Portuguese ambassador. 'The Dominican Father, the archbishop of Goa, has returned from Portugal, being sent into this court by that king with a considerable sum of money'. The nuncio adds cautiously, 'this is not to be presumed true as if the ears were to take all as being true'.[53] Following close on the Friar's departure to Paris came the unexpected death of João IV on 6 November. He had gone out hunting a week previously and had been seized by sudden pain. Subsequently, it was diagnosed as a serious rupture, and after lingering for several days fully conscious, he died with great self-possession and tranquillity on the evening of the 6th. He was fifty-three years old.

João IV, the first king of the Bragança dynasty, died without the satisfaction of seeing his kingdom at peace or recognised formally. Although he was not a brilliant monarch, João IV gave his country reason to think well of him, and re-examining his handling of foreign policy has resulted in an ever-growing appreciation of his great qualities. He brought his country through a trying period, and while he could not save the entire Portuguese colonial empire, he saved more than any of his contemporaries expected. He had been forced to go, hat in hand, to the European powers begging favours and assuming the status of a poor relation. His own life was as insecure as his throne because Spain had waged a personal vendetta against him. In 1647, a Spanish-inspired plot failed only because the hired assassin lost his nerve at the critical moment. João's brother Prince Duarte, an intelligent and able administrator, was arrested in Austria by the Hapsburg relations of Philip IV, turned over to the Spaniards and imprisoned in Milan where he died of neglect.

On the evening of the fourth day after the death of João IV, the council of state, the officials of the royal palace, and certain other dignitaries assembled to hear Vieira, the secretary of state, read the last will and testament of the late king. In a deep silence, the listeners learned that João IV, according to the law of the kingdom, had nominated the queen, Luisa de Gusmão, tutor and guardian of his children during their minority:[54]

> And because of the great prudence which I have always recognised in the queen, and her awareness and experience in matters of this kingdom, and because of her love for all my subjects, I trust she will govern as well as she ought, administering to all impartial justice, in which I have understood the defence and conservation of the kingdom to consist, more than in arms. I nominate her as regent and governor of this kingdom, the prince not being of age, in conformity with the laws and customs of this kingdom as required in royal persons. And to govern the kingdom, the queen shall have all the jurisdiction and power which I hold today, until such a time as the prince comes of age ...[55]

The reading of the will finished, in deference to the prerogatives of the supreme authority, the captain of the guard was ordered to pass from the king's quarters to those of the queen-mother.

The regency had begun.

NOTES

1   Caix de Saint-Aymour, *Recueil des instructions donné aux Ambasaduers de France despuses les traits de Westphalia*, pp xix–xx. (This is usually referred to as *Recueil*).

2   I.S. Revah, *Le Cardinal de Richelieu et la Restauration du Portugal* (Lisbon, 1950), p. 23, where he suggests Fernao Cabral. R. Cavalheiro, *1640. Richelieu e o Duque de Bragança* (Lisbon, 1942) where he puts forward Pinheiro, chancellor of the three military orders. Visconde de Sanchas de Baena, *Notas e Documentas inedites para biographia de João Pinto Ribeiro*. This is a rare 92-page book kept in Reservados, Lisbon National Library, classed B.N.L. 14537.

3   J.P. Ribeiro, *Discurso sobre os Fidalgos, e Soldados Portuguezes não militarem em conquistas alhoes* (Lisbon, 1632).

4   *Recueil*.

5   For a brisk discussion of the problem see L.F. Almeida, 'Rodrigues Cavalheiro-1640, Richelieu, e O Duque de Bragança', in *Revista Portuguesa de Historia,* iii. 458–62 (Coimbra, 1944–47).

6   E. Brazäo, *A Restauração,* p. 9.

7   G. Marañón, *El Condo-Duque de Olivares,* p. 316.

8   *Ibid.* p. 141.

9   D. Jose de los Rios, *Historia de la villa y corte de Madrid,* iii. 357.

10   B.V. Barb. Latin MS 8564, ff. 10–13.

11   V. de Santarem, *Quadro Elementar das relacoesões politicas e diplomaticas de Portugal,* iv. 5. This book is usually referred to as *Quadro Elementar.*

12   M. de Matos, 'Vinte annõs de batalhas', in J. Cayolla (ed.), *A Restauracaõ e o Imperio colonial,* pp 479–507.

13   F. Meinecke, *Machiavellism* (trans. D. Scott, 1957), p. 194.

14   L. d'Azevedo, *Historia de Antonio Vieira, S.J.,* i. 30–140.

15   E. Brazão, *Uma Velha Alianca,* pp 56–76 (for texts of various treaties).

16   M. de Matos, *op. cit.,* p. 507.

17   *Recueil,* p. xxvi.

18   L.B. de Castro, *Collecão de Tratados, convencoes e contratos celebrados entre a Coraõ de Portugal e as mais potencias desde 1640 até o presente.* This monumental work is known as *Tratados.*

19   L. de Azevedi, *Historia de Antonio Vieira, S.J.* i. 106–131.

20   E. Prestage, *Diplomatic Relations of Portugal during the 17th Century,* pp 40–45.

21   J. Tessier, *Le Chevalier de Jant,* p. 66.

22   Amsterdam, 1719.

23   *Recueil,* p. 13.

24   *Ibid.*

25   *Ibid.*

26   Bibl. Nat. (Paris), Fr. 5853, f. 12–17.

27   ATdoT, Miscell. MS 170, ff. 402–3.

28   For a full discussion of this episode, see J. Tessier, *Le Chevalier de Jant,* p. 240.

29   *Loc. cit.,* p. 243.

30   L. d'Azevedo, *Historia de Antonio Vieira, S.J.* i. 156.

31   Bibl. Nat. Fr. 5853, f. 27.

32   *Ibid,* f. 31.

33   E. Prestage, *Diplomatic Relations of Portugal,* p. 56. This is not in Jant's own version.

34   Bibl, Nat., Fr. 5853, f. 41–4.

35   J. Tessier, *Le Chevalier de Jant,* pp 246–50.

36 A.V. Nunz. Di Francia 109, ff. 500v (for Coutinho); f. 636v (for Jant).

37 Bibl. D'Ajuda (Lisbon), Mss. cod. 51–vii–29, ff. 262–3.

38 O'Daly to Mazarin, 18 February 1658 (*Correspondencia de Portugal*, iv 143).

39 Bibl. D'Ajuda, MS 51–v–41, ff. 7–10 (Findings of Council of State for 2, 8, 20 March 1656).

40 Quoted in J. Tessier, *Le Chevalier de Jant*, p. 65.

41 Bibl. D'Ajuda, MS 51–iii–58, f. 586.

42 A.TdoT., MS de S. Vicente, xiv, 63.

43 A.V. Nunz.di Francia 110, ff. 200–206.

44 De Brienne to João IV, 20 May 1656 (*Correspondiencia de Portugal*, lv. 71).

45 *Ibid*, p. 60.

46 Bibl. D'Ajuda, COD. 51–v–41 f. 41v. (Findings of Council of State, 11 July 1656).

47 *Loc. Cit.*

48 *Ibid*, f. 43 (Findings of Council of State, 26 July 1656).

49 A.TdoT. Ms de S. Vincente, vol. 22, f. 190.

50 *Ibid*, ff. XIX–XXX. 413–414.

51 De Souse Coutinho to João IV, I April 1656 (*Corpo Diplomatico Portugueza*, xii, 280–282.

52 The *Instructions* for O'Daly's second mission are to be found in several published sources, that of Sancho Baena, *Notas e Documentas ineditos*, p. 71 and that of E. Prestage, *Frai Domiingos do Rosario, Diplomata e Politico*, pp 70–3.

53 A.V. Nunz. Da Francia 110, f. 465v.

54 National Library Lisbon (Reservados), V. de Gusman Soares, *Ultimas Accões de Rey D. João IV/ Nosso Senhor*, Lisbon MDCLVII.

55 H. Raposa, *Luisa de Gusmão*, pp 226–9.

V

ROYAL MATCHMAKING

Brave Cromwell (and his valiant blades)
Who hath conquered Kingdoms three
And made the war the best of trades
And made it like to be.

His actions 'tis I do intend
T'expose unto your view;
Therefore no Muse I need to friend,
Nor ought but to speak true

Jockey's Defeat makes all the earth
Abundantly to know Him;
His fame yet finds a second birth
From Zim, and Gim, and Chim.

O would he keep but his command
For one half file of years,
I'd lose my head he'd clear the land
Of Teigs and Cavaliers.[1]

This ballad appeared in a Cork-printed newspaper of 1649,
the first of its kind in Ireland. Only one number of *The Irish
Monthly Mercury* exists, and it remains a literary curiosity

with its faulty orthography and quaint punctuation. In tone it bids high for Cromwellian favours by eulogising, in unmistakeable terms, the career of that general, but its merit lies in the amount of social history it contains.

Though broadsides and news sheets had been appearing on the continent since the beginning of the century, it was only with the abolition of the Star-chamber in 1641 that the free exercise of the press began to manifest itself in England, Scotland and Ireland. To Rinuccini is given the credit, erroneously, of introducing the idea of newspapers into Ireland, but in fact intense pamphleteering activity went on throughout the whole decade of the confederate wars, representing the political propaganda of each of the parties.[2] These pamphlets found a wide circulation both at home and on the continent, and in their limited way, they make interesting reading as they show evidence of a political consciousness among the common people. In a sense they make vocal the uncomplicated, even misguided, political aspirations of the popular mind. The south was particularly active during the confederate wars, and a marked feature of this type of journalism was that the cities tended to represent the prevailing political creed. So in Waterford, the cause of the native or 'old' Irish was manifested most strongly. Cork, when not parliamentarian, was purely royalist while Kilkenny championed the cause of the Anglo-Irish of the Pale.

Apart from the political pamphlets that were printed in Ireland, many more were printed abroad and were offered to the continental public in various European languages. In 1644, a twenty-page pamphlet in Portuguese was issued in Lisbon. It was printed by the reputable Lisbon printer Craesbeecka, and its anonymous author set out to give 'a short, true account of the present kingdom of Ireland, together with letters of important persons, and information of certain men of credit'. It succeeded in being a sober account of the causes and progress of the '41

Rebellion to the close of 1643 as viewed from the standpoint of the 'old Irish'.[3] From Frankfurt in 1647, came a pamphlet entitled *Political Manifestations de Jure Regni Hiberniae*, which received wide circulation. In England, Thomason, the tract-collector, added *A Bloudy Fight in Ireland* to his monumental collection.[4] Examining pamphlets such as these, one gets a vivid impression of what may be termed 'the popular mind', and the attitudes of different sections of the people towards politics, religion and law.

One other stream of folk-thought in Ireland at this period has not received its due consideration from the historian: the Jacobite poetry that seemed to rise spontaneously from the people after the collapse of the native hegemony in 1607. The term 'Jacobite' for this poetry is indicative of its predominant quality: its hope in the Stuart cause. The sombre *'Muscail do mhisneach, a Bhanba'* appeared in 1646, ushering in a kind of love poetry whose subject was no mortal woman but the spirit of Ireland, the *spéirbhean*, whose fortunes were bound up with 'the coming of the prince', who was always a Stuart. Unlike the political pamphlets of this time which were written in an execrable style, this poetry flowed in remarkable and beautiful rhythm, appealing to the emotions and to the intelligence. The poems were eagerly received and retained by a semi-literate peasantry who passed them down orally to the succeeding generation. The Stuarts were not regarded by the Irish people in the same light as the Tudors. James I was the son of the martyred Mary, Queen of Scots. His son, Charles I, had married the Catholic Henrietta Maria. Instinctively, the mass of the Irish people feared the anti-monarchical forces in England, a dread realised in the person of Cromwell. Welded into unity by the Cromwellian persecution, Ireland was to be found defending the English monarchy, eventually supplying the last military effort for James II at the close of the century.[5]

By 1652, O'Daly seems to have been the acknowledged representative of Charles Stuart in Portugal, as there are two fleeting references to him in that year. The first is a grudging tribute from Ormond saying that he had written to Father O'Daly, 'who, I am told, is in good credit in that court (Lisbon) to employ his endeavours in obtaining what is desired by the king'.[6] The other reference is a rather trivial one to a sum of English money confiscated by the Portuguese ministers, 'none of whom are disposed to favour King Charles except Father Domingos Rosario, a loyal and true subject'. What makes it interesting is that it was written to Charles Stuart himself.[7]

The execution of Charles I in January 1649 focused the interest of all royalists on his eldest son, Charles Stuart. In Paris, as Nuncio di Bagno notes, he was immediately given the title of King of England, though his mother, Henrietta Maria, still treated him as a schoolboy and kept him in pocket money.[8] He had inherited from her grace, charm and a certain Gallic levity. His dark sardonic looks were a reminder of his Italian grandmother, Maria de Medici. Unfortunately for him, he had derived much of her capricious irresponsibility too. Gifted with an acute intelligence, he had been given as tutor William Cavendish, Lord Newcastle, who had allowed his young charge every gratification of his sensual nature, and had given him complete licence in carrying out his own will. A bewildering mixture of races, he had a genuine appreciation of honesty and virtue while his pretended indifference to things of the spirit masked a religious sensibility that oscillated between Catholicism and Protestantism.

He had an assured position in the French court by reason of his talent for witty conversation and his rare distinction of manners; however, the Vatican ambassador shrewdly observed that Charles Stuart was an unhappy man:

> The Prince of Wales does not find here all satisfaction and pleasure. Adversity has made him accustomed to dissimulation and to patience. At certain times he is prone to moodiness and grieves because he has not been able to procure the promised aid and that his financial embarrassment, as a king, has rendered him powerless to make peace overtures.[9]

From April 1649 onward, he had been persistently besieging his mother to consent to his departure for Scotland or Ireland, whither he had been invited. George Digby, the royalist agent, had worked for years on his own cherished scheme to bring Charles Stuart over to Ireland, hoping that his mere presence there would make it possible to launch a united confederate-royalist assault. He urged the queen-mother to allow her son to go to Ireland and had been put off with a vague promise at some unspecified date.[10]

In Edinburgh, Charles Stuart was proclaimed king on 5 February 1649, and public opinion in Scotland was with him. Ormond followed suit and issued a proclamation in those parts of Ireland under his control. The Scots in Ulster also acknowledged the new king. France maintained no diplomatic relations with the commonwealth, and by 23 July it was common property in St Germain that the King of England was believed to be going to Ireland on the instance of Colonel Preston and the Marquis of Ormond. On 24 September, the French nuncio reported the departure of Charles for Jersey; on 31 October, Charles issued his declaration of rights. Cromwell's lightning campaign in Ireland effectively closed the country as a base, and when a parliamentary fleet from Portsmouth appeared off Jersey on 13 February 1650, Charles set sail and took refuge in Breda.

There followed six months of intense royalist activity on the continent and in those parts of Ireland and Scotland that still held for the king. At Ostend, Windham was the agent; in Sweden, Robert Meade was busy on the Stuart cause in that court which had come to life under the young Christina. In Spain, five royalists had set upon the parliamentary representative of the commonwealth there and recently received covert sympathy from the partially-embarrassed King Philip. In Portugal, Mr Vane, Cromwell's resident, was withdrawn in June 1650. He had met with a cold reception there because he was thought by the English parliament to be of no political value. This was not surprising in view of the fact that Prince Rupert's declaration urging the Portuguese to help the cause of Charles Stuart had appeared two months earlier in Lisbon and had received an enthusiastic reception.[11]

Not only were the Portuguese sympathetic to the Stuart cause but João IV had tacitly allowed the queen's confessor, Frei Domingos do Rosario, to act as an agent for Charles Stuart. This is borne out by a letter of de Sousa Coutinho to João IV when the former was ambassador at Paris. Though undated, it has been calendared as January 1649. He wrote:

Yesterday, with the dispatch I received from Your Majesty, I saw the king of England (Charles II). He was very pleased with the proposal. I also mentioned to him that Your Majesty was sending a religious to Ireland under the pretext of raising troops, but the real reason was to see if anything could be done to serve His Majesty (Charles), whom your Majesty highly esteemed, and he wished to know the name of the religious. I told him Frei Domingos do Rosario, although Your Majesty had not mentioned his name to me but my wife had told me ... The king wished me to write to Frei Domingos and for him to bring a letter I would direct to Prince Rupert and to the Marquis of Ormond, Viceroy of the kingdom, and I shall warn Frei Domingos to take the necessary precautions. The king is resolved to go to Ireland but under no circumstances to go to Scotland.[12]

Neither Charles Stuart nor O'Daly went to Ireland that time. The King was dissuaded by his friends as a memorial drawn up by a certain Colonel Price serves to illustrate:

That His Majesty should weigh well what assurance he depends for his army in Ireland, and because we here suppose it to be an army united of several interests; that the generals have had particular animosities one towards the other, and the greatest design is by money to continue these jealousies, and at last secure one party, to the betraying of the rest of Scotland ... His Majesty's party in England is so poor, so disjointed, so severely watched by both the other factions that it is impossible for them to do anything on their own score ... We propose, first, for Ireland whether His Majesty can with safety go thither; first by reason of the jealousies before mentioned; next if he goes with no force, he will appear too little to his friends and discourage them. If he draws a considerable power thither, he is sure to encounter all the power that these people can throw on him, and engage so far off, and, perhaps so long a time, that all his friends will be ruined here, and the present government acknowledged and habitual ... Whether if it be not possible for His Majesty to go (to Scotland and deal) so with the Presbyterians in England with just ... Whether if His Majesty yields to their ambassadors, it is not probable that his power will soon rise again, if once he appear acknowledged by his three kingdoms and his people have liberty to repair to his service.[13]

In January 1650, James Graham, 2nd Marquis of Montrose, set up the royal standard in Scotland. Before the news of his overthrow had reached Charles, he accepted the commissioners' terms, which imposed the covenant on him and upon the entire Scottish nation so that all civil affairs would be determined by the parliament. Charles arrived in Scotland at Cromerty on 16 June 1650 and pledged himself to support the Presbyterian religion in both England and Scotland.[14] Though he was crowned king of Scotland on 1 January of the following year, Cromwell defeated him decisively at Worcester nine months later, and after an amazing series of adventures Charles sailed from Brighton for France on 15 October.

Frei Domingos O'Daly did not go to Ireland either, though his master general had given him a permission which was entered in the Registers, and which stated that the friar could go to Ireland with the power of nominating a substitute vicar in his absence from Lisbon.[15] It was dated 6 January 1649, and in fact O'Daly was absent from Portugal for most of the following year, Father James Arthur, O.P., acting as vicar in his stead. In a letter to Ormond, undated but received by Sir James Preston, 28 August 1650, O'Daly is explicit in stating why he did not go to Ireland. Though written in a rather florid, sonorous style, it repays scrutiny as the letter conveys certain nuances and shades of meaning made popular by the pamphleteering activity of those years:

> Most excellent Lord Lieutenant: I am extremely sorry I cannot have the happiness to kiss your hands having failed to convenience His Majesty, who was pleased to appoint me, the time limited for my appearance to Rome being near expired, which depriving me of fully filling my intentions for Ireland, constrains me to be troublesome to Your Excellency with these lines.

> I was employed by the king of Portugal to His Majesty of Great Britain, who by reason of the correspondence I had before with his father and himself grounded on my past endeavours in his affairs in the court of Lisbon.

> I presume to signify Your Excellency how His Majesty commanded me to deliver my mind plainly to him in all I understood in the cause of Ireland. And I possessed H.M. (according to my opinion) that the agreement and settlement of that kingdom consisted principally in the fruition of the privileges of a free kingdom, as Ireland is deserving it better than any of H.M. dominions for to show themselves more loyal in their later revolutions for which they should not be of worst conditions, rather enjoying larger privileges for the future example and consequence. I added how it was against natural law that a kingdom should be under another but only

dependent from their king immediately, according to the conditions of all nations. Whereunto I found His Majesty well-disposed, but his council most adverse, whom I cannot blame herein for not concurring to deprive themselves of the government and disposition of that kingdom.

If what I offer here for commission in lieu of moneys may seem to Your Eminence to merit the charge of an express, Mr. King may be entrusted therein who hath instructions how and where to find me, who humbly craves Y.E.'s pardon for the liberty I assume to express myself, and the desire I have manifest by some better testimony my zeal to serve the country and Y.E. in pursuance of the resolution I have taken to purchase by my uttermost endeavours the esteem and title of Milord.[16]

Several interesting facts emerge from this rather pompous letter. From the first line it is evident that O'Daly received a commission from Charles to go to Ireland. He did not go because he had to be in Rome by a fixed date in 1650 for the general chapter of his order. He was empowered by King João IV of Portugal to act for His Majesty of Great Britain, Charles II. He had previously done some business for Charles I and the then prince of Wales in Lisbon.

He is deferential toward the Marquis of Ormond despite the fact that Ormond had shown such little faith in the confederates and in his Catholic countrymen. 'They hold continual intelligence and dangerous correspondence with foreign nations and have at this time amongst them a nuncio from the pope and agents from France and Spain', Ormond had written sourly, and here was one of these very agents meddling in the affairs of Charles Stuart at this critical juncture. His own reaction to O'Daly's letter is typical – a line of horrified comment. 'Father Daniel O'Daly … with his demands for a free Ireland, and this friar was rewarded by the king and queen and Lord Jermyn as having very good pretensions'.[17]

Was the friar merely making vocal the 'popular mind' of a certain class of his fellow countrymen?

> The agreement and settlement of that kingdom consisted principally in the fruition of the privileges of a free kingdom as Ireland is deserving it better than any of H. M. dominion ... it was against natural law that a kingdom should be under another but only dependent from their king immediately, according to the conditions of all nations.

The idea of one king ruling over three kingdoms seems to have been acceptable as the prevailing political theory about the relationship of Great Britain and Ireland in the seventeenth century. O'Daly uses the phrase, so also does Colonel Price in his *Memorial,* and later the Venetian ambassador in London employs the term continually in his reports back to the Doge. When O'Daly used the phrase, 'dependent from their king immediately, according to the conditions of all nations', was he speaking as a Thomistic theologian familiar with *De Regimine* of Aquinas, or merely an Irishman with a strong pro-Stuart bias, to whom the idea of one king reigning over a loose federation of sister-kingdoms, so far from being repugnant, was most desirable?

Of his personal qualities we have formed some opinion and there seems to have been no end to his many-sided interests. His social contacts were everywhere and represented all walks of life. For one who played a relatively hidden and unspectacular part in the various negotiations with which he was concerned, O'Daly takes up far more space in state papers and diplomatic correspondence than the scattered references indicate. There is one other factor that contributes to a man's personality, especially as it expresses itself in political activity, namely group behaviour. O'Daly's position as an Irishman emerges clearly. It is obvious from his letter that his years in Portugal had not made him less an Irishman, and his claim for a 'free Ireland' was in keeping with the manifestation of the popular mind as exhibited in the prevailing political pamphlets. But to what group did O'Daly belong?

It is only from occasional remarks in Rinnucini's correspondence, or from almost casual observations thrown out at random by some thoughtful contemporary observer that the modern mind forms some idea of the actual political atmosphere of a period as viewed through the eyes of one living at that time. So the prevailing mood in Ireland was caught and held like the proverbial fly in amber by just such a casual observer in 1650. Writing from Rome concerning the abbot of Newry, the Spanish ambassador, the Duque del Infantada, gives a thumbnail sketch of the political situation prior to Cromwell's landing. For sheer comprehension and condensation, it is admirable in its brief way.

He described the two factions; one mainly consisting of the Old Irish headed by the O'Neills who looked to Spain for help; the other, chiefly the Anglo-Irish, claimed dependence on England and France. Their leaders were Ormond and Inchiquin. Cardinal Mazarin, on behalf of the king of France, solicited the support of the second group and had an agent in Ireland for this purpose, but, added the duke, Crilly, the abbot of Newry, had sought to checkmate their plans saying that help from Spain was expected shortly. To further Mazarin's design, the queens of England and France sent Father Daly, a Dominican, to treat with King Charles in England, and to pass from thence to Ireland where he was to continue those negotiations.[18]

No help for Charles Stuart came from Spain, uncertain whether political etiquette demanded they recognise the commonwealth or the son of the executed king. Unexpectedly, support came from Portugal in the shape of a small fleet. On 29 September 1650, the nuncio in Paris reported a clash between twenty-three English and

Portuguese vessels with twenty-five vessels of Cromwell outside the harbour of Lisbon. The nuncio reported that the king of Portugal had financed the Stuart expedition. Even before the expedition had taken place, O'Daly had gone to Rome ostensibly to take part in the general chapter of his order, and secretly with a commission from Henrietta Maria to treat with the pope for her son. The nuncio had interested himself in the project and had written privately to the cardinal secretary on O'Daly's behalf. 'Among the most capable Irish subjects I know', he had written on 10 April:

> it seems to me that the Reverend Father Master Dominic of the Rosary, the Dominican, is most zealous for the preservation and union of good Catholics in that kingdom. I know Master Dominic is greatly esteemed and very powerful in his country. Hoping to be of use to it, he did not hesitate to use all means which could succour it in any way. Motivated by the highest zeal he has considered it well to go and to give an account to His Holiness and to Your Eminence.

There was far more at issue in Rome just then, a matter to which the carefully-worded letter of the nuncio conveyed subtly.[19] It was urgent that Father Dominic have an audience with the pope, *prima facie* to treat the affair of Charles Stuart. In fact, he hoped to lay before Pope Innocent X the true and miserable state of the Church of Portugal without arousing the suspicion of the Spanish ambassador. Meynell, royalist agent in Rome, resumed the story. For him, it was his prime concern and he obviously had no inkling of O'Daly's other business with the pope. Writing to Cottington and Hyde on 24 June, he noted that:

> Daniel O'Daly, the Irish Dominican, was with the present king at Jersey and came from him extremely satisfied ... there is small hope of his effecting anything at Rome as the queen's authority is much on the wane here.

Some weeks later he reported that:

a flat answer had been given to Fr. Daniel O'Daly that he cannot at all meddle in this business. Apparently the pope will not be persuaded to part with money.[20]

Meynell's ironic second report seems most probable that the 'flat answer' referred to O'Daly's mission from João IV on church matters, while the refusal to part with money alluded to the Stuart mission. O'Daly returned to Paris with his report for Henrietta Maria. It was in keeping with his personality that wherever he went, he became involved in adventure. This time he was entrusted by the master-general with the care of young Philip Howard, grandson of the earl of Arundel and destined to restore the Dominican order in England. Philip's flight from home and entry into the order had caused the master-general some embarrassment, and in November 1650, he seized gratefully the opportunity of sending the young Englishman away from the trying Italian climate and the badgering of relatives to Rennes to complete his studies.

O'Daly also carried letters with him in French from the master-general to Henrietta Maria. In one letter, he stated that Father Dominic of the Rosary would give her an account of his journey to Rome. Evidently the friar was acting not merely as the agent of Charles Stuart, but also in a semi-official status which had the full approval of his sovereign and the approbation of his master-general. At least three documents in the chancery of João IV refer to the Dominican's absence on government affairs from Lisbon. The dates given are 13 March 1649, 27 January 1650 and 2 March 1655. The documents are orders for four measures of corn for his friars during his absence.[21]

'A loyal and true subject', Robert Cooke had called O'Daly, when writing to Charles Stuart in March 1652. In the years that elapsed between that observation and the return of O'Daly to Paris as Portuguese ambassador in November 1656, 'to propose in the name of the infanta of Portugal to the king', as the nuncio observes maliciously, the Irish friar had not forgotten the cause of Charles Stuart. Nor had Luisa de Gusmão. As early as 1644, she had envisaged a marriage between Joanna, eldest daughter of the Bragança house and the then prince of Wales. The project had to be reluctantly abandoned because of the political insecurity of the English throne. Joanna died in 1653, and the queen of Portugal fixed her hopes on Catherine, her second daughter.

Few figures of this era are as pathetic as Catherine of Bragança. Brought up in a court which was austere and gloomy, under the severe tutelage of a strong-minded mother, the young princess had received no formal education, and remained gauche and timid at an age when most young girls are consciously aware of their charms and are achieving some measure of social success. To the end of her life, Catherine was to suffer from an overwhelming shyness. Yet, Luisa de Gusmão lost no time in furthering her cherished scheme of marrying her daughter to Louis XIV, not realising that to the fastidious young French king, Portugal lagged behind in the world's race. Her court was stiff, formal and hedged in with iron conventions. Her nobles were sombre and unbending in a rut of outmoded codes of behaviour. Her women were secluded in a privacy that was a reminder of the days of the Moors. Certainly the young princess was taught to embroider delicately, to sing sacred music, to assist with devotion at long religious ceremonies, but she was unschooled in any of the arts and graces which were a prerequisite for the first lady of France. Outside the palace walls existed a world of which she knew nothing and for which she always had a minimum curiosity.

Without great beauty, as many of her contemporaries testify, the portrait now hanging in the Museu Nacional dos Coches in Lisbon reveals a face that is both pretty and intelligent, and a slight graceful figure which is full of dignity. Black curling hair springs away from a forehead too high for the contemporary conventions of beauty. Her magnificent eyes have a sad expression that deepens with each portrait by later court-painters in England. Her mouth has a certain primness and a hint of sulkiness, a trait which unfortunately manifested itself quite often in the early years of married life, until Catherine's intelligence warned her to change her tactics. Her untried prettiness in the Portuguese portrait painted when she was seventeen contrasts with the later portrait by John Husyman as queen of England where her expression seems to be one of disciplined suffering. According to the Venetian ambassador to England, Giovanni Sagredo, she was 'bela'. Mde de Motteville, perhaps the most delightful of all court-gossips, who wrote *Memoires*, recalled that Anne of Austria was captivated by the Nocret miniature, (now lost), of the young princess and confided to her, Mde de Motteville, her hopes of gaining Catherine as a daughter-in-law. Unfortunately, Mde de Motteville added irrepressibly that it was common tattle in Paris that Queen Luisa was offering large sums to make her daughter queen of France.[22] It was not that Catherine's looks were at fault but rather that her personality seemed colourless and undeveloped in comparison with the scornful assurance of a Barbara Castlemaine.

O'Daly landed at Le Harve and reached his post in Paris early in November. His arrival there was heralded by rumours founded on fact but exaggerated out of all proportions. Sir Richard Browne, English royalist resident at the court of St Germain, voiced the gossip then current in the French court:

> I saw yesterday letters in a Frenchman's hands newly come from Rouen, which have Father Daily (the Irish Dominican) being put ashore at Harve le Grace by an English ship come from Lisbon. This is true for if he came not hither last night, he is expected here this day. But what truth there is in the letter, or, in case it is true, how it should come to be some merchant's news I much doubt; namely, that he brings the offer of the

king of Portugal's daughter for this king with three million of ready money, thirty tall ships entertained in the service of this crown for six years, and a quadruple league offensive and defensive between France, Sweden, Portugal and England; in which last article God forbid any subject of His Majesty (Charles II) who pretends – as this man doth – to be loyal, should ever prove instrumental.[23]

A few days later Browne was again writing to Nicholas. Cromwell was rumoured to have provided the means of transportation for the Portuguese envoy and to have given 'particular orders' to the ship that brought him.[24] Browne's concern about the colour of O'Daly's English politics serves as a timely introduction to a problem which must have troubled the Irish friar from time to time, as he became increasingly identified with Portuguese foreign policy abroad.

In the previous March O'Daly had a long talk with Monsignor di Bagno, papal nuncio at Paris. The nuncio had asked him outright what was his attitude and his patron's towards joining the league between England, France and Sweden then being mooted. From January 1655 onwards, it was clear that the Holy See was perturbed by the idea of a league between the Protestant countries of Europe, Sweden and England, and the Catholic countries, France and Portugal. Frequently, in his letters to the nuncios at Paris and Madrid, the cardinal secretary had expressed the Holy Father's concern with the continued disharmony between the Catholic powers of Europe which, as a consequence, obliged alliances between Catholic and Protestant countries.[25]

Looking back from the vantage-point of the twenty-first century, one can understand something of the changing pattern of politics in the post-Westphalian period, and the emergence of France as a primary power with an entirely new concept of statecraft. To many monarchs, and in particular to the Holy See, France seemed deeply involved in the double struggle of the Fronde and the Port-Royal heresy, and for some time yet they were to look on Spain as a hidden menace. In truth, Spain had been a waning power for nearly half a century, and Rocroi (1643) had smashed her one claim to prestige, her infantry. Her small Portuguese neighbour, by persistent defensive war at the frontiers and diplomacy abroad, completed, more effectively than has been assessed, the decline of Spain.

João IV's position in regard to the commonwealth of England was delicate. Until the death of Charles I, there had been sympathy for the Stuart cause in Portugal, and in the months following his execution, the royalist cause in Lisbon had prospered. Prince Rupert and Prince Maurice, who were initially received by João IV with kindness, began early in 1650 to make Lisbon a base for semi-piratical operations. The parliament of England sent its representative, Charles Vane, to make an appeal to the king of Portugal. Though the king had received him courteously, he had not acceded to the demands of the English parliament and Vane departed. In May of the same year, Cromwell sent a squadron under General Blake to blockade the harbour of Lisbon, thus forcing the Portuguese into the position of giving battle. Much to their own astonishment they were victorious and Blake retreated, but the impression remained that the Portuguese were covertly supporting the royalist cause.[26]

João IV was a realist. With a war at the frontier and an unsatisfactory ally in France, he could not afford to have a fractious naval power in his harbour. He resolved to establish relations with the *ipso facto* government of England and sent an envoy to London, 27 January 1650, to open negotiations with Cromwell for a treaty. The mission was a complete failure. With that quiet tenacity which was the cornerstone of Portuguese foreign policy, João IV dispatched another envoy to England and was rewarded when the Speaker introduced the preliminary articles to the English parliament on 29 December 1652. The treaty was finally signed at Westminster in July 1654. For England it was a complete diplomatic victory. It had become evident in the two years that Mazarin was abandoning Portugal, and the English alliance became increasingly desirable. But Cromwell made João IV pay dearly for it.

The treaty was only ratified by Portugal in June of 1656. João IV, a religious man and a lover of liberty, had grave doubts about the two articles concerning religious freedom. The Holy See had not recognised Portugal as a monarchy separate from Spain and had maintained a disapproving attitude towards the small country ever since the Castracani affair, breaking off formal diplomatic relations shortly after the accession of João IV. It was of major importance for Portugal to get papal recognition. Signing a treaty with Cromwell was hardly the best way to conciliate the Holy See. Yet, João IV knew that if he refused to sign that treaty of alliance, he would plunge his county into greater danger. The treaty offered was prejudicial to his country's freedom, and in his slow, careful way, he searched for a solution to his dilemma. A few months before his death an answer presented itself to him. With deliberation and in spite of the remonstraces of Don Diego de Lima, he selected Frei Domingos do Rosario as the man best suited to his mission. O'Daly was dispatched a second time to Paris as his accredited minister and his written *Instructions* were to negotiate the '*liga formal*', and to effect a marriage alliance. It was clear by the following May that Portugal would have to abandon completely its demands as laid down by the first *cortes* of 1641. It was then that O'Daly played his second card.

The year 1656 had ended badly for Portugal. The Spaniards, thinking that the country was enfeebled by the death of its king, and by the regency of a woman – a Spaniard at that – planned an extensive operation, offensive in nature, to be carried out in the following spring. The Dutch, too, had been growing restive. In 1653, they had been reduced to the last extremity in Brazil and held only one city Pernambuco and four ports. Pernambuco capitulated early in the new year. After some hesitation, the united states of the Netherlands, under pressure from the Dutch company of the West Indies, decided on war with Portugal, even though Friesland and several towns in the Netherlands protested. In April 1657, the Dutch began to prepare a fleet to bombard Lisbon. O'Daly in Paris gave Mazarin serious warning that a Spanish invasion of Portugal seemed imminent. The veteran troops of Catalonia, he declared, were being ordered to march into Portugal and Philip himself rumoured to be at the head of the army. O'Daly suggested that the French stage a diversion in Catalonia because the United Provinces were tending to unite with Spain. Immediately, the French government rushed instructions to its minister at The Hague, de Thou. Hot upon the French heels came a query from Cromwell to The Hague. Bluntly he demanded to know if the Madrid cabinet was at the back of the recent Dutch activity.[27]

The Netherlands stated that their only object in sending a fleet to Lisbon was to demand reparation for the injuries suffered by them in Brazil and had nothing to do with Spain. With this doubtful assurance Mazarin and Cromwell had to be content, but it forced them to consider seriously the alternative João IV and O'Daly had both seen as a possibility: a quadruple alliance. Previously, in February, the nuncio in Paris had written a long worried letter to the cardinal secretary, saying that there was a meeting of ministers in Paris just then: the Dutch ambassador, the Portuguese (O'Daly), the secretary of state from Sweden and a gentleman from Cromwell. 'It does not auger well for peace' he wrote anxiously and went on to discuss the vanishing chances of a universal peace.

Evidently he did not let the matter rest there. In two later reports, he tells how he remonstrated first with Mazarin and then with O'Daly on the pernicious effect of an alliance between Catholic and Protestant powers. He was pleased to tell the cardinal secretary that his words had made an impression, Mazarin being temporarily embarrassed, and O'Daly confused and harassed by the conflicting demands of church and state policy in Lisbon.[28]

That was in April. Cromwell was still uneasy. Mazarin recovered his composure which had been ruffled by the reproaches of the nuncio. O'Daly, though passing through the most trying period of his diplomatic career, remained on the whole impervious to the censures of the nuncio. On 23 June, Afonso VI, acting through his mother, sent instructions to O'Daly to negotiate the inclusion of Portugal in a quadruple alliance consisting of France, England and Sweden as the other parties instead of the former elusive league between France and Portugal. Simultaneously, the Lisbon *cortes* decided to send the Marquis de Sande, hero of the Alentejo frontier, to London to work towards the quadruple alliance from that end. If the proposals in London were well-received, negotiations would then be opened directly with France and Sweden. O'Daly was ordered to delay all transactions in Paris pending the results of Sande's mission to London.[29]

It was Sande's first diplomatic mission. A soldier by choice, he had distinguished himself in the war against Spain. He had received a good education, was polished and cultured in manner, and was favoured with many natural gifts. He became one of the finest Portuguese diplomats of this period. His *Instructions*, given 10 July 1657, were as indicated in Afonso's letter to O'Daly: to speak to Cromwell on the advantages of including Portugal in a quadruple alliance, and to offer Portuguese harbours to the English fleet as bases of operation.[30]

It is at this juncture of English politics that the urbane and ubiquitous personage of the Venetian ambassador insinuates himself into the scene. Always in European affairs, the Venetian ambassador stands apart and comments in a detached way on the passing cavalcade. He is especially proficient in giving magnificent character sketches of the great personages he observes, but he has little use for the lesser fry whom he rarely mentions. He sums up with skill the implications of the contemporary political scene. He is wise, acutely observant, with a mind for, and grasp of, the most minute details which he narrates selectively and judges without passion. The Venetian ambassador is indispensable for an understanding of European history. He had centuries of tradition and training to guide him.

Although in general Venice was in decline during the seventeenth century and was preoccupied with the Turks, her diplomats were still a powerful influence in every court. At this period she was in opposition to Spanish policy and was concerned to get Cromwell's help against the Turks. Therefore, the Venetian ambassador in London, Giovanni Sagredo, one of the most valuable and well-informed representatives of the republic just then, gave full reports on the change that was taking place in England during the closing years of Cromwell's regime. Sagredo's analysis of Cromwell and his pretentions to monarchy is pitiless but masterly. The 1654 treaty between England and Portugal, which had been such a humiliation to the troubled conscience of João IV, began to yield its long-term dividends towards the end of 1657. Imperceptibly it had begun for Portugal the transference of power from Paris to London, and by 1657, it was clear to the observant that for Portugal, two broad streams of foreign policy were converging. Charles Stuart would be restored as king of England. Peace between France and Spain was imminent. By the English alliance, Portugal would steer clear of

Spanish absorption or French integration. To O'Daly goes the credit for keeping open friendly relations between the Portuguese monarchy and the shabby king without a throne. To Sande was entrusted the precarious task of harmonising the official status between the restored English monarch and the Portuguese government which could have been destabilised by a reminder of its Cromwellian associations. The adjustment was effected by the wedding alliance between Charles II and Catherine of Bragança.

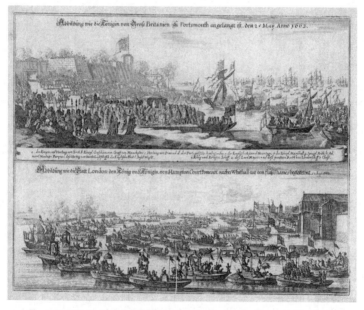

Engraving of the arrival of Catherine of Bragança in England
courtesy of the National Portrait Gallery, London

Maried May A°1662

Marriage of Catherine of Bragança and Charles II
courtesy of the National Portrait Gallery, London

'This was not a simple marriage between the king of England and a princess, but of the kingdom of England and the kingdom of Portugal', the Venetian ambassador remarked thoughtfully.[31] Frequently in the course of history the marriages of a monarch's children have been arranged to serve the interests of a dynasty rather than those of the persons concerned. All matrimonial settlements in the immediate family of João IV were directed towards the strengthening of Portugal's position by alliances with the leading royal families of Europe. At various times, schemes were put forward to unite the Portuguese and French royal houses. The untimely death of Theodosio, oldest son of João IV in 1653 ended, or rather rescued him, from a projected match with the elderly duchess of Montpensier, niece of Louis XIII. In the same year, 1653, Joanna, eldest daughter of the Braganças died, and all hopes were centred on Catherine.

When the Jesuit Antonio Vieira returned from Brazil two years later, he suggested to the king the desirability of an alliance between Catherine and Louis XIV. The king incorporated the projected match into O'Daly's *Instructions* as the friar was on the point of leaving for France. No hint is given about O'Daly's private feelings on the matter. In a letter to the queen, when his mission had failed, he assured her with dignity that 'his sole desire was to serve Her Majesty in any place or capacity'.[32] Nevertheless, his heart was not in the projected marriage. That an alliance with the house of Bragança was entertained seriously in Paris, especially by Anne of Austria, is evident from the reports of the Venetian ambassadors in Madrid and Paris who arrived at the same conclusions independently from observation. The French interests were running in counter direction with the young king proving unexpectedly restive with the decisions being made about his future queen.[33]

Henrietta Maria, exiled widow of Charles I, had spoken to O'Daly on the subject of a marriage between her son Charles and one of the Portuguese princesses. By Joanna's death, Catherine became the infanta of Portugal and one of the richest heiresses of Europe. There were other English and Irish exiles on the continent who had the projected Stuart-Bragança marriage at heart. Peter Talbot, close friend of Charles Stuart and later the archbishop of Dublin, was in contact with O'Daly in Paris, and they discussed the matter as a means of furthering the Stuart cause and of bringing about the conversion of Charles Stuart to the Catholic religion. A letter of Talbot's to Charles Stuart from Paris, 5 May 1656, confirms this and shows O'Daly still 'a loyal and true subject'. He guaranteed supplies from the king of Portugal as Charles Stuart needed them.[34] Richard Russell, S.J., the superior of the English college in Lisbon, greatly desired this alliance too, and he played his part in due course to bring about the successful completion of his cherished ambition in 1661.

But Mazarin saw in O'Daly's *Instructions* for his second mission to Paris a heaven-sent opportunity, and while he had no intention of making Catherine of Bragança queen of France, he simulated a deep interest in the offer O'Daly brought. Indeed, to judge by the parallel reports of the Venetian ambassadors in Paris and Madrid at the close of 1656, Mazarin was by no means in favour of the Spanish match, fearing that the nation as a whole had what Giovanni Nani described as a 'natural aversion' for the alliance. Louis himself, the papal nuncio was not above reporting, was plunged in misery by the removal of his cherished *amanta*, niece of Mazarin, ruthlessly plucked from the French court by her uncle and married off to the duke of Savoy.[35] As early as 1655, Mazarin had decided on Marie Therese of Spain as the future wife of Louis, but no hint of his plans ever appeared in the official French documents of those years.

On reading the file of correspondence that passed between Luisa, acting regent of Portugal, and her ambassador in Paris for the months following the king's death, it is clear that a French marriage was uppermost in the queen's mind in an anxiously maternal way. One senses in the reproaches she hurls at the friar from time to time her keen disappointment over the non-realisation of this match. Her letter of 10 April 1657 to O'Daly still glows with her indignation, and she scolds her ambassador with an energy that raises a smile in the reader.[36] When O'Daly returned to Lisbon in the following July with the newly-appointed French ambassador, the Comte de Cominges, he had failed in his mission, but he had received an urgent communication from Sande to drop all negotiations and return to Lisbon before he, Sande, set out for London.[37]

What passed between the two has never been disclosed. In August, Sande travelled to England in an English ship, his companions being Father Richard Russell, S.J. and a certain 'Father Patrick' recommended by O'Daly. This Father Patrick was none other than Patrick Ghines or Maginn, later queen's almoner to Catherine, and 'to become chiefly useful for procuring access to His Majesty (Charles II) and conveying a message to him'.[38]

The event which made the Restoration of Charles Stuart a genuine possibility was the death of Oliver Cromwell, 'about three o'clock in the afternoon of Friday 3 September 1658'. In May 1660, came the official Restoration, one of the great watersheds in the history of the British Isles. Hardly were the celebrations of that event over when Afonso VI wrote to Charles II that Sande had powers to confirm existing treaties. Sande proposed immediately that Charles should marry Catherine, securing thereby the support of England in the struggle against Spain and Holland. Catherine's dowry was to include Bombay, Tangier and 500,000 *pistoles*. Despite the strenuous opposition of Clarendon, and the threats of the Spanish ambassador, Charles accepted both princess and dowry in the spring of 1661. Sande was rewarded for his services in this matter by being created Baron of Mullingar. Richard Russell was nominated bishop of Portalegre in Portugal in 1672, and six years later was still drawing wages as almoner of

Queen Catherine in Somerset House. His part in the marriage was noted by Charles in his first letter to Catherine: 'likewise, not forgetting the good Richard Russell, who laboured on his part to the very end'.[39] Father Patrick Maginn remained in London as almoner and though he was given a grant of a manor house, town and lands of Kilcowan, County Wexford in 1675, 'in consideration of his many and faithful services', he appears to have remained on at his post in London where it was reported that 'the king willingly listens to Ghines, in whom he places entire trust'.[40] According to Vincent Baron, the Dominican, then acting as Visitator in Lisbon for the master-general, Charles II wrote to O'Daly at his wife's instigation, and invited him to accept the posts of chaplain in her suite, a post the friar did not accept.[41]

With the signing of the marriage contract on 23 June 1661, a new chapter opened in the history of the Catholic church in England, and the sympathetic leanings of the king towards Catholicism led him eventually to profess that faith. There can be little doubt that O'Daly shared the conviction of his fellow countryman, Talbot, that a Catholic marriage for Charles II was most desirable and to be furthered in every way. Many of the Irish exiles on the continent showed a like attitude towards the restored Stuarts and were concerned deeply in promoting Catholic royal alliances: hopes which culminated with the coronation of James II.

What of Catherine herself, the pawn in all these negotiations? Frei Domingos had belonged to the intimate family circle that had known and watched Catherine grow up to become one of the most eligible heiresses in Europe. Had he no feelings of compassion for this young girl, educated so narrowly, submissive, retiring and untrained to take her place in the most corrupt court of Europe? Despised by many there because of her religion, a caricature full of spite and malice has been handed down to posterity; only in recent years has an attempt been made to assess her rightful place and to present her with her Portuguese heart and character.[42] To educate as a Portuguese one who was destined to be a queen in a foreign court was a cruel mistake on the part of her mother and those immediately concerned with her upbringing. There was present from the very beginning of her married life in England a dangerous duality in Catherine's behaviour: to live as Portuguese, and to act as queen of England. The initial mistake, together with her limited peninsular education and its narrowing cultural effects on her mind, were the main reasons for the antipathy of the English court, and they contributed more than she realised to her unhappiness as a young bride.

Yet the marriage was a success! From the outset, Catherine was utterly devoted to the graceless Charles. Most reliable women historians are agreed that her affection was reciprocated in as much as the complex nature of Charles allowed. She grew to tolerate his many misdemeanours, and to enjoy, in her rather prim way, his good humour and his irrepressible witticisms. A view of the two is given in 1675 by the Venetian ambassador, Morosini, who took a keen interest in the proceedings and reported them graciously from time to time. 'The king, Charles II', he noted:

> is approaching the age of forty-five, schooled to adversity, he shows nothing of it, or of good fortune, in his expression. A generous and intrepid soul, he is vivacious and frank, full of strength and scientific knowledge, to which he unites a natural affability which conciliates all. Possessing many languages, he usually speaks French and though he listens to Italian, prefers not to speak it.

Of Catherine he says:

> the queen is the sister of the king Don Afonso and of Don Pedro of Portugal, having come to England with a rich dowry; she is a princess endowed with remarkable gifts of soul and

possesses the greatest strength and prudence. She remains aloof from business and does not meddle in the public or private affairs of the kingdom. Loved by all, even the enemies of Catholicism admit her goodness, but she gives no son to the realm and this diminishes somewhat the applause she might otherwise get. The good results of her piety are most important for the Catholic religion here because she maintains the full splendour of the liturgical functions, and among the persecutions of this heresy, the free exercise of the Roman church shines out.[43]

Much more compelling is her own quiet testimony to her favourite brother, Pedro, in 1681 when she had come through the terrors and humiliations of the Popish plot. In a letter to this companion of her childhood and her closest confident, she wrote, 'I have all that I can want to make me completely satisfied with my life, nor do I wish to think that I have anything to desire'.

Politically, the alliance between England and Portugal yielded a rich harvest. David Ogg, in his study of the reign of Charles II, observed:

by 1662, Portugal had assumed a position of triangular importance in European diplomacy. She succeeded in maintaining the old alliance with England in the inter-regnum. She was a unit in the calculations of French diplomacy, and she succeeded in preserving the friendship of the exiled Stuarts.

That Daniel O'Daly had a large share in winning this position for Portugal seems clear. Sousa de Macedo, one-time secretary of state for João IV, writing in 1662, singled out this particular negotiation of Frei Domingos as his greatest contribution to Portuguese diplomacy; even though he remained at heart an Irishman whose hopes were placed in the Stuart cause.[44] The murmurs of disapproval which had been stilled by João IV's decisive action in sending the friar back to Paris as official ambassador were again becoming vocal during the troubled regency that followed the king's death.

NOTES

1   B.M. E595(5), *The Irish Monthly Mercury* (Cork, 1649).

2   J. Buckley, 'The First Irish Newspaper', in *Journal Cork Hist. and Archael. Society*, 2nd Series, iii, no. 28, pp 136–46 (April, 1897).

3   National Library Lisbon (Reservados), B.N.L. 95.

4   B.M. Thomason Tracts E.632 (9).

5   B. Corish, 'The Church and Irish Nationalism', in *Iris Hibernia*, 1957, p. 11.

6   Ormond to Mennes, 11 February 1652 (*Ormond Mss*, New Series, i. 258).

7   Robert Cocke to Charles Stuart, 2 March 1652 (*Clar. C.P.*, ii 124).

8   A.V., Nunz. *Di Francia*, 99, f. 103.

9   N. Barozzi-G. Berchet, *Relazioni degli stati europei lette al Senato dagli ambasciate veneti nel sec. 17*, Francia 2nd Series, ii, 464. Report of Giovanni Nani. These volumes are usually referred to as *Ambasciatore*.

10   V. Gabrieli, 'La Missione di Sir Kenelm Digby alla corte di Innocenzo X, 1645–8', in *English Miscelleny*, iv. 247–88 (Rome 1954).

11   *Cal.S.P.Dom. 1650*, pp 94, 116, 184, 341, 610.

12   De Sousa Coutinho to João IV, ? January 1649 (*Corpo. Dipl. Port.*, xiii. 280–82).

13   *Cal. S.P.Dom. 1650*, pp 69–70 (Copy of paper brought by Colonel Price to Beauvais endorsed by Nicholas).

14   Some sources give 23 June.

15   AGOP, IV, 87, f. 94. *Concessum P. Mag. Fratri Dominico del Rosario possit ire in Hiberniam cum facultate substituendi aliquem loco sui in vicanium colegii S. Rosarii e miniales B. Sucesso ejus earum commissorum donec redeat ex Hibernia.*

16   O'Daly to Ormond, recd. 28 August 1650 (*Carte Papers*, xxix, 506, addend. 642, new paging).

17   *Loc. cit.*, p. 506.

18   Simancas, Estado leg. 3020. Letter of Duke of Infantado, giving a summary of a report from Abbot Patrick Crilly, February 1650.

19   A.V., Nunz. Di Francia 101, f. 106.

20   Meynell to Cottington, 24 June, 31 July 1650 (*Clar. S.P.* ii. 66 *et. Seq.*).

21   A.TdoT., Chanc. De João IV, xxi. 151–3; xxvii. 99.

22   Mde. De Motteville, Mémoires in Michaud's *Collection*, xxix. 448.

23   Browne to Nicholas, 17 November 1652 (*The Nicholas Papers*, iii. 289).

24   *Ibid*, p. 291.

25 A.V., Nunz. Di Francia III, f. 97.

26 C.S.P. British and Foreign, i. 480–92.

27 E. Prestage, *Diplomatic Relations of Portugal during the 17th Century*, pp 214–16.

28 A.V., Nunz. Di Francia IIIA, ff. 56, 90, 129.

29 Afonso VI to O'Daly, 23 June 1657 (Mss de S. Vincente, vol. 22, ff. 192–3 in A.TdoT.).

30 *Ibid.* See also E. Prestage, *Diplomatic Relations of Portugal*, p. 228.

31 *Ambasciatore*, Inglaterra 4th Series, p. 383.

32 O'Daly to Luisa de Gusmão, 1 May 1657 (*State Papers Foreign*, iv. I58, Record Office London).

33 *Ambasciaatore*, Francia 2nd Series, I, 39; *Spagna* 1st Series, ii, 303.

34 Talbot to Charles Stuart, 5 May 1656 (*Clar. S.P.* iii. 122).

35 A.V., Nunz. Di Francia III, f. 136.

36 Luisa de Gusmão to O'Daly, 10 April 1657 (Mss de S. Vincente, xiv. 64–66 in A.TdoT.).

37 E. Prestage, *Diplomatic Relations of Portugal*, p. 135.

38 Brady, *Episcopal Succession*, iii. 117 (Agretti Report, 1669).

39 J.C. Weale, 'Registers of Portuguese Embassy Chapel', in *C.R.S.* 38, pp xi–xxxi. See also L.C. Davidson, *Catherine of Bragança*, p. 63. Letter of Charlies II, 2 July 1661.

40 Brady, *Episcopal Succession*, iii. 117.

41 T. de Burgo, *Hibernia Dominicana*, p. 493.

42 Virginia Rau, 'Catherine of Bragança', *O Instituto* 98 (Coimbra, 1941), pp 18–258. Augusto Casimiro, *Dona Catarina de Bragança*, (Lisbon, 1956), p. 110. Caettano Beirão, 'As negociacões para o casamento da Infant D. Caterino com Carlos II da Inglaterra', in *Anais 7* (1942). Ciclo da Restauração, Academia Portuguesa da Historia.

43 *Ambasciatore*, Inghilterra, 4th series, pp 451–2.

44 Bibl. D'Ajuda, Cod. 51–v–39, f. 10. Cf. J. de Torres, 'Antonio de Sousa de Maçedo' in Ar v. 364 (1863) .chiv. *Pittoresco*.

VI

POLITICAL AMBITIONS

Monsignor Coelio Piccolomini was clearly nonplussed by the tall Irishman who was representing the affairs of Portugal at Paris. Piccolomini had taken up residence at his post sometime in November 1657, replacing the benign and astute Guido di Bagno as papal nuncio. It was only in the new year that he began to consider Frei Domingos do Rosario. Perhaps the most tantalising aspect of his scrutiny was his concealment of the name and identity of the man who for the next few months he persisted in calling 'the gentleman', or 'the mandate', or 'the resident' from Portugal. Yet, his dispatches concerning O'Daly were directed mainly to the cardinal secretary at Rome, Rospigliosi, later to become Pope Clement IX, who was well-acquainted with the Irish friar whom he had met in Rome the previous year.

Despite Piccolomini's reluctance to disclose the Dominican's identity, O'Daly does not remain a mere cypher in the prosy dispatches that went so regularly from Paris to Rome. Quite the contrary, Piccolomini succeeds in giving glimpses of the Portuguese ambassador which are fascinating precisely because they are set in such dull surroundings. In a series of small word-vignettes, we see the mandate from Portugal, which is the nuncio's usual expression, carrying out his social obligations with a splendour that set Paris buzzing during the early summer of 1657.

On a Saturday morning in mid-April, the cathedral of Notre Dame was filled to overflowing with the court, the diplomatic corps and important members of church and city to do honour to the memory of the dead king João IV. Even Cromwell's representative and his wife came out of curiosity, and 'not wishing to appear in a public church because of their religion' hid discreetly. Caught in a dark corner without means of exit, they were subjected to a funeral oration in which the bishop of Vennes referred energetically to the late lamentable happenings in England and the usurpation of the rightful monarchy there.

A month later, all Paris flocked to the windows on both sides of the river to watch *'un belissimo fuoco'* (a great fireworks), apparently in midstream, which was one of the means the Portuguese ambassador used to celebrate his young monarch's fourteenth birthday. That night, in conjunction with Cardinal Antonio Barberini, O'Daly gave a superb banquet at the house of the Genovese ambassador to a large gathering which included the nuncio. The following day Frei Domingos left Paris in the company of the new French ambassador to Portugal, Lieutenant General, the Comte de Cominges, to the annoyance of Piccolomini who wanted a few words with him before he departed. O'Daly was back within the week having been overtaken by a special courier en route with fresh orders from his monarch that necessitated his immediate return.[1]

The overall impression that Piccolomini gives of O'Daly at this period is of a colourful personality who had many audiences with Mazarin and who made no secret of his master's affairs. Though purely superficial, Piccolomini's dispatches show O'Daly as one possessing the power to call attention to what he wanted: the existence of a king in Portugal.

Perhaps the clearest account of O'Daly's mission in Paris comes from the pen of de Brienne, the French secretary of state. No great admirer of Mazarin, de Brienne gave a brief and succinct account of the Portuguese negotiations for the year 1656–7. He wrote in his *Memoires:*

> the Portuguese, who had made it obvious since the previous year that they were incapable of playing a part that would be advantageous to them, sent away the two secretaries of their ambassador. The latter continued to demonstrate the weakness of Portugal by saying that he was ready to let us have the money, provided that it was being used against the common enemy and that assurances were given that no terms would be made without His Majesty of Portugal's consent.
>
> Then the ambassador asked me concerning a matter which, he said, had been granted by the late king (Louis XIII) and I told him to show me the relevant document. He thought to satisfy my demands by showing us a recommendation which the supreme council had made the king his master. There it appeared that Louis XIII had exhorted him to uphold his just rights and offered his troops to maintain those rights on condition that a treaty should be made beforehand, regulating what each of the kings would be bound to. The treaty was not settled, so I concluded we were not bound to anything. However, to show the Portuguese ambassador that the king had the intention of assisting Portugal, I said to him: 'Since you have money, give us some and I will give you all possible assurances that it will be returned if your master does not wish to subscribe to a treaty which I will draw up for you'. I even reduced myself to a demand of only 50,000 ecus, but this ambassador who knew well that the money was not at La Rochelle, but only its value in sugar, excused himself and I thus concluded that the king of Portugal was our friend provided that our affairs prospered, and that he would never do anything to the disadvantage of France.

The ambassador often asked me why immense sums had been given to the Swedes, the Dutch and the Landgrave of Hesse, while on the contrary the Portuguese were asked for money. I had no trouble in assuring him that they acted for the common cause, while the king, his master, remained inactive. Then the ambassador persuaded me that it was permissible for his master to recover what belonged to him, but that he could not, without committing an enormous crime, encroach on the goods of others and, far from making conquests of his enemies, his only concern was to defend his own country.[2]

De Brienne conveyed the impression that O'Daly was a shrewd bargainer and an ambassador alerted to the possible dangers of a false move. There is no hint that he was a pensioner of France; indeed, the French secretary of state showed that O'Daly succeeded only too well in making the French government aware of Portugal's financial embarrassment, while at the same time he maintained a sturdy independence on behalf of the country he represented.

So far O'Daly's career as a diplomat has revealed little of his inner self; yet, in another way, it shows him much as contemporary Europeans saw him. To the Portuguese courtiers of Don Diego's variety, who watched his gradual climb to the post of Portuguese ambassador to Paris, the Irish Dominican was an object of resentment. He seems to have moved in an atmosphere of suspicion. At Lisbon he was thought to be a pensionary of France. To English royalists like Browne in Paris, he caused uneasiness because they believed that O'Daly was an unofficial agent of Charles Stuart; yet, in his capacity as Portuguese ambassador he was obliged to make overtures to Cromwell's government. To Mazarin and de Brienne, O'Daly was just one more of the Portuguese envoys sent by João IV to negotiate a formal alliance which France found inconvenient. For all that, O'Daly did not act imprudently as did Vieira in 1646. Neither did he infuriate the cardinal as the forthright Coutinho had done three years previously; instead, he managed to placate Mazarin to such an extent that he determined to send an ambassador to Lisbon formally. He paid O'Daly the doubtful compliment that:

> the friar was entirely in accord with His Eminence in all things he professed, and had been so moved by the reasons given him he (O'Daly) had resolved to make the journey with Cominges in order to uphold him and speak freely with the queen and persuade her that the only salvation of Portugal lay in conforming to Louis XIV's wishes, making all possible efforts to assist France.[3]

The significance of this passage is its place in the *Secret Instructions* issued to Cominges on 13 May 1657. It remained for Cominges to complete through his dispatches the story of O'Daly's activities as a friar at court.

In the perfection of its organisation, the diplomatic service of France was without an equal. Under the exacting administration of Mazarin, and even more so of Louis XIV later on, the labours of the diplomatic agents of France, as shown by existing archives, were often enormous. The zeal of men like Cominges is necessary to understand because they were sacrificed to the glory of France. The long distance traversed, the slowness of communication, the expenses that went hand in hand with their meagre pay, usually in arrears, the isolation in moments of decision made the life of a French ambassador burdensome. His only reward for so much labour was a word of praise, or a preferment to a post of increased importance and honour.

The value of Cominges's dispatches is twofold. It enables us to observe the vast machinery of French diplomacy narrowed down to one insignificant cog, and to comprehend that France completed her ascendancy over Europe by means of organisation. The real value of his dispatches, however, in the present context lies in the information he supplied about O'Daly. In so far as Nuncio

Piccolomini provides an unusual perspective of the friar by his casual references, Cominges exposes the schemes and ambitions of the Irishman in a wholly unexpected way. The nuncio shows us the smooth exterior of the man; Cominges removes the mask.

'To have the perfect ambassador you must first have the perfect prince', remarks the author of *El Embajador*, the most popular seventeenth century book on diplomacy, and O'Daly might have echoed the work of another contemporary, Jean Hotman: 'sometimes in the service of the king there is no choice'. The statesman João IV was dead. A regency is always a calamity for a nation, and Portugal was particularly unfortunate in the person of the young Afonso, eldest surviving son of João IV and Luisa.

On the death of Theodosio, João's eldest son, in 1653, the *cortes* had confirmed the succession of Afonso, then aged ten. As a child Afonso had contracted a disease which left him partly paralysed on his right side. The degree to which he was incapacitated is difficult to determine. At times his acts were those of an idiot, but there were occasions when he displayed normal intelligence. The English ambassador, Sir Robert Southwell, described him as being pitifully stupid, though on occasion sound in the head.

A few months before he died, the king had discussed with the friar the desirability of allowing Pedro, his younger son, to rule in preference to Afonso the heir, but died without effecting the alteration he had in mind.[4] In his will, João IV had nominated his wife regent and the *cortes* ratified the nomination immediately. But it was doubtful that Luisa would sustain the prudent grasp of affairs she had shared with her husband. She was a queen by temperament, ambition and destiny. Daughter of one of the great Spanish houses, the duke of Medina Sidonia, she had been trained in the severe Spanish formation of perfect conformity to her father's will and of maintaining a strict outward composure. Both had been tested when her father suddenly announced at the close of 1631 that it was the wish of Philip IV and of Olivares, her cousin, that she marry the young duke of Bragança, constable of Portugal, whom she had never met.

So closely identified did she become with her husband and his people in the following decades that her transition to the role of regent caused no uneasiness. Though strong-minded and decisive in the pursuit of a policy, her early training and harmonious married life had attuned her to playing second fiddle. While she was wholly admirable in her loyal support of her husband's efforts to win recognition for his monarchy, and indeed was his chief inspiration, as regent she leaned heavily on her councillors, and too often exhibited an emotional pre-occupation with problems which required a logical approach. Later she was to confess how trying she found this period of her life: 'my life is irksome to me, because as a ruler I am regarded as having two heads'. Besides consulting her two councillors of state, the counts of Odemira and Cantanhede, she was deeply influenced by Vieira da Silva, the secretary of state, and by her confessor Father Daniel O'Daly, who as well as being in the powerful position of spiritual director to the queen, also advised her on domestic and state matters.

To create a better understanding between the ministers who enjoyed her trust, Luisa established the Junta Nocturna, composed of eight members with whom she met nightly in the palace. Theoretically, the Junta was meant to help the queen by peaceful co-operation; in fact, it became a torment of wrangling and discord to her. There is a bizarre unreality about the proceedings of the Junta which is conveyed in a contemporary description of the scene: the flaring torches and the sharp rattle of the queen's escort breaking the hush of the Paço; the dark figure of the regent hurrying by, her face completely hidden by its black veiling; and finally, the sound of altercation behind closed doors.

The regency which followed the death of João IV was accordingly a period of court intrigue and dissension at Lisbon. Ericeira, the official historian of the Portuguese Restoration, was mainly concerned with the factual recording of events between 1640–68, in a style reminiscent of the Four Masters. He made no effort to present a clear picture of the circumstances surrounding the eclipse of Luisa de Gusmão, and the installation of her son, the inept Afonso as king of Portugal.[5]

The minutes of the councils of state extending over the regency period supply many details as to the nature of the divisions that rent the *cortes* and placed the queen-regent and her immediate circle of advisors effectively outside the arena of politics in Portugal.[6] By far the most interesting account of this complicated time comes from the pen of Cominges who accompanied O'Daly to Lisbon in July 1657. His correspondence with de Brienne gives valuable information about events as they were seen and partly understood by a stranger; due allowance was made for the fact that he was acting solely in the interests of his country and that his every move in Lisbon was controlled by Mazarin to whom he owed his preferment. Nothing that occurred in Lisbon was unimportant to be recorded by Cominges's observant, if acid, pen, and thus a clear picture emerges of the events following his and O'Daly's arrival in the capital.[7]

In normal conditions the regency should have lasted only a few months, that is until Afonso had completed his fourteenth year. According to Ericeira, some of his advisors thought it prudent to wait until it could be determined whether Afonso was fit to rule before proclaiming him king, while others considered that the perils of the time were too great for Portugal to be without a king. Luisa de Gusmão accepted the second view and the *cortes* put all power into her hands while, at the same time, declaring her son Afonso lawful king of Portugal.

In his letters from Paris to the queen-regent, O'Daly had repeatedly asked for news of affairs in Lisbon and he suspected trouble in that quarter. When he arrived in the Portuguese capital, he found the queen hedged in with difficulties. Apparently, she was very relieved to see him and the new French ambassador. Cominges wrote to de Brienne that he had been received by her 'as a man sent from Heaven', and that his very presence there had soothed the people of Lisbon who were murmuring against the nobles.[8]

On the frontiers, the Spaniards had again massed their troops. The knowledge that João IV was dead, that the minor was incapable and that the government had passed into the hands of a widow, a Spaniard at that, roused the Castilian army to renewed vigour. The acquisition of Prince Condé, a fugitive from the French court, was a further incentive. Philip IV seized the opportunity to plan an extensive operation by land and sea against the Portuguese in the early months of 1657. Behind him was Don Luis de Haro, nephew of the Conde-Duque Olivares who continued his policy. The threat of a Dutch fleet suddenly appearing in the Lisbon harbour seemed very real in July when O'Daly and Cominges came from France. Indeed, open hostility broke out in the autumn. In the *cortes* a division detrimental to the power of the queen was fast becoming a formidable faction. The minutes of the council of state for the second half of that year reveal only too clearly the disharmony of that critical period. The sessions on the defence of the country were particularly stormy, and sectional interest weakened the nation's welfare.

This was particularly evident in the appointment of the count of Sao Laurence as commander in the key position of the Alentejo frontier. Precipitately, the queen had dismissed the cautious da Costa, whom her late husband had placed as commander there, and who was an experienced and tried soldier. His rival, Sao Laurence, immediately threw over the now traditional defensive policy with disastrous consequences. The Spaniards captured the border town of Olivenca and retained their hold on it. The affair split the court into two factions, and even though Sao Laurence was dismissed and the defensive policy resumed, the dissonance continued at Lisbon.[9]

A letter signed by Afonso VI to O'Daly written some time previous to Cominges's *Instructions* ordered the friar to press for the following:

> above all, fleet and cavalry have to be produced ... and if not possible to obtain both, then begin with the fleet and then the cavalry; and if you cannot get that, ask for financial aid which Portugal will never get from France as Holland, Sweden and other allies have got in large sums and for continued intervals. Put it to the minister that the time is opportune for creating a diversion in Catalonia rather than in Flanders or Italy.[10]

In the previous March when the treaty had been concluded between Cromwell and Louis XIV, Mazarin had thought the time was opportune to sign the *'liga formal'* with Portugal. Prompted by the fair-minded de Brienne, and by O'Daly, he had allowed it to be known publicly that he was sending a French ambassador to Lisbon for that purpose. Piccolomini alone, the papal nuncio, was distrustful of Mazarin's promises and voiced his suspicions to Rospigliosi. Three months later Mazarin coolly changed his tactics as his *Secret Instructions* to Cominges reveal only too clearly. France, or rather Mazarin, needed money and Cominges's main task was to bargain.

The French ambassador, in his second audience with the regent, made known the terms Louis XIV was prepared to offer, adding that he was sent to Lisbon 'in view of Frei

Domingos O'Daly's urgent solicitations to his master'. Louis hoped that his representative would meet with a better reception this time as past experience had shown little sincerity and help from Portugal. O'Daly was present during this speech and acted as interpreter. It took place publicly and the queen was uneasy. She bade Cominges speak softly and requested the friar to draw nearer so that he was the only other person in the room who heard what Cominges was saying. Finally, she directed that he open negotiations with the count of Odemira, O'Daly and the secretary of state, but he was to keep in touch with herself by calling on her often. With customary French gallantry, the ambassador, when taking his leave, complimented the mother on her daughter Catherine 'who seems to me so beautiful that I cannot believe she is a human creature, but somehow divine', a gallantry, wrote the complacent diplomat, that much pleased the mother.[11]

Louis XIV desired peace with Spain that summer, but he feared that any alliance with Portugal just then would be detrimental to the general peace so ardently wished for by the reigning pope. Consequently, he dallied with both Spain and Portugal. His cousin, Condé, hero of the Fronde, was living in Spain and had prevailed on Philip not to enter into an agreement with France unless he, Condé, received ample satisfaction for the slights he had endured from Mazarin and from Anne of Austria. A deadlock followed. Louis, though he realised that Spain would never sanction the inclusion of Portugal's independence as an article of the peace treaty, decided that summer to continue the war and signed an offensive alliance with Cromwell. The terms which Cominges laid before the three commissioners chosen by the regent were therefore matters of intense concern to her.

Of the three commissioners selected to meet Cominges, the count of Odemira, according to the French ambassador, had the most authority in the council of state. He was also the most clamorous in the Junta Noctura. Most Portuguese historians give an unfavourable account of Odemira's political career and blame his negligence as king's tutor for Afonso's misbehaviour at this period:

> A man as attentive to his own convenience as he was heedless of the prince's instructions, judging that he would best forward himself in the king's good graces by leaving him to give rein to his appetites rather than by restraining him and educating him.

Such is the judgment passed by the anonymous author of the *Anti-Catastrof* which is a defence of Afonso.[12]

In their first conference together, Cominges submitted the proposals offered by Louis XIV to the three commissioners. In return for signing an alliance between the two countries, Portugal was to pay France two million in gold payable over a period of two years, and two hundred thousand crusados each year as long as the war lasted. Cominges then listed his other demands as instructed: offensive operations against Spain, a supply of Portuguese ships for the French fleet, facilities for raising a corps of infantry and cavalry in France at the expense of Portugal and finally the fortress of Tangier to be held by a picked force chosen by Louis.[13] No mention was made of a marriage between the two royal houses. O'Daly immediately objected to the terms proposed by Cominges. In his conferences in Paris, he said he had spoken of the cession of Tangier in a different context, as a part of the Infanta Catherine's dowry. Although he realised the advantage of an alliance with France, yet the French ought not demand what Portugal could ill-afford to concede.[14]

Cominges had been instructed to abandon French pretensions to Tangier if it jeopardised his chances of success. Now when O'Daly voiced his objections, the Frenchman changed his tactics, and he never mentioned the subject again. He maintained cordial relations with the friar whom he asked to discover the views of his colleagues. On 31 July, he had a visit from O'Daly. Nothing favourable might be expected from the commissioners because they were hostile towards France or in bad faith with their own government. Cominges noted in his dispatch to de Brienne that the population of Lisbon was pro-French and had accused the authorities of putting obstacles in the way of an agreement. Apparently the mayor of Lisbon with the city councillors went officially to the French embassy and offered help, declaring that some of the ministers were at the service of Spain and were trying to ruin the kingdom. O'Daly had brought something else to Cominges that last day of July: the written refusal of the commissioners to the French demands. The conditions asked for were impossible to fulfil, although the queen would have liked to satisfy French demands.[15] Clearly O'Daly was acting under instructions, and in the reply written by Vieira da Silva, the commissioners pointed out that when the friar had first gone to Paris, João IV had instructed him not to resort to bribes, and in his second mission, he was allowed the sum of one million cruzados as bribes for those who carried through the marriage negotiations successfully. Da Silva further stated that Portugal had two armies at the front and might reasonably have expected aid from France; instead, the requests from France exceeded all previous ones.

The reply of the French ambassador was a storm of rhetoric which he duly set down for de Brienne. The newly-restored monarchy would be able to live in peace 'while we, (the French), poured out the noble blood of France'. He protested vigorously against the use of the word 'bribe', and declared that the friendship of Louis XIV was without price. If it were for sale, not all the riches of India would suffice to buy the least part of it.

In his account of O'Daly's visit to him the comte goes on to speak of other things. The count of Castelmelhor was forming a strong anti-monarchical party and was rapidly gaining ground, partly because of the distinguished role played by his father in the war and chiefly because of his own undoubted energy and ambition. He was known to be bitterly hostile to France, a fact, said Cominges, which carried weight with many of the discontented nobility. There was dissatisfaction everywhere. In the army there was no general of experience; the soldiers were undisciplined and the general maintenance was extravagant. Even if enormous sums were spent on the fortifications of Lisbon harbour, it would still take generations to complete them. In Cominges's opinion, the Portuguese were marking time while maintaining themselves securely in Lisbon, and he advised de Brienne to threaten them with the ultimatum of breaking off negotiations within eight days.[16] This last suggestion was impractical seeing that the very minimum for an exchange of notes between Paris and Lisbon was two months.

The second conference took place on 22 August. O'Daly acted as intermediary, and probably interpreter between the two parties, and arranged for the meeting to take place. At the back of his mind was the knowledge that Sande was setting sail for England with counter proposals upon which he and Sande had agreed. Again the conference ended in disharmony. At a subsequent meeting the commissioners yielded cautiously on the matter of payment, but they refused to cede Tangier or to lend warships to the French navy. Bargaining now began in earnest, O'Daly still acting as the go-between. The only surviving account of what followed comes from the pen of Cominges as Ericeira remained silent on these issues and the council of state was not informed of the proceedings.

O'Daly had also arranged for a private meeting between the queen and the ambassador while he remained the third party present. Cominges complained to the regent of the impossible situation that had arisen in the last two meetings with the commissioners and sketched the lamentable condition of Portugal, 'this kingdom afflicted on all sides'. Then Luisa promised to entrust the whole matter to Frei Domingos who would explain the position more clearly to herself, especially the causes of Cominges's complaints, and would endeavour to remove them. In his dispatch to de Brienne, the French ambassador wrote enigmatically that he then became suspicious of the friar, because he saw in the queen's answer yet another delaying tactic.[17]

In his September dispatch, Cominges throws further light on his mysterious statement. The members of the council of state had spoken to the regent, he wrote, and accused O'Daly of being an ignorant and untrustworthy traitor. 'The friar found it prudent to retire for a few days to his monastery'. The Portuguese ministers were not, according to Cominges, very able; they had no practice in diplomacy and were always changing their minds.[18]

Was O'Daly a traitor? Vieira da Silva referred to him as a good subject in the session of the council of state for March 1656 even as he made the request that a Portuguese noble be appointed ambassador to France. Frei Domingos seemed to be devoted to his sovereign's interests at this time, a fact which Donna Luisa acknowledged. His account of his negotiations at Paris in the previous year appeared over-optimistic in the light of subsequent events, and his efforts to secure an alliance was a failure. The role he assumed as matchmaker between Catherine of Bragança and Louis XIV ceases to be a riddle in the light of his Stuart activities. The whole problem of O'Daly's career as a diplomat hinges on the question of his trustworthiness, since it was widely suspected in Lisbon that he was given to playing a double game between Portugal, to which he had pledged his allegiance, and France, from which it was reputed he had received financial aid. This seems to be the charge most often brought against him.

On 21 September, queen Luisa reinstated the friar as her intermediary. The conferences had continued in his absence but no decision was reached. The commissioners instructed O'Daly to try and draw up a settlement on favourable terms, and when that failed, he proposed sending a Portuguese representative to Paris to explain the situation to Mazarin. Cominges promptly rejected that proposition, but it was the conclusion ultimately reached by all parties after several more months of haggling. Nevertheless, Cominges's dispatch of 28 September was kinder in tone, and he did justice to the difficulties of the Portuguese:

> They have two armies in the field; the Dutch with forty vessels are off the bar of Lisbon and demand five million cruzados and leave to trade with Brazil; the Portuguese have lost Ceylon which gave them their best revenues from the east; Goa is invaded, and the Brazil fleet is in danger of being attacked. They are hard-pressed and cannot grant what we demand.

The dispatch shows a good grasp of affairs, and if Cominges saw the defects of the nation through the jaundiced eyes as his later correspondence indicates, he recognised its difficulties at this early stage. He was plainly ill-at-ease in his role as prevaricator and was to suffer, for he came to be regarded as little more than a spy, a position that was daily to become more intolerable to one whom Mde de Motteville has described as a gallant of the French court.

Meanwhile, Mazarin was keeping in close touch with his ambassador in Lisbon. In a letter of 17 August, he rejoiced at the safe arrival of Cominges and wished him every success. In a letter of 28 September, he instructed him to set in motion an agreement between the United Provinces and Portugal and desired news of his main transactions.[19] Cominges was changeable and moody. At the end of August, he wrote to de Brienne that he had suddenly grown suspicious of O'Daly. Now in September his attitude had undergone another change, and he gives the friar praise for his concern about the French alliance and the proposed marriage, though Sande had at that very time sailed for England with O'Daly's approval of the Stuart match:

> Le Pere Dominique has a great regard for France and works with energy in the French interest. He has much power over the queen's mind, but as I have said before, he is disliked by all the ministers who are jealous of the fact that these negotiations pass through his hands. More especially the matter of the marriage has especially increased their dislike because they knew that he alone holds in his hands all the details of the negotiations, and to him alone the queen entrusts every particular of it.

There is unconscious humour in the fact that what the unsuspecting Cominges said was true, but not in the manner he believed.

By September, O'Daly was beginning to doubt the sincerity of Cominges and to mark his moody alternations. O'Daly wrote privately to Mazarin outlining how in the previous meetings the regent had tried to get the ministers to agree to the French proposals and to work harmoniously together. O'Daly again assured Mazarin that the country could not pay the sum proposed, but that Donna Luisa's magnanimity was such that she had the courage to promise payment.[20]

Those were sorrowful days for the queen and she had to summon every ounce of courage to sustain her as mother of the irresponsible Afonso and the rejected Catherine. It was a bitter humiliation to her proud and dignified nature to witness the physical and moral miseries of her son worsening with each birthday. By modern standards, his outrageous conduct and his association with a band of disreputable youths would class him now as a juvenile delinquent. In general, his misdeeds, though reprehensible, may be passed over in silence; yet, they aroused disrespect and damaged the prestige of the royal family. Abroad Philip IV redoubled his efforts to win back Portugal. At home there were those in the *cortes* who saw in the defective Afonso a means of overthrowing Luisa's government and of furthering their own ends. The queen refused to acknowledge Afonso's incapacity as bordering on lunacy and would not have him deposed. Thus arose the curious position of this unhappy king born to be ruled first by his mother, then by the count of Castelmelhor and finally for the last sixteen years of his life (1667–83) by his younger brother Pedro.

As well as keeping de Brienne informed on the ebb and flow of the Dutch menace, Cominges was recounting the usual court gossip. The queen fell into an illness from anxiety and was bled nine times, but the only person who succeeded in soothing her was her confessor, 'le Pere Dominique'. He continued to enjoy her confidence and, added the ambassador, to nourish ambitions to be a minister:

> He is assuredly the most capable and most intelligent man at this court, the most devoted to the crown and to the royal family of Portugal, but in order to serve it in a more beneficial manner, he would like to enter the ministry. He had proposed that I should speak to the queen of it, without letting her know that he had any part in it. (I have not done so because it appears to me too delicate a matter to be dealt with before the league is concluded and without a positive order from His Majesty.) However, I did not refuse outright; I spoke kindly to him and promised to make known in France the capable and obliging fashion in which he takes care of the queen's interests. I am writing personally to S.E., (Mazarin) about this matter. I beg you to look over the letter, so that in your answer to it, you may be careful not to show that the whole idea has come from the friar. Since I did not show this part of my reply he suspects that I did not speak to S.E. about it, or else that I

deceived him in promising him not to speak without his consent. He deserves to be humoured in the interests of France and his obvious goodwill towards us ought to be recognised. He has the marriage of the Infanta always at the back of his mind, and it is that which draws upon him the dislike of all the ministers. They think that since he had the honour of furthering the first proposal of the match in France, to him will go all the credit, if the negotiations are to succeed.[21]

Here indeed is a merciless exposure of Daniel O'Daly's hopes and secret ambitions for a political career. The fact that the French ambassador reported this conversation to his chief in Paris would indicate that it actually took place. Cominges's remarks on life in Lisbon deteriorate in proportion as his character becomes suspect to the court there. At the same time, unless O'Daly were speaking in a very childish or naïve way, the report of the conversation throws light on the friar's ambitions at court.

On 22 November 1657, there was a serious crisis in Lisbon. The Dutch fleet was outside the harbour. Secret rivalry between Odemira, the king's tutor, and the count of Cantenhede, one of the ministers, had exploded and split the court into two factions. In a previous dispatch, Cominges had outlined the beginnings of the quarrel. Odemira held the balance of power in the council of state, because he enjoyed the queen's confidence, and also had strong supporters. He was an opportunist. At the crucial moment when the duke of Bragança had been proclaimed king, Odemira had 'simulated madness', thus avoiding the necessity of taking an active part in the revolution. He was now in opposition to the party of the secretary of state who usually joined with Frei Domingos on all important issues. The Dominican was not popular with the Portuguese nobles who said he was a friar and therefore ignorant, but he was firmly entrenched in the queen's favour. O'Daly's unpopularity, explained Cominges, was due to the fact that he rarely shared the opinions of the nobles on any subject, and they opposed him in everything.[22]

Queen Luisa was in an awkward position. While her sympathies patently leaned towards a French alliance, she was doing her utmost to lighten their demand for money. The common people shared her partiality and were not unwilling to contribute, but the nobles avoided all payments. So far the clergy had not been approached, and the people were clamouring for a full assembly of the *cortes* which the regent was more than willing to convene. The nobles, said Cominges, did not desire a convocation of *cortes* because they would be obliged to pay taxes; the minister wanted it even less since they would have to render an account of their administration to it. The clergy also opposed the popular demand. There was a determined coalition led by Odemira who intended to weaken the power of Luisa de Gusmão by removing her advisors, notably da Silva and O'Daly.[23]

The coalition met with some success. In December the queen was approached and requested to solicit the Provincial of the Dominican order in Portugal for permission to allow Frei Domingos do Rosario to proceed to Goa as archbishop. What the French ambassador really thought of the proposal was:

> le Pere Dominique remains fixed in his desire to enter the ministry, and does not lose a single opportunity of telling me the benefits France will thereby receive. He is in alliance with the secretary of state since he cannot stand alone against the other ministers What I deduce from his behaviour is that he is ambitious, and that he would not object to being bishop of Evora, so that sheltering behind that title, he could proceed on equal footing with the great ones of the kingdom and be assured of his ministry through that dignity.[24]

This ruse of the cabal was to culminate in a resolution of the council of state, seven months later, in the session of 9 July 1658, demanding that Frei Domingos be nominated in the first place for the archbishopric of Goa, 'seeing that by his learning and virtues, he is fully competent for that post'.[25]

It was not the first time that Frei Domingos had been associated with the archbishopric of Goa. More than two years previously, his name had been forwarded as a most worthy candidate for the see to king João IV by members of the council of state. João IV ignored the recommendation because he was intent on sending the friar to Paris. But the report persisted and followed him to the French capital. Nuncio di Bagno, on the point of leaving, took time off from packing to note on 24 October 1656 that 'the Dominican Father, the archbishop of Goa, had returned from Portugal as ambassador'. That was one of the few occasions that the urbane nuncio was wrongly informed.

For an ambitious and active man, the archbishopric of Goa was a post teeming with possibilities; for a zealous churchman, it was a position bristling with difficulties. Rather O'Daly was approaching his middle sixties. He suffered from periodic gout. He stated that he felt he was needed in Lisbon; however, the attempt to oust him from politics was not abandoned.

Meanwhile France had again started peace negotiations with Spain, and at the end of March 1658, Cominges reported widespread dissatisfaction with Mazarin's duplicity. Cleverly the cardinal had maintained crossfire letters to his representative, to O'Daly, and to Afonso VI, urging on all three the necessity of taking the offensive against Spain. Now it was felt in Lisbon that he had used Cominges's presence in Portugal as first official ambassador to that country as a lever to wrest terms from an alarmed and battle-scarred Spain. Consequently, his representative rapidly lost prestige there and was reduced to the disagreeable role of playing second fiddle to O'Daly who was treating directly with the French government, and was pressing for the appointment of a Portuguese envoy to Paris. In his spring correspondence to de Brienne, Cominges adds a new note of grievance: Mazarin failed to keep him informed on his mode of procedure while the Irish friar had intimate knowledge of current affairs in France, England and Rome. This was typical of the heartless way the course of French diplomacy took under Mazarin's direction. When negotiations broke down or failed the French envoy was expected to become the scapegoat, even if it was his master who was at fault.

In a series of petty complaints to de Brienne, Cominges vented his chagrin which was mainly directed against the friar:

> And as hope is the passion which flatters us most agreeably and comes to life first within us and is the last to die, as the queen is filled with fresh hope which Frei Domingoes had given her. There is nothing she will not attempt to carry out. Frei Domingos is still most anxious to enter the ministry, but as he desires to appear modest, he is anxious that King Louis should marry the Portuguese princess when he has brought the political alliance to a successful conclusion. He is ambitious to the last degree and on better terms than ever with the queen.[26]

O'Daly was indeed on better terms than ever with the queen. She had very generously paid over eight thousand cruzados for the site of Corpo Santo, and the following year, she accepted the invitation to be present at the laying of the foundation stone. And apparently Cominges heard nothing of what was afoot between Charles Stuart and his agents in Lisbon.

The summer of 1658 was a tense one for the Portuguese. They made one final bid for the French alliance after seventeen years of bargaining. In the field, they made a supreme effort to drive out the Spaniards. The elder Duke Odemira laid siege to Badajos without marked success, and the siege dragged on until autumn plunging the whole court into gloom. It became increasingly clear that Spain and France were determined on peace, and Cominges's position became daily more untenable. He remained without instructions, another Mazarin tactic when he did not wish to commit himself. In letter after letter Cominges pressed for leave to return home, considering his stay discreditable to the honour of his country. He had not, moreover, received a salary for eight months and owed money to tradespeople in the city. He was, he concluded poignantly, penniless.

In between his requests for money and permission to return home, he gave a detailed account, written with a certain elegance and grace, of O'Daly's removal from public affairs.[27]

Towards the end of July, the younger Odemira, whose star was temporarily in the ascendant since his father had just commenced the siege of Badajos, and all Portugal was hopeful, convinced the regent that the archbishopric of Goa needed a man like Frei Domingos do Rosario. If we are to believe Cominges, Odemira apparently jibed at the friar when he refused the honour saying that he aspired to the office of grand inquisitor and first councillor of the realm whereupon O'Daly well and truly lost his temper and retired fuming.

Queen Luisa gave way to despondency. She, whose courage and ability had aroused the admiration of two successive Venetian ambassadors to write of her in glowing terms, lost heart at this critical stage. The Franco-Spanish negotiations were in their concluding stages. The marriage between the young king of France and Marie Therese was now a certainty. Afonso, king of Portugal, was bringing shame and disgrace on the Bragança dynasty by his latest escapade. With a group of wild companions on horseback, he had battered down the door of the Jesuit novitiate at midnight and ridden into the hall with much noise and ribaldry, an adventure which was recounted with glee in the Spanish court.

Temporarily, Luisa abandoned her husband's nominees in the government and allowed herself to be swayed by her son's tutor Odemira's Rasputin-like influence.

Immediately the secretary of state and the ministers who had made the revolution of 1649, the marquis of Niza, Cantanhede and de Albranches, went into opposition, and chose O'Daly to be their spokesman. They resolved to remonstrate with the regent, and the friar was asked to make representation on behalf of the others. He was again laid up with gout, so he wrote to the queen declaring that he was acting out of motives of patriotism, though Cominges cannot resist adding that the friar's real motive was to be revenged on Odemira. On her receipt of the letter, Luisa received a deputation of the protesting ministers who requested her to make some changes in the government. From their point of view, the result was satisfactory. Cantanhede was sent to take over the army at the frontier; da Silva resumed his post as secretary of state with the full confidence of the queen, and O'Daly became more firmly entrenched than ever in the queen's esteem.[28] Jestingly, he used to call her Zenobia, in memory of the good queen of Palmira, wife of the duke Don João II who had long been venerated in Portugal as the exemplar of queens.

Acting on his advice, though contrary to that of Cominges, queen Luisa decided to send an envoy, Ferreiro Rebello, to Paris to represent the country's desperate need for military assistance. Though Cominges had described Cantanhede as a man without experience or talents, and as one who had never left the precincts of Lisbon, Ericeira, the official historian of this period, gives the impression that it was Cantanhede who was responsible for the victory of the line of Elvas, which though a defensive battle, raised the prestige of the Portuguese army considerably. Whether O'Daly had warned the queen to be aware of the French ambassador, or whether it was becoming painfully clear to her that Mazarin's protestations of friendship were insincere, her manner towards Cominges changed. The general atmosphere of resentment and suspicion which enveloped the forlorn Cominges is well conveyed in his report of 9 October 1658:

> The queen has taken every precaution to surround our interviews with secrecy; the ministers strive always to keep me away from her, and they spy on her every action and on my every word. There is very little security in conversing with them, and their intentions do not seem to have that sincerity which is desirable for the good of the state. I see malice in some and presumption and ignorance in all ... If you want to know my feelings I will tell you simply that they are sick people who must be saved in spite of themselves, from whom must be extracted as much money as possible, money, which can be used in some enterprise which will keep the enemies away from their frontiers.[29]

There is only one other reference to Daniel O'Daly in Cominges's correspondence after the summer of 1658. It consists in a bitter attack, conveyed to de Brienne in a dispatch dated 27 November 1658. It is worth quoting in full as it represents the extreme opposition to the friar which may be first remarked in Don Diogo's remonstrance to the king in 1655. Cominges wrote:

> I return to le Pere Dominique, who is the most presumptuous, the most inconstant, and the craftiest of all men that ever existed. Presumption appears in all his designs; inconstancy in all his actions, and malice is apparently in his whole behaviour. I have felt their effects ever since I came into this kingdom in my dealings with him and in my own person. Someday I will give you a full account of it all. Take good care not to trust too much in his words. He never says what he thinks, and never thinks what he says. It is true that with it all he is so stupid that if only he is bribed and flattered in his vanity, he always says more than he wants to. He desired to persuade the queen of Portugal and all the ministers that he ruled absolutely; that he had convinced S.E., you, de Guise, Furenne, de Gramont, and the bishop of Frejus, on whom the count of Harcourt had brought pressure to bear though the Abbe of Champagne, and of the necessity of supplying commanders to the armies of Portugal, and that the information I had given had changed their plan to help

Portugal. He said that he would make you revoke your decision quite easily and that a few words would destroy what I had written. I keep on good terms with him; I could not refuse to keep up appearances without injuring my mission, but as soon as it is finished, I will tell him my sentiments.[30]

One wonders if the Frenchman ever got the opportunity of telling the friar what he thought of him! It would seem that Monsieur le Comte, who had so favoured Frei Domingos in the early days of their acquaintanceship which, because of his zeal in the French interest, now reviled him as presumptuous, inconstant and even malicious. 'He is ambitious of power' observed Cominges, and 'he is so stupid that if only he is bribed and flattered in his vanity he always says more than he wants to'. On the other hand, Cominges contradicted himself when he wrote: 'he never says what he thinks or thinks what he says'. Though his mission was only an episode in the kaleidoscopic series of negotiations which filled Mazarin's regime, Cominges's correspondence is by no means negligible as a close-up of French diplomacy just then. As a professional diplomat, he possessed little news value for the vast machinery of de Brienne's foreign department; yet, it was the slow, inexorable piling up of reports such as his, a closely-written mass of documentation which gave France her pre-eminence in this field.

As for O'Daly, his subsequent career magnificently established him as a successful careerist, if he had wished to impress Cominges. On 4 May 1659, there took place the colourful ceremony of the laying of the foundation stone of Corpo Santo which crowned his years of patient negotiation. Then too, he preserved a certain political influence because the Marquis de Chouppe, who succeeded Cominges as French ambassador to Lisbon, transacted all business matters with Luisa de Gusmão through the friar. De Chouppe mentioned in a dispatch that the Portuguese ministers brought him on one occasion to the friar's room in his monastery there to confer with him on matters of state.[31] As usual the Dominican was laid up with gout.

In January 1662, O'Daly was nominated bishop of Coimbra, mainly through the instrumentality of the queen. It was a position that carried with it such benefits and so handsome a revenue as to make the bishop of that see, *ipso facto*, one of the most important men in Portugal. On paper, his last years read like a legend and evoke the white-robed figure of Dominic of the Rosary some twenty-five years before. It was a relationship seized upon with delight by his earliest biographers who presented him as reluctantly accepting the high dignity with every show of hidden grief. It would be tempting to remark that 'to die in exile with a stranger soil for grave was, for the Irish monk, the extreme of abnegation and the crown of religious life', and to point out as Frei Lucas has done, that the Irish friar had not completed the sacrifice exchanging the monastic for the episcopal life because he died as bishop-elect.[32]

It must also be borne in mind that O'Daly carved out for himself a highly-successful career in Europe and that he died as bishop-elect of one of the wealthiest sees in Portugal. He ensured that his relatives were well-provided for. A document in the state archives sanctioned the bestowal of a legacy of 3000 cruzados to 'well-deserving relatives of the Irishman, together with one quarter of the revenue of the see of Coimbra'. The document bears the seal of king Afonso and is dated 20 October 1661. The friar died the following year, 30 June 1662. His brother's family were accepted into the ranks of the heredity nobility, and so Denis was repaid in full for his loyalty to his brother. In 1683, a grand-nephew Don Charles O'Daly was still in receipt of a handsome pension for the services rendered to the state by Frei Domingos more than twenty years before.[33]

While each version of the legend contains an element of truth, neither conveys the sense of tragedy which was present in the heart of the priest in those last years of his life. Only recently has Portuguese historical research succeeded in revealing an intensely dramatic chapter of Portugal's relations with the Holy See in the years immediately following the Restoration. It was a problem which tormented the religious soul of João IV until death relieved him of the burden. That burden, though shared by several, seemed to weigh more heavily on the spirit of O'Daly than on any of those directly concerned. So finally, in the last analysis of European diplomacy, the vast, seemingly effortless, infinitely resourceful machinery of papal diplomacy is exposed. Again one single negotiation is isolated as affording a miniature of its ecclesiastical organisation. This time the true facts emerge from a complicated mass of documentation involving the secret reports of many agents, and it is not the career or reputation of one single person that is being examined, but the political existence of a nation.

NOTES

1   A.V. Nunz. Di Francia 110A, ff. 247, 248, 259, 286, 303–305, 310, 416. *Ibid* III A, ff. 129, 146, 186.

2   Comte de Brienne, *Mémoires,* in Michaud's *Collection,* xxxiii. 151–2.

3   *Recueil*, p. 38.

4   João IV to O'Daly, 6 May 1656 (Mss de S. Vincente, vol. 24, f. 63 in A.TdoT.).

5   L. de Menezes, Conde de Ericeira, *Historia de Portugal Restorado,* vols. I–iv (ed.), A. Doria (Liveraria Civilizacaõ Lisboa, 1945).

6   Bibl. D'Ajuda, Cod. 51–v–41.

7   Cominges's correspondence is collected and preserved in the British Museum dept. (Harl. MS4547). It is now available in microfilm in the National Library, Dublin, neg. 4274.

8   B.M., Harl. MS 4547, ff. 9–10v.

9   Catastrophe de Portugal, MDCLXIX, p. 17 in National Library, Lisbon, Reservados. Fortunata de Almeida, *Historia de Portugal,* (Coimbra, 1918), p. 273. Damião Peres, *Historia de Portugal,* (Barcelos, 1934), pp 58–125.

10 Afonso VI to O'Daly, undated 1657 (MSS de S. Vincente, vol. 12, ff. 629–30 in A.TdoT.).

11 B.M. Harl. MS 4547, ff. 19–20.

12 Anti-Catastrophe, *Historia d'El-rei D. Afonso VI de Portugal* (ed. Lisboa, 1854), p. 120 *et. seq.*

13 *Recueil*, p. 28.

14 B.M., Harl. MS 4547, f. 21.

15 *Ibid.*

16 *Loc. cit.,* ff. 45–6.

17 *Ibid.*

18 *Ibid*, f. 72.

19 Mazarin to Cominges, 28 September 1657 (Lettres de Mazarin, viii. 117).

20 O'Daly to Mazarin, 26 September 1657 (*Correspondencia de Portugal*, iv, 100).

21 B.M., Harl. MS 4547, f. 106v.

22 *Ibid*, f. 28v.

23 *Ibid*, f. 116.

24 *Ibid*, f. 129.

25 Bibl. D'Ajuda, Cod. 51–v–41, f. IIOv.

26 H.M., Harl. MS 4547, f. 172.

27 *Ibid*, f. 197.

28 B.M., Harl. MS 4547, f. 247 *et seq.*

29 *Ibid*, ff. 227029.

30 *Ibid*, f. 273.

31 Bibl. D'Ajuda, Cod. 49–x–13, f. 453; of. *Recueil*, pp 63–5.

32 Quotation from 'Martyrology of Tallaght', Frei Lucas, *Historia de S. Domingos,* iv. 739.

33 A.TdoT., Chanc. d'Afonso VI, vol. 24, f. 262. See also: V. de Juromenho, *Familia de O'Daly,* f. 3 in same archives.

VII

A QUESTION OF BISHOPS

Although war and diplomacy had been the principal concerns of the European states since the 1490s, none of them had developed a foreign office as efficient as that of the Venetian signory of its time or the Vatican. With the Council of Trent (1545–63), papal diplomacy climbed to its zenith and remained long in the ascendancy, reluctantly making room for a new star in the following century, the French secular diplomacy of Richelieu. The introduction of permanent nuncios as part of Roman diplomatic practice was not the decision of any one particular pope, although Paul III laid the foundations of a department of foreign affairs in 1537 when he placed Cardinal Farnese in charge of foreign correspondence in the Roman Curia. Historical events speeded on the development of papal diplomacy, and after the Council of Trent, nuncios to the different European countries began to be appointed regularly. By the end of the century, a foreign office and permanent nunciatures were operating efficiently and smoothly.

Permanent nuncios were bound to reside in the country to which they were appointed. The scope of their mission embraced all matters connected with the Holy See. On their recall or transfer, other nuncios succeeded them, giving the position its permanent character. Nuncios were expected to communicate with the cardinal secretary of state at least once a week, and usually they wrote to Rome more often.[1] In the correspondence between nuncios and the Roman Curia ciphers were used. If the information were of a secret nature, the nuncio took the further precaution of using a personal cipher.

With the establishment of Propaganda Fide in 1622, the nunciature took on a further responsibility. To each nuncio was allotted a number of 'persecuted' or 'mission' countries whose interests he had to watch on behalf of Propaganda Fide. As the nuncio at Brussels was charged with the Low Countries, Denmark, England, Scotland and Ireland, his post became that of an inter-nuncio who exchanged and passed on international news items to Rome and to other nuncios. The nuncio in Paris had the advantage of situation. The distance which separated Madrid from Vienna or from Rome gave Paris the benefit of swifter intelligence and more rapid action. Because of its proximity to England, Brussels, The Hague and Portugal, the nunciature at Paris became a rendezvous for secret envoys who desired to negotiate with the pope without incurring the suspicion of the Spanish ambassador at Rome.

It was the nuncios who always noted the comings and goings of diplomats; their interminable discussions of treaties never signed. With an unwearied perseverance, the pope and his agents attempted to weave a chain of peaceful negotiations, patiently renewing the links even as they broke. Rome became the listening post of Europe. There a whispered word in the corridors might be of more consequence than threat of war in one of the Spanish dominions. To Rome, therefore, came the most accomplished diplomats and the most promising jurors. The best-equipped legations were maintained in Rome. In effect, the Vatican became the most important determining influence in international politics in the period between Trent and Westphalia and in its courts aired the principal matters of European governments.

During much the same time, the prestige of the Spanish ambassador rode high, and Europe witnessed the paradox of a nation whose power was little more than a husk even as the Spanish genius for diplomacy came to its fullest flowering. The Spanish ambassadors moved on the stage of European politics with a formidable independent life which commanded respect and frequently intimidated.

In Rome, the Spanish ambassadors enjoyed a special influence in the political destiny of the Christian states. During the reign of Charles V, the ambassadors of Spain were also those of the Empire. Those of Philip II ranked first in precedence in the papal court with the right of privileged audiences. In the decadent period of the third and fourth Philips, negotiations with the Low Countries, Savoy, Franche-Comte, Portugal and the French Crown were approved or vetoed arbitrarily by the ambassador of His Most Catholic Majesty at the Holy See. Through his chancery passed all matters concerning the Spanish clergy because the king of Spain was 'patron and defender of churches, religious orders, and members of the clergy'. The Spanish ambassador exercised this prerogative in the Roman Curia so tyrannically that he had been accused of dictating policies to the successors of St Peter. It was he who sent to the bishops of Spain the ordinations of the pope. He implemented canonisations, concessions of the 'Cruzados', the imposition of 'Millones', and other donations by which the king of Spain graciously allowed his coffers to be filled at the expense of Holy Mother Church.[2]

It was only after 1631 that papal diplomacy interested itself actively in the reconciliation of the great Catholic powers, France and the House of Hapsburgs. Their mutual hostility, personified in the persons of Richelieu and Olivares, prolonged the war that lasted thirty years. This division of the great Catholic Houses was a matter of deep anxiety to the papacy.

But because Urban VIII wished to be the common father of all, he was suspected by all. At Madrid and at Vienna it gave scandal because the Holy See continued to maintain friendly relations with Richelieu and Louis. The least favours shown to the House of Austria in the interests of religion provoked lively protests from Paris. Harsher than either has been the judgement of history. 'No sounding line of historical enquiry can reach the motives of his actions, and the actual foundation of his character', has been said of Maffeo Barberini, elected pope in August 1623. Relying too much on the testament of Venetian ambassadors, an unfavourable and prejudiced portrait of this pope has come down to posterity. Leopold von Ranke, historian of the popes, affirms that indirect alliances had existed in 1631–32 between the Holy See and Protestant Germany and Sweden.[3] The German historian Gregorovius (1879), claims that Urban VIII tolerated the alliances of Louis XIII in order to weaken the Hapsburgs. Schnitzer (1899) in an examination of the politique of the Holy See during the first part of the Thirty Years War claims that Urban's foreign policy was dominated by fear of a Swedish invasion of Italy. Moritz Borsch (1906) makes the bold statement:

> to judge by all that has come down to us with the warrant of unimpeachable evidence concerning his anti-Spanish and anti-Imperial policy, he would have liked nothing better than that Richelieu and his confederates should have wrested from the grasp of Spain, the possession of Milan, Flanders, and, if possible, Naples as well.

Jedin (1948), historian of the counter-reformation, frankly admits the prevalence of Machiavellianism in this period, and cites Pallavicino, the official chronicler of the counter-reformation, who, writing in the middle of the seventeenth century, justified papal procedure by applying the general doctrine of casuistry in cases of bribery and deceit. Vatican diplomacy in Urban's time had acquired the name of being dilatory and over-cautious, calculating and deceitful, best summed up in a contemporary fulmination: *'le tergiversazioni e gli intrighi della corte romana'*.

Urban's greatest defender, Auguste Leman, concedes his failing as a temporal ruler: his secret pro-French sympathies, his propensity for nepotism, his role of strict, but passive, neutrality, points out justly that Urban was the patron of a lost cause.[4] In the quest for universal peace in Europe, he was indefatigable, and he succeeded in passing on to his two immediate successors, Innocent X and Alexander VII, his own sense of urgency to achieve this goal almost, one would say, at any price.

When on the night of 1 December 1640, João IV was acclaimed king in the great square of Lisbon, the relations between Portugal and the Holy See were far from cordial. Mainly as a consequence of the religious policy of the Spanish monarch in Portugal, Lisbon had been penalised by a general interdict on its churches for over a year. The situation was further complicated by the flight of the bishop of Leiria to Spain, by the manifest irresolution of the archbishop of Evora to accept the new king, and by the imprisonment of the archbishop of Braga and of his confederates, the bishop of Martiria and the bishop-elect of Malaca for entering into conspiracy against the newly-elected king a few months after his enthronement. For João IV, it became, and remained, his chief care to restore harmony between the Church in Portugal and the Vatican.

It is not easy to obtain a comprehensive view of João IV's dealings with the papacy, because the problem was essentially a political one involving Spain as the antagonist and France as the protagonist. Much of the material for this sketch is to be found among the correspondence of the papal collectors at Lisbon, the French and Spanish nuncios, and among the replies and directives of the cardinal secretary of state.[5] Another source of information is the massive collection of letters and documents that passed between the Braganças and their ambassadors in Rome, principally de Sousa Coutinho.[6] Yet another stream of letters passed between Philip IV and his ambassadors at the Holy See. It consists of reports and copies of letters from pro-Spanish cardinals in the Roman Curia and of documents and correspondence from Spanish agents of Philip in the different courts of Europe. These the Spanish ambassador forwarded with his own reports, receiving, in due course, answers from Philip and from his council of state.[7]

According to traditional procedure in the kingdom of Portugal, bishops were beneficed *ad supplicationem* or *ad nominationem*. This privilege of *ad nomationem*, which was the process employed by the Datario in the seventeenth century, belonged to the king of Portugal not as a special prerogative, but uniquely *'ex consuetudine tamquam regem Portugallise'*. In practice, this had meant that the appointments of bishops were achieved simply by supplication or nomination of the king of Portugal, without specifying expressly that the king had the power of nominating bishops, and the Holy See usually confirmed the nominations. When Portugal was incorporated into the possessions of Philip II in 1580, this method of appointing bishops was adopted by the Spanish monarchy, and Philip IV used it as an incontestable weapon in his war against what he termed 'his rebel of Portugal'. João de Bragança could not hope that the cautious Urban would risk a breach with Spain by conceding back to him this ancient privilege. Instead, he urged the provision of bishops *de motu proprio* (on his own impulse) by the pope himself, and in ordinary circumstances this suggestion would have been sanctioned promptly by the Holy See. In this case, however, there was the formidable hostility of the Spanish ambassador in Rome to be reckoned with, and Rome soon discovered that, theoretically, João IV still clung to the ancient privilege. If the pope nominated bishops *de motu proprio*, it must be with the approval of the king of Portugal. The question of bishops should have been a mild domestic tiff between the father of Christendom and one of his sons; instead, it assumed the alarming proportions of imminent schism.[8]

In the few days that elapsed between the revolution of 1 December and the arrival of the duke of Bragança in Lisbon from Villaviciosa, the archbishops of Lisbon and Braga were entrusted with the interim government. Their first concern was to lift the interdict that lay over the city. They appealed to the vice-collector and petitioned him to suspend the interdict for at least six months. On their side they guaranteed, in the name of the new king, Portugal's loyalty to the Holy See, and full exercise of his former function to the papal collector.[9]

João IV confirmed the pledges of his archbishops and wrote immediately to the cardinal secretary stating that he wished 'to expedite all negotiations proper to the jurisdiction of the collector as heretofore'. On the same day, 8 January 1641, he published a decree ordaining that the benefices accruing to the Holy See were not to be molested. Clearly he was showing his determination to terminate the abuses which had arisen over the usurpation of chapels. The cardinal secretary, Barberini, recognising the turn for good which events in Lisbon were taking, approved the proceedings of the vice-collector. The Curia renewed his faculty to suspend the interdict for a further six months but warned him to exercise the maximum prudence. He was not to proceed without orders from Rome, or compromise the Roman Curia in any way.[10] Barberini was, of course, thinking of Madrid.

So the first six months of João IV's reign passed peacefully in direct contact with the Holy See. The first hint of difficulty came unexpectedly from the nuncio in Paris. He refused to receive the bishop of Lamego, Portuguese ambassador to Rome, who was passing through Paris and desired to meet him. The nuncio said he had received no instructions from Rome.[11] Already the immense influence that Spain exercised over the Roman Curia was at work. Even before the bishop of Lamego reached Rome, Philip IV had presented an ultimatum to the pope: if Urban VIII received the Portuguese ambassador, Spain would break off all diplomatic relations with the Holy See.[12] The pope referred the matter to a commission of cardinals who found there was nothing to prevent the bishop of Lamego from entering Rome as the representative of a Christian prince at the feet of the vicar of Christ. Some, however, prudently suggested that the Portuguese envoy reside outside the city in the event of a Spanish attack on his person. On 17 November, the bishop of Lamego arrived in Rome and was housed in the palace of the French ambassador. His entry and place of residence did, in fact, provoke a passionate and stormy protest from the Spanish ambassador who began an intense campaign with Urban VIII presenting long memorials in his weekly and extraordinary audiences.[13]

Meanwhile, João IV was faced with a situation in Lisbon. A group of disconsolate nobles, under the leadership of the archbishop of Braga, had entered into conspiracy with several members of the newly-appointed council of state, to exterminate the Bragança family and restore Portugal to Philip IV. The plot was discovered and the leading conspirators were condemned to death. In the case of the archbishop and other ecclesiastics, the sentence was mitigated to imprisonment. It was necessary in his own defence and that of his kingdom, João IV told the vice-collector, to commit to prison the chief conspirator who was put in custody of the vice-collector.[14]

In Rome, the tone of the Spanish ambassador became more menacing. If Urban VIII recognised the duke of Bragança as king of Portugal, the papal nuncio in Madrid would be expelled. A change of ambassadors did not lessen the hostility. The new ambassador's *Instructions* were clear; he was to hinder the Portuguese representative in every way possible, using force if necessary. He could rely on getting soldiers from Naples.[15] In the Roman heat of mid-August, a street encounter took place between the household of the French and Spanish ambassadors. In reality, it was an assault on the retinue of the bishop of Lamego. The Portuguese envoy made one last appeal to Urban who offered him an audience behind locked doors. The bishop of Lamego, who felt that this reception was unworthy of his master, refused, and he departed on 11 December 1642. His failure to co-operate on what, after all, was a small point of procedure cost Portugal dearly. With his departure the nomination of bishops to Portuguese sees escalated into a major problem.

Officially, the Holy See continued to address Philip IV as king of Portugal and Algarve, but it was not prepared to appoint Philip's nominees to ecclesiastical benefices in those territories. In Lisbon, according to the vice-collector, a wave of disillusionment had swept over the city when the details of Lamego's mission and its failure were made public. All could yet be righted if the Holy See confirmed the nominations of João IV.[16] The Spanish nuncio thought otherwise. It is not easy to understand the attitude adopted by Nuncio Panziroli in this affair. From his dispatches to Rome during these years one gets the unfavourable impression that his mission as papal representative had been completely disoriented by the strong personality of

Conde-Duque Olivares, so frequent and so full of adulation was his flattery of the prime minister. His appointment as secretary of state to Urban VIII poses an interesting problem: to what extent did the official correspondence of the cardinal secretaries of state reflect their personal views or those of the pope? Barberini, nephew and secretary of state of Urban was also cardinal-protector of Spain. Indeed, it was this continued effort of Barberini to safeguard his own position and that of the Roman Curia with Philip IV that delayed settlement of this question in the early years.

There were now fourteen sees in Portugal and overseas without bishops. It troubled the conscience of Urban VIII in the last months of his life.[17] Yet true to his nature, he temporised to the end. He set up a commission to examine the problem. Their findings were favourable to João IV. The appointment of bishops in Portugal was achieved simply *'ad supplicationem o ad nominationem regis'*, without specifying further. The commission recommended the following line of action to Urban VIII, not to approve the nomination of persons unsympathetic to the nation which had elected the duke of Bragança its king and notify Philip IV accordingly.[18] Still Urban VIII hesitated. He was a temporal ruler and needed the Spanish alliance against Parma. It would not do to hurt the susceptibilities of Philip just then. Even Barberini was conscious of the injustice, and he wrote a letter full of uneasy excuses to Panziroli.[19]

Baffled by the obsequious explanations of the cardinal secretary, João IV called a council of theologians in his kingdom to study the religious situation and offer a solution. On 22 January 1644, they presented their findings. They warned the king of the danger of a national council. Only the pope in the circumstances under survey could appoint bishops, and they reminded his Majesty that this was only a passing misunderstanding. Eventually the Holy See would confirm his nominations.[20] It was excellent advice. If João IV had but considered, his best card was to shed all responsibility for the vacant sees. Instead, he voluntarily assumed a burden which grew heavier with the years. The same year Urban VIII died. He had refused vehemently to excommunicate the 'rebel' of Portugal though Spain had brought much pressure to bear, but he was haunted at the end by the thought of so many vacant sees.

The new pope, Innocent X, was greeted with misgivings by the various political parties. A man of great talents, he was timid and hesitant and wilted before any manifestation of violence. Ademola, who made a study of his reign as pope, described him as inconsistent, ('variable') and Von Pastor deplored the deleterious family influences which undermined the government and prestige of Innocent X. His reign as pope was plagued by the incessant and overweening ambition of his sister-in-law, the masterful Dona Olimpia Maidalchini, and by the greed of the cardinal nephew, Camilio Pamfili. For the next few years, the Spanish ambassador at Rome refers frequently to private audiences with Dona Olimpia and to hard bargains struck.[21]

Towards Portugal, Innocent X manifested a certain dubious cordiality which was rendered ineffective by an exaggerated deference to Philip. Secretly he was pro-French. The result was unfortunate. He created an attitude of suspicion between Rome and Lisbon which hardened João IV in his resolution to wrest the nomination of bishops *de motu proprio* from the Holy See. Yet another Junta took place in Portugal. Again its findings were couched in similar terms, but it added a new note of appeal: under no circumstances to expel the vice-collector.[22]

Surprise had deepened into resentment as the years passed and no collector was appointed by the Holy See. The king now resolved to send Jerome Bataglia, the vice-collector, to Rome in November 1646. The time was propitious. Innocent X had been shocked by the brutal attack made on the person of Nicholas Montiero who had come to Rome on behalf of the Portuguese clergy some time previously. It was quite obvious to everyone in Rome who was the instigator of the crime. Therefore, João IV sent the vice-collector; no-one would represent more fully the true state of religion in Portugal; no-one would be more certain of gaining a hearing. But he underestimated his adversary. The departure of Bataglia was construed as the official expulsion of the vice-collector. Both von Pastor and Ademolo present this interpretation which has been generally accepted.[23] Never did the Portuguese come so near the actualisation of their hopes as when the vice-collector went to Rome. Unfortunately, Innocent was changeable. In the Münster preliminaries to Westphalia that went on during the year 1647, the Portuguese fought a hard and fruitless battle to win recognition of their country's independence at the coming peace negotiations. They were opposed relentlessly by Spain and by the pope's representative, Fabio Chigi.

Feeling that all recognised diplomatic methods had failed, João IV again played with the idea of a national council. On this occasion, he turned to the universities and singled out the Sorbonne as lending a sympathetic ear. In extreme necessity could he the king, permit the consecration of bishops without having recourse to the Holy See? The Sorbonne's answer was dangerously equivocal. If the pope continued to defer the solution, and if the imminent perils of the Church necessitated such, the king could, and ought to, appoint the bishops of his kingdom who would be consecrated in virtue of the ancient right of the community to elect, by reason of willful delay by the pope or without just cause. Having established this strange principle, the Sorbonne encouraged the king of Portugal to summon a national council. In the circumstances he could not be accused of schism since the consecration of the bishops would be made according to what appertained to the Church by legitimately-chosen bishops.[24]

According to Ericeira, João IV had a profoundly-religious conscience. In ecclesiastical affairs he sought the opinion of learned men, and he read all the documents connected with the matter in question. He was a slow, deep thinker, and he never acted impulsively. He rejected the recommendations of the Sorbonne, though with reluctance and set about working through diplomatic channels again.

The nuncio at Paris, Guido di Bagno, was undoubtedly sympathetic to Portugal. That much is clear from his lucid dispatches. It was natural that João IV, barred by the powerful Spanish ambassador at Rome, would enlist the help of the nuncio in Paris. From 1650 on, he adopted the tedious process of treating indirectly with Rome through the Paris nunciature, while Portuguese agents in Rome sought to gain an audience with the unwilling pope. Throughout the whole of 1650, the Spanish ambassador complained peevishly to Philip IV of the Portuguese 'lizards' who were seeking auditions with the pope. He reports with satisfaction the failure of the mission of Antonio Vieira, S.J.; the father-general of the Jesuits guaranteed him personally that he would have Vieira removed from the political scene. Yet another Portuguese Jesuit who penetrated the Vatican wrote the fretful Infantado a little later. He feared the pope would react to all this pressure by acting intemperately. He requested Philip to write again to the general of the Company.[25]

But the duke of Infantado failed to note the presence of the Irishman, Frei Domingos do Rosario in Rome the summer of 1650, though in the previous February he had drawn Philip IV's attention to 'Father Daly, the Dominican, who previously helped the faction of the

Portuguese rebel' and was then engaged as agent for Charles II. Infantado apparently never suspected that O'Daly succeeded in having an audience with His Holiness ostensibly to treat the affairs of Charles II, and with the cardinal-protector of Spain as O'Daly gratefully testified in a dedicatory letter to the Barberinis.[26] The mission of O'Daly would have gone unrecorded were it not for a brief letter of Nuncio di Bagno from Paris, and the reports of two English royalist agents, Meynell and Cottington. Cottington assumed that Charles II was the subject of O'Daly's audience with the pope, whereas it is clear from his mixed report that the friar was also representing the plight of the Portuguese church. He too was unsuccessful, being told roundly by Innocent X 'on no account to meddle in this business'.

In Paris, Francisco de Coutinho, the blunt, self-confident ambassador of João IV was trying different tactics. In an assembly-general of the French clergy at the Augustinian monastery in Paris, he made known the lamentable situation and the perplexity of his master. His appeal for support was cordially received and a letter of supplication from the French clergy went to Rome. It was supported by recommendations from Louis XIV, a boy of thirteen, from the impulsive Cardinal d'Este, and from the unpopular Cardinal Antonio Barberini. It was coldly received, and after a lapse of nearly a year, Innocent X, acting through his secretary of state, directed a long letter to Nuncio di Bagno. He regretted what had passed in the French capital and drew the nuncio's attention to the political consequences of Portugal's exclusion from the Münster peace. Simultaneously, he sent a brief to the archbishops, bishops and clergy of France acknowledging the receipt of their petition and politely advising them to attend to their own problems.[27]

Some months earlier Nuncio di Bagno had reported a rumour in Paris that the bishop of Belem, a learned and pious man, was going to Lisbon to consecrate bishops. After an interval he wrote saying that despite his remonstrance, the French clergy were sending the bishop of Belem to Rome to represent the urgency of the matter to Innocent X. The whole idea had originated in the French court.[28]

Spain acted promptly. Dona Olimpia was notoriously avaricious. In a laconic letter to Philip IV, the duke of Infantado reported that he had had several satisfactory audiences with her. He advised the king to offer the cardinal-nephew a wealthy benefice. With his dispatches he enclosed several adulatory letters from Cardinal Trivulcio, assuring the king of his support and that of the pro-Spanish cardinals in the consistory which Innocent X threatened to convene about the problem.[29]

The bishop of Belem, however, had several audiences with the pope and with Cardinals Spado and Lugo. It seemed at last that Innocent X would yield to the many petitions. With perfect timing Philip IV offered the wealthy benefice of Grandeza to the cardinal-nephew, and it was accepted. João IV retaliated by nominating Cardinal Ursino protector of Portugal and the pope was not displeased. Influenced by the new protector, by the many appeals and by his talks with the bishop of Belem, Innocent X sent secret instructions to his nuncio in Paris to treat directly with the Portuguese representative in Paris on the nomination of bishops. The sentiment of the pope was one of anxious desire to do his duty as universal pastor of the church. With quite extraordinary courage for such a timid man, he offered three nominations *de motu proprio* to João IV acting through the Paris nunciature. With incredible obstinacy, Coutinho, without consulting his master, rejected them because he considered them inimical to his sovereign's rights. Despite the prudent advice of Vincent de Paul, Coutinho recklessly broke off negotiations with the nuncio in 1653, and the favourable moment passed. Dona Olimpia reasserted her malign and grasping influence over the Vatican, and palace intrigues assailed the unhappy pope until he died on 17 January 1655.[30]

With the death of Innocent X all negotiations which had been paralysed by his feebleness in the closing years of his life converged hopefully on the election of his successor. The college of cardinals was divided. On one side were ranged the pro-Spanish faction; on the other side were the French cardinals. In between was a group free from political influence who wanted the best pope for the church. On 20 January 1655, sixty-nine cardinals went into conclave, and after eighty days, Fabio Chigi was elected, taking the name of Alexander VII.

Fabio Chigi was a learned, experienced and upright man. He was universally esteemed. But to Portugal his election was a bitter blow. There was the painful memory of his relentless opposition to the Portuguese delegates at the Münster congress of 1647. Politically, the new pope posed as neutral, but allowing for the grave difficulties that existed just then between Paris and the Holy See, he was drawn almost inevitably to range with Spain, and a jubilant letter from Philip IV to Terranova, his ambassador in Rome, is full of plans for 'aiding or serving the relations of the new pope'. Terranova acknowledged receipt of the king's letter on 22 November 1655, and he discussed the line of action the national cardinals were to take in case the pope approves the *motu proprio* of the Portuguese churches.[31]

Alexander VII had acted as cardinal secretary of state for Innocent X and was fully alive to the ramifications of the bishop question. He had transacted business with Coutinho through the Paris nunciature and was a man with a conscience, as Terranova warned Philip IV. When he began his reign in 1655, he was determined to find a solution. In six months he had won a grudging consent to issue a *motu proprio* from the king of Spain.

In Paris, Francisco de Sousa Coutinho had incurred the displeasure of Mazarin, and he was transferred to Rome. O'Daly took his place in the French capital. Prior to his departure, Coutinho contacted Nuncio de Bagno to ascertain if his mission would be favourably received by the Roman Curia. The nuncio held out every hope.[32] In the fifteen years that had elapsed, the attitude of the Curia towards Portugal had softened considerably. For one thing, the influence of Spain was diminishing; for another, the 'rebel' of Portugal had gained unwilling recognition as an able administrator fully justifying the expectations of the nation that had acclaimed him king. All was set for a reconciliation.

The account of the next few months with its mass of documentation marked the peak of the activity which centred around the nomination of Portuguese bishops and illustrates the bewildering luxuriance of diplomatic intrigue that was to be encountered in Vatican circles of that century.

In a long letter to his king, Coutinho gave an account of his first meeting with the cardinals in Rome, Cardinal Palotti and Sacchetti being most cordial, but his major concern was to gain an audience with the pope. Ursino, cardinal-protector of Portugal, had taken a dislike to Coutinho and refused to exert his influence to get him a hearing.[33] Coutinho was not to know that an urgent series of letters had passed between Philip IV and Terranova. In five letters sent between 13 October and 18 December, Terranova reported how he was received in audience by Alexander, and he protested strongly against the proximate arrival of the envoy of the rebel of Portugal. The pope listened to him attentively but seemed oppressed by the thought of so many bishoprics without pastors, especially in India and overseas. With his dispatch of 25

October, Terranova enclosed a copy of a letter he had sent the pope:

I have received notice that Francisco de Sousa Coutinho, Chevalier and Gentleman of the House of the Rebel of Portugal, comes to this court. He was ambassador in Holland for one year, in Paris three, and was also in Sweden. He is expected here on November 10 and brings with him two nephews called Don Manuel and Don Gaspar Pereyra. He is a widower. He has in his service a secretary called Julian Hiebado, who has been in Rome a long time, a Castilian but partial to France. Also, I understand that Father Master Domingo del Rosario, the Irishman, of the order of St. Dominic, comes from Portugal sent by the duke of Bragança to treat with You Holiness on the question of the bishoprics of that kingdom and that he brings the opinions of universities and theologians who are not subjects of His Majesty (Philip IV). In which case, Your Holiness will not yield on the issue of creating a Patriarchate for that kingdom. Also, this religious may arrive in France, travel to Paris to confer with Francisco de Sousa and it is possible that he will make the journey here with him.

To this, the pope replied guardedly that he would not accede Coutinho the credentials of a minister or impede his arrival in any way. As to O'Daly, he knew nothing of his coming, but would accord the same treatment to the one as to the other.[34]

From the other end, Philip IV had dashed off a letter to his ambassador on 2 November. It was in cipher warning him:

that he had received intelligence that a Dominican was going to Rome to treat of the provision of bishops on behalf of the rebel of Portugal, and that he, Philip IV, renewed his orders on that subject.[35]

The pope, too, had his own channels of information. In an intercepted letter from an agent in Paris, which Terranova copied for Philip IV, Alexander VII was appraised of the political situation there, of the failure of

Jant's recent mission in Lisbon, and of Coutinho's unpopularity with Mazarin. 'It is this same man who has left Paris and waits upon you in this court'. Whether as in 1650, O'Daly managed to see the pope without the knowledge of the Spanish ambassador is not recorded. He was in Paris in late December and reported an audience with Mazarin toward the end of the year, as we learn from one of his own dispatches. The French nuncio had calendared the return of Jant and the departure of Coutinho in October, but he did not mention O'Daly until early in 1656.

The new year saw Alexander VII resolved to settle this thorny question which had gone on too long. He wrote a brief full of warmth to Philip IV on the urgency of nominating bishops for the vacant sees, and he appealed to the well-known piety of the new king. It had the effect of a gentle softening breeze. Philip's reply of 19 February 1656, was much milder in tone, and he cautiously ceded to the pope the right of nominating bishops *de motu proprio*.[36]

In the same month Nuncio di Bagno wrote with disturbing news. João IV intended to join a detestable league composed of France, Sweden and England as the other partners. It revived all Alexander VII's prejudices against the 'rebel' of Portugal which had been so manifest at the Münster congress. For the papacy, as for Spain, politics still remained theology-minded. Though the toleration for permission of two or more religions within a state had been laid down finally at Westphalia, Alexander VII's sentiments could be summed up by the tenth century dictum; permission is not the same as approval. He was not prepared to accept with equanimity political alliances between Catholic and non-Catholic states. During the spring of 1656, the Portuguese ambassador at Paris once again became the subject of letters that passed between Rome, Madrid and Paris. O'Daly was interviewed repeatedly by the French nuncio whose report of 17 March described O'Daly as an agile and subtle diplomat:

> The Dominican Father, Dominic of the Rosary, who is in this court on business of the duke of Bragança, claiming to be king of Portugal, asked me to see him for the third time. Our meeting took place on the 13 of this month in the convent of the Jesuit Fathers in Father Draceti's room. Father Draceti pretends to much familiarity with Cardinal Mazarin, and told me the cardinal called him to Florence during last year, when he was there himself. However, the results of this confidence in which we placed our hopes, were never seen. After some compliments between Father Dominic and myself – (I had met him at other times, when he was in this court before, and in Rome some years ago) – he told me that his master, like every good Catholic, was greatly distressed about the proposed union between France, Sweden and Cromwell because of the injury to the faith and to the Holy See. His master felt that the great misery of this century was that Catholic princes rather desired the friendship and approval of heretical princes instead of making peace between themselves. He also pointed out that English navigation to India was inimical to Portugal's interests and that he had come to Paris for a final decision about what his master could hope from France. He had spoken with Cardinal Mazarin who had shown no interest complaining that he had seen no beneficial results in the past and did not feel obliged to protect the king of Portugal. O'Daly thought that this contempt for Portugal was the reason that H.E. was turning to Cromwell or that possibly Cromwell was seeking the alliance. O'Daly suggested that if His Holiness were to intercede on his behalf to procure a Spanish passport, he would go and propose terms between Spain and Portugal that would not have to be altered by the Spaniards. Willingly he, Dominic, would come to Rome and lay these conditions before His Holiness. His master gave him perfect confidence and full authority to go ahead in this matter, hoping that such a union (Spain-Portugal) would be useful and profitable to the Catholic Church and the Holy See. I answered him very generally, feeling rather doubtful about the cardinal's reaction to Dominic's scheme. However, I had every reason to believe the sincerity of what he said. Father

Draceti informed me that Dominic had also treated for the Catholics of Ireland and transacted other matters.[37]

Promptly, on 10 April, the answer came from the cardinal secretary of state: His Holiness was perplexed about the whole business and requested his nuncio to keep to very general terms when speaking with the Dominican.[38] From the nuncio files it is obvious that Alexander VII had his heart set on universal peace in Europe and as with his predecessors the ponderous demands of Madrid paralysed his efforts as vicar of Christ. In June of that year, João IV finally ratified the 1654 treaty between Portugal and England. With an accurate sense of timing Philip IV wrote to Alexander VII a month later. He requested a renewal of the 'Millones' by papal brief which he had been receiving for the past six years to be employed against the enemies of Holy Religion. Now with the unique finality he petitioned Alexander VII for 'help in the war against the rebel of Portugal'.[39]

O'Daly, helped by the French nuncio, was still seeking a Spanish passport. The death of João IV on 6 November kept him busy in Paris and after 18 October we hear no more of his projected visit to Madrid.[40] Alexander VII, too, was extricated from an awkward predicament by the death of the 'rebel'. On 14 November, the instructions the pope sent to his nuncio in Paris concerned Portugal and were conveyed accordingly to Frei Domingos do Rosario. Nowhere had the pope stated his position as regards Portugal so precisely as in this document. His basic attitude of disavowal and disengagement was apparent; Alexander VII was still Fabio Chigi. His nuncio was to try and prevent any reaction in the French court in the event of the Portuguese ambassador being asked to leave Rome.[41]

João IV's first concern in 1641, when he accepted the thorny crown of Portugal, was to settle the rupture with Rome peacefully. He had not been responsible for the break. When João IV died, sixteen years later, the breach had widened considerably; yet, few monarchs had gone to such lengths to safeguard the faith of his kingdom and keep united with Rome. Seldom in the history of monarchy had a king sustained a diplomatic campaign so hard fought, so persistent, and with so many odds against him. Many factors contributed to defeat his efforts: the Spanish intransigence, the Roman Curia's distrustful conservativism and João IV's own secular outlook in his dealings with European states. In fact, three popes had been ready to nominate bishops *de motu proprio* and were foiled on two occasions by the official representatives of João IV. By a singular unhappy choice, both ambassadors that the king of Portugal sent officially to Rome on this important mission failed through personal action. The bishop of Lamego in 1642 and de Sousa Coutinho in 1653 acted impulsively without orders. On reading Coutinho's correspondence, one is left with the impression of a man pre-occupied with the recognition of his rank as ambassador, of one who had too large a vision of his own talents.[42] He had come to Rome full of diplomatic experience, ready to patch up all misunderstandings between Portugal and Rome, but he lacked the wisdom of adapting himself to the extremely-subtle atmosphere of the soft-footed Vatican.

One can advance the view also, that the Roman diplomacy of this era which witnessed the rise of the secular states was impeded by the political authority of the papacy, and in many cases was gravely culpable by reason of that very authority. Officially, the principle of political toleration was laid down at the peace of Westphalia. In practice, Alexander VII refused to admit it. To princes who viewed their own particular interests, he urged the higher interests of the Christian republic.[43]

Not until peace was finally signed between Portugal and Spain did the Roman Curia resume official relations with the son of João of Bragança. In March 1658, Coutinho received an order from Afonso VI to leave Rome immediately, Cardinal Ursino having brought pressure to bear.[44] In July 1659, the cardinal secretary of state notified the Spanish ambassador, Sobremonte, that 'His Holiness could not reconcile an action so contrary to justice and the clear rights of His Majesty as to set up as patron of the churches of Portugal – a rebel'. In a twenty-page report on the Roman Curia the same year, Don Gaspar de Sobremonte describes Alexander VII as:

> one who has no love for negotiations, trusts no-one, and allows problems to solve themselves … as regards His Majesty's affairs at Rome, he need neither fear much adversity, nor hope for prosperity. As for external affairs, I do not know which of the two, France or England, is detested more by the pope.[45]

It was to France and England that João IV inclined in his foreign policy. After his death, O'Daly, as counsellor of the queen-regent, assumed responsibility for maintaining that policy. Despite Alexander VII's obvious displeasure conveyed through his nuncios, O'Daly persisted in his efforts to conciliate France, even to the point of joining the quadruple alliance the following year (1657). Again he worked towards the realisation of a union between the Stuarts and the Braganças brought about by the wedding of Charles II and the Infanta Catherine. It was these two operations which vexed Alexander VII most sorely and hardened him against Portugal. It was these two factors which politically put Portugal on the map of Europe again. By 1663, France was secretly helping Afonso VI in his war against Spain with money, arms and officers sent by way of London. O'Daly, much more than Coutinho, carried on and implemented the foreign policy of his master. That he might have been embarrassed by his allegiance to a master more sacred than his king, forces us to consider him more attentively.

There was his concern to keep the balance of power between England and France and the consequent secular nature of Portugal's diplomatic alliances which so annoyed the pope. More arresting than either, was the undeniable fact that like the greater Richelieu, O'Daly abandoned diplomacy as an instrument of religious propaganda. In this he was a man of his age and diplomatic practice of the seventeenth century had lost any overtones of religiosity in the decade after Westphalia. In fact, Richelieu was the real architect of modern diplomacy, and the age which ushered in the peace of Westphalia saw the complete and permanent organisation of the art and technicalities of political negotiations. To Richelieu goes the credit of founding this great structure of French politics, this ever-present sense of the necessity for diplomatic action. Diplomacy, he says, tacitly in his *Spiritual Testament*, ought to know no boundaries; no zone ought to be closed to it. After Westphalia France served as a model to all other states, because her diplomatic institutions formed an organism, homogeneous yet compact, posited to the total service of the state, differing radically in its constituent parts from Roman diplomacy and from the decaying Venetian diplomacy. O'Daly was a man of his age; it was to this school he belonged. It remained to be seen what talents he possessed as a diplomat.

To determine O'Daly's gifts of diplomacy, it is necessary to ascertain what were the prevailing ideas on the subject, and what were the qualities sought for in a diplomat of Mazarin's era. These are best exemplified by Gabriel Naudé in his 'Coup d'Etat', written in 1639 and analysed by Meinecke in his study *Machiavellism*.[46] Naudé idealised Richelieu and advised rulers to follow the example of Louis XIII and put themselves in the hands of one strong minister, making the freest choice of individuals, and not excluding even foreigners, even monks, even scholars. He had, according to Naudé, to possess three qualities: force, justice and prudence. Strength (*la force*), Naudé defined as a mental disposition which would always be uniformly heroic and firm, capable of seeing everything, hearing all, and doing all without being agitated. The second virtue, justice, would seem to refer rather to political justice. 'Never', says Naudé:

> let oneself be used as a tool for the passions of one's master and never propose anything to him which one does not oneself believe to be necessary for maintaining the state, the welfare of the people, or the safety of the ruler.

Prudence was the queen of the political virtues and consisted in the ability to keep something secret, if it were not suitable to express it. 'It consists in letting one's speech be prompted rather by necessity than by ambition; of not treating anyone badly, or despising them'. This seems an idealised picture of the perfect Christian diplomat, and Meinecke comments on it as a 'remarkable and contradictory combination of arrogance and immorality, of heroic grandeur, spiritual strength and superficiality'.

The decade following the peace of Westphalia was what Meinicke termed 'the classic period of Machiavelli'. It was the diplomat, sending in his reports, who was the acknowledged discoverer of the theory of the interests of states. If he was one of those who took his work more seriously, he could not rest content with merely reporting what had occurred and what had been achieved, with sketching the characters of people and collecting statistical material about the force of the foreign state; he also found himself compelled to try and bring events, plans and possibilities at any particular time, over one common denominator, the interests of state.[47]

The theory of the interests of the state would seem to imply for Naudé the Machiavellian principle:

> that the interests of the state may, in case of need, be made to override every principle of morality and the ruler is free to lie,

deceive, betray, rob and murder if he thinks his country is
profited thereby.

Coming back to an examination of Daniel O'Daly's
political career, it is well to recapitulate briefly the chief
points of that career. He was sent on a mission to France to
make demands which she was not prepared to give and in
which others had failed before him. If he urged the French
alliance, as he undoubtedly did, it was because that unless
Portugal had France as her ally, her own position between
Spain and Holland was critical.

Was he ambitious? The charge rests on the evidence of
the fretful Cominges who gave an account of
conversations which he and O'Daly had on the possibility
of a ministerial post in the government for the friar.[48] It
would seem that Daniel O'Daly enjoyed having a finger in
political pies and had a flair for diplomacy. It was no
accident that such diverse characters as Philip IV of Spain,
the master-general of the Dominican order, Henrietta
Maria and her son, Charles Stuart, the king and queen of
Portugal employed the Irishman to carry out negotiations
which required tactful handling. His role as envoy in the
question of bishops was a hidden one. It was a dangerous
matter for a member of the regular clergy to meddle in,
and there was the example of Vieira, the Jesuit, to remind
him of the power of the Spanish ambassador. Yet, O'Daly
was idealistic enough to risk his vindictiveness on at least
two occasions and expressed his willingness to walk into
the lion's den if one could procure a Spanish passport.
That he was capable of enlisting Nuncio di Bagno's co-
operation in this delicate matter is for reflection. Again, he
succeeded in maintaining cordial relations with Mazarin,
even while disagreeing with his line of conduct.[49]

Prestage in his monograph on O'Daly advances the view
that the Irishman's desire to enter the ministry of Portugal
was influenced by the example of Mazarin, an Italian, who
governed France.[50] Unfortunately, Prestage does not

elaborate on this point and there seems to be no direct evidence to show that O'Daly modelled himself on the cardinal. Nor do his letters to Mazarin give any indication of admiration; they were curt and businesslike. If O'Daly were deficient in political virtue, as described by Naudé, it was in 'the ability to keep something secret if it is unsuitable to express it'. If we are to believe Cominges's dispatches, O'Daly was indiscreet and even imprudent in his choice of subject when conversing with the French ambassador.

Yet the picture Vincent Baron gives of the Irish friar in Paris would seem to tally with Naudé's concept of the king's minister:

> I would wish that the statesman should live in the world, as if he stood outside it, and move beneath heaven as if he were above it; I would wish him to devote himself to a noble poverty; to a freedom which was philosophical and yet, nevertheless, that of a man of the world. I would wish him to treat the court as if on loan, and that he be in the service of a master for the sole purpose of giving him proper satisfaction.[51]

Daniel O'Daly first went to Spain from Louvain on business for the Irish province of his order. He was employed by Philip IV on a recruiting expedition to Ireland as a necessary condition for gaining the required permission to erect a monastery for Irish-born nuns in Lisbon. The Portuguese Restoration occurred while he was actually employed in this task in Lisbon, and he supported the weaker party, that of the duke of Bragança. Without influence and a stranger, the Irish friar gained the confidence of both king and queen, and continued to hold it until his death. He was admitted into the family circle and entrusted with their hopes and anxieties for their children. He became a fully-accredited ambassador, a pioneer in the long and honourable history of Portuguese diplomacy. On 7 January 1662, he was nominated bishop of Coimbra by Luisa de Gusmão, one of the most powerful positions in the Portuguese church. He died six months later on 30 June, the day following the *coup d'état* of Castelmelhor which was successful in ousting the queen-regent from power and in placing the county under the personal dictatorship of Castelmelhor who then appointed himself private secretary to Afonso VI. His dictatorship was to prove beneficial to the country in the long run as he regularised and controlled both the army and the economic situation. It was during his dictatorship, too, that peace was finally signed between Portugal and Spain in 1668.

There are two letters addressed to the canons of the chapter of Coimbra referring to the appointment of the Dominican friar as archbishop. One letter, dated 13 January 1662, was written in Afonso's name, but it was from Queen Luisa apprising the canons of Frei Domingos' nomination. The other letter, dated 31 January 1662, was from the Dominican saying that he was 'good for nothing, possessing neither spiritual nor physical strength to rule a diocese', and he thanks the canons for their goodness in welcoming a stranger.[52] Among the correspondence of the master-general of the Dominican order, John Baptist de Marinis, there is to be found a letter from him to the friar with whom he was on familiar terms, authorising him to accept the honour. Possibly the letter could be regarded as a sample of those polite insincerities which are employed on such occasions, except that John Baptist de Marinis was a man of intense sincerity, loyal to his friends, out-spoken and straightforward in his dealings, with perhaps an excessive fondness for caustic criticism. His letters were never merely on the conventional level but also expressed his personal concern for the particular problem of the subject he was addressing. He wrote:

> We, on our part, considering not without great pity and paternal sympathy that even at your advanced age no loophole can be found by which you can justly refuse the will

of God as you confess openly. Yet begin to have less fear for your safety, especially since those outstanding gifts of mind and heart have become known to us, which King of kings has bestowed on you for prudent government and administration. We have the greatest trust in your integrity, zeal and prudence, and now promoted to a higher office, you will redouble by your high-mindedness all the qualities of piety, erudition, constancy, and uprightness of which you have given proof for so many years.[53]

That the nomination of Daniel O'Daly as archbishop of Coimbra would not be approved by the Holy See is only too clear from the foregoing pages. His appointment to that see seems to be ignored for the most part by Portuguese ecclesiastical writers. The *Historia Ecclesiastica Coimbra* regards the see as vacant from 1646 to 1671 when Don Manuel de Noronha became archbishop. Yet neither O'Daly nor any of his contemporaries seem to have doubted that the nomination was genuine. If he had lived, would he have succeeded in getting his nomination approved by Rome?

Notes

1   A complete copy contained the entire letter. A partial copy known as a *Regestum* gave the body of the letter, with the date at the end. The volume in which they were kept was known as *Registro*. Before the actual letter was written, a rough draft of it was often made; this was known as a *Minuta*, and contained amendments or corrections. Those had no signature at the end, but were usually written on the right-hand side of the page, leaving the other half free for additions or corrections. On the top left-hand side were the date and a short directive. If the *Minuta* was to be converted into cipher, the word *cifrato* appeared also. These *Registri and Minute* are sometimes the only records of letters sent from the secretariat, or from the different nunciatures. Cf., C. Giblin, *Collectanea Hibernica* I (1958), introduction. Fink, *Vatican Archives*.

2   R.P.D. Luciano Serrano, *Indice Analitico de los Documentos del Siglo XVI*, vol. I, pp vii–xxvii. G, Mattingly, *Renaissance Diplomacy*, pp 255–268. In a scholarly and fascinating study,

N.G. Martin shows the interdependence of the Holy See on Spain economically from the time of Alexander VI on, and points out that the question of *'spoliorum'* was at the core of relations between the Holy See and Spain during the following centuries. N.G. Martin, *La aportación económica de España a la Santa Sede por medio de los espolio y vacantes durante la nunciatura de César Monti (1630–34)* (Madrid, 1959).

3   For a full treatment of this aspect see: M. Brosch, 'Papal Policy', in *C.M.H.* iv. 682 *et seq*; Ranke, *History of the* Papacy, iii. 168.

4   A. Leman, *Urbain VIII et la Rivalité de la France et de la Maison d'Austriche de 1631–35* (University of Lille, 1919).

5   A.V. Nunz. Di Port., 24, 24 A.Nunz. di Spagna, 84, 86, 87, 88, 89, 94, 99A, 113, 346. Nunz. di Francia, 87, 103, 105, 279, 309. Nunz. Div., 86. Fondo Pio 275. Miscell. Arm. I. vols. 64, 65, 74; III, vol. 65. Letters de Principi, vols. 65, 79, 84, 85. Epistolas ad Principes, vols. 53, 55, 56, 57. B.V. Barb. Latin MSS., 8476, 8477, 8487, 9562, 8561, 8562, 8563. Chigi, O.I. 12; R.I. 4; F. VI. 149. Nicoletti A., Vita di Urbano VIII (Barb. Lat. 4730–4738). Vat. Latino 8350, Pts. I, II.

6   *Corpo Diplomatico Português* (Lisboa, 1842–1936). *Cartas de El-rei. D. João IV* (Lisboa, 1940). Arnauld-Henri, *Negociactions a la Cour de Rome*, vol. 1 (1748).

7   Archives General Simancas, Estado Legs. 3006, 3008, 3011, 3107, 3030, 3032. Archives Ministry Foreign Affairs Madrid, Archivo de la Embajada de España en Roma, Legs. 62, 70, 96. This source is usually referred to as *Fondo Santa Sede*.

8   The term *'motu proprio'* is unusual as applied to the appointment of a bishop. Here in the context, it would suggest 'by absolutely free nomination' as contra-distinguished from an appointment after *commendation* by the local clergy or bishops; or from an appointment after *nomination* or *presentation* by the civil authority; or from an appointment after *election* by the diocesan chapter. For the most complete treatment of this question cf., P.A. Borges, 'Provisão dos Bispados e Concilio Naacional no Reinado de D. João IV', in *Lusitania Sacra* ii (1957) pp III–219; iii (1958) pp 94–164.

9   B.V., Barb. Latin MS 8563, f. 2.

10 Barberini to vice-collector, 26 February 1641 (Barb. Latin MS 8561, ff. 61–61v in B.V.).

11 A.V., Nunz. Di Francia 87, ff. 140–140v (report of 19 April 1641). In the previous February, the nuncio had asked the king of France and Richelieu on behalf of the pope 'not to foment rebellion among the subjects of other princes', and Nicoletti in

his life of Urban declares that 'His Holiness made all diligence possible in France to put off (dissuade) the mission of the bishop of Lamego'.

12 Simancas, Estado legs. 3006, 3107.

13 B.V. Miscell. Arm. I, vol. 65, ff. 420–428v.

14 B.V. Barb. Latin MS 8561, ff. 16–18v (report of Jerome Bataglia, 10 September 1641; idem 8476, f. 14).

15 B.V., Chigi, O.I. 12, ff. 150–65v. Instructions given by Olivares to Spanish ambassador in Rome.

16 B.V., Barb. Latin MS 9562, ff. 22v–26 (Report of J. Bataglia, 10 April 1643).

17 Corpo. Dipl. Port. Xiii. 377–78 (Report of F. Brandão, 5 March 1644). For Panziroli's attitude, cf., Nunz. Di Spagna 86, ff. 143–43v; 205–06.

18 B.V., Chigi R.I. 4, ff. 246–50.

19 A.V., Nunz di Spagna 86, ff. 220–24 v.

20 B.V., Barb. Latin MS 8560, ff. 75–8. A.V. Miscell. Arm. I, vol. 64, ff. 178–80 (Reply of junta to João IV translated into Italian).

21 Simancas, Estado leg. 3107, letters for year 1649 and that of 18 November 1648.

22 Ericeira, Histsoria de Portugal Restorado, ii. 244–68. A.V., Nunz. Di Port. 24A, ff. 114–15; 138–9. Von Pastor does not agree with Ericeira in his interpretation of these years.

23 Von Pastor, History of the Popes, xiv, pt. I, p. 60. A. Ademolo, La Quuestionedella Independenza portoghese a Roma dal 1640 al 1670 (Florence, 1878), p. 73.

24 A.V., Miscell. Arm. I, vol. 74, ff. 83–93.

25 Infantado to Philip IV, 2 July 1650; 15 October 1650 (Estado leg. 3107 in Simancas). Findings of Council of State, 21 December 1650, loc. Cit.

26 Simancas, Estado leg. 3020 (O'Crilly's report, 20 February 1650); O'Daly's Geraldines, p. 3, author's dedication.

27 B.V., Vat. Lat. 8350, pt. I, ff. 19–22v. Corpo. Dipl. Port. Xiii, 189–91. Secretary of state to nuncio in France, 21 August 1651 (X. Nunz.di Francia 279, ff. 97–99 in A.7).

28 A.V. Nunz. Di Francia 105, ff. 36–36v (report of 9 February 1652).

29 Simancas, Estado leg. 3107, letters of Cardinal Trivulcio for 16 January, 28 January and 18 February 1652. Findings of Council of State, 25 March 1652.

30 Corpo. Dipl. Port., xiii. 205–223. For closing years of Innocent's reign, viz. von Psstor, op. cit. pp 33–7; 283.

31 Philip IV to Terranova, undated 1655 (Fondo Santa Sede, leg. 62, f. 143.)

32 A.V. Nunz. Di Francia 279, f. 2250v.

33 Coutinho to João IV, ? January 1656 (*Corpo Dipl. Port.*, xiii. 211–23).

34 Simancas, Estado leg. 3107, letters of 25 October, 20, 22 November, 18 December 1655.

35 Philip IV to Terranova, 19 February 1656 (Fondo Santa Sede, Leg. 95, f. 187).

36 *Corpo. Dipl. Port.*, xiii. 269–70 (Brief of Alexander VII to Philip IV, 18 January 1656). A.V. Nunz. Di Spagna 113, ff. 405v–07. Simancas, Estado leg. 3107, Reply of Philip IV, 19 February 1656.

37 A.V., Nunz. Di Francia III, f. 97.

38 *Ibid*, f. 287v.

39 A.V., Principi 79, ff. 218–19.

40 A.V., Nunz. Di Spagna 104A, f. 202; f. 206. These consist of two requests dated 13 September and 18 October respectively, from Nuncio di Bagno to the nuncio in Madrid to procure a passport for Frei Domingos do Rosario.

41 *Corpo.Dipl.Port.* xiii. 375–80.

42 *Loc. Cit.*, letter of 28 January 1656. Even from his own report it is obvious that Coutinho was too categorical and self-important in claiming the prerogatives of the king of Portugal. According to a report of the Spanish ambassador, Coutinho's first audience antagonised the pope. Simancas, Estado leg. 3107, letter of 18 December 1655).

43 For counter-reformation viz., J. Lecler, *Toleration and the Reformation*, 2 vols., T. Westow (Longmans, 1960).

44 *Corpo. Dipl. Port.* xiii. 597.

45 Simancas, Estado leg. 3032 (report of Sobremonte, 8 February 1659).

46 F Meinecke, *Machiavellism*, trans. D. Scott (1957), pp 197–203.

47 *Op. cit.*, p. 149.

48 B.M., Harl. MS 4547, f. 100v.

49 To judge by his own version, later reported by Nuncio di Bagno, 23 June 1656 (Nunz. Di Francia III, f. 189); 'Domenico del Rosario answered the cardinal that the princes would not be worried about such an agreement (between Spain and France) but that they are troubled about the alliance with Cromwell and the king of Sweden. The cardinal was much put out and embarrassed and said he had to answer to no-one for his actions, and he concluded by saying the conditions of his (Domenico's)

demands were too great. Domenico insisted on having a written testimony, but this he refused to give'.

50 E. Prestage, *Frei Domingos do Rosario: Diplomata e Politico* (Coimbra, 1926), p. 52.

51 F. Meinecke, *Machiavellism*, p. 197.

52 Afonso VI to Canons of Coimbra, 23 January 1662; O'Daly to Canons of Coimbra, 31 January 1662; both these letters are classified *Entre os papeis Rice Cartorio do Cabido*, unfol. in Archives Coimbra University.

53 AGOP, John Baptist de Marinis.

VIII

O'DALY:
THE MAN AND HIS WRITING

'May I not', wrote O'Daly:

> indulge old and hallowed remembrances even in the solitude
> and darkness of the night-time, while you are wrapped in
> slumber. I admit the Geraldines are dead and gone; I call them
> not up from their graves. Oh would to God I could!

In these few lines the man, Daniel O'Daly, revealed
himself. They are to be found in the last chapter of his
book *Initium, Incrementum et Exitus Geraldinorum*.[1]

Both the subject matter of his writings and their purpose
command interest. He who seemed, in the summer of 1655,
completely absorbed in political affairs chose to publish, in
Lisbon, a popular version of the Geraldine family and of
the persecutions that followed its downfall. Here was a
man who had schooled himself to act in a deliberate and
methodical way indulging 'old and hallowed memories'
and committing them to paper during the busiest period of
his career. Furthermore, this same account was begun in

1650, as we learn from a permission given to him at the general chapter of his order held that year.[2] It was completed by 1653 and published two years later. It seems reasonable enough to believe that *Initium, Incrementum, et Exitus Geraldinorum* served a deliberate, if now almost indefinable, purpose.

In any assessment of O'Daly's writing several problems present themselves. Was he merely recording for his own intellectual and emotional satisfaction the story of his patrons? Was his main object to hand on to posterity the history of this family as accurately as lay in his power? On the other hand, was he just using the subject of the Geraldines as a means of getting into print the story of the Irish persecutions after 1583? There is finally the question whether he was selecting for public scrutiny various favourable aspects of his country's story, because he felt the Ireland he knew was at an end.

To Irish scholars who lived and wrote during that century the native culture seemed in danger of extinction, while paradoxically, the breakdown of the bardic system released hidden springs of genius which made the whole century an age of national scholarship, never since been equalled. The Irish language passed into a new phase and took on a limpid quality with the advent of Keating's prose. In Latin a polished style of prose was used by Irish writers of this century; while the English language, as William Molyneux and Sir James Ware used it, became a competent medium of expression for polemical and antiquarian works of Irish interest.

History and theology appear to have been the main interests with which Irish scholars were concerned in this century, and it was no accident that a printing press for Irish type was set up in St Anthony's Franciscan college, Louvain, in 1611. There was a close connection between the seminary movement on the continent and the prevailing fashion among Irish exiles to write popular accounts of some aspects of their country's misfortunes. To them it seemed the sun was setting on her literary tradition, and the compelling need was to record for the benefit of posterity the story of Ireland's past glories and her present tribulations. The pessimism of Irish exiles and the realisation of the need to write the authentic facts as they knew them, or the 'legend' in which they believed, led a considerable number of Irishmen to write history. The century abounds in historical writers, annalists, chroniclers and storytellers including O'Sullivan Beare, the Four Masters, Duald Mac Firbis and Geoffrey Keating.

Simultaneously with this wave of pessimism among the literary coterie abroad, the Irish nation was being formed at home. Shared calamities, particularly the Cromwellian confiscation, welded Gael and Norman together and gave them a sense of belonging to a common national fellowship. It was not so much the actual shared experience as what they believed they had shared which drew them together in the first beginnings of a national consciousness. Such beliefs are the very stuff of local history, and from them come the popular legends which mould the national community.

O'Daly may have wished to present Ireland's story in the best possible light for posterity, and unconsciously perhaps, he may have created a 'legend' out of the Geraldine chapter. In the preface to his *Initium* he makes the claim that 'the history of the Florentine Family has been my special study', and he adds that he was bound by the twofold obligation of truth and history to write the deeds of the Geraldine earls of Desmond. His account ends on a note of deep gloom. All the great families of Ireland are dead and gone; persecution had followed their extinction. Finally, he returns to his main argument:

> I could not separate my country's ruin from that of the Geraldines ... it was my intention to have written chiefly of the persecution which my religion had sustained under

English tyranny, but where could I find more tragic illustration of it than in the family of the Geraldines?[3]

Reading the *Initium* one gets a clear picture of the writer himself. From an appraisal of his sources, one gets an idea of his value as an historian.

O'Daly's book was completed sometime in 1653. The first letter of approval from a Father Thomas de Aranha, O.P., Prior of Amaranthem in Portugal is dated 18 Kal. Oct. 1653, and a second from a Father Domingos de S. Thomas, O.P., Prior of Sao Domingos in Lisbon is undated. A third letter, dated 15 October 1655 was from Father Fernando Sueiro, O.P., who afterwards preached at the laying of the foundation stone of Corpo Santo. The bishop of Targas, also present at this function, gave his approval on 6 September 1653 to the publication of the book. The Inquisition, always tardy in such matters, gave its permission only on 4 December 1654, and the book, complete with these documents, made its appearance in 1655. The publishers were the Officina Craesbeeckina, who had previously published O'Sullivan Beare's *Catholic History* in 1621.

The heading *Relatio Geraldinorum ac persecutionis Hyberniae* appeared on the title page. The work is usually referred to as the *History of the Geraldines* to avoid confusion with Russell's loyalist *Relatio Geraldinorum* which appeared in 1638. Subsequently, a French version by the Abbé Joubert made its appearance in Dunkirk. The English version was translated by C.P. Meehan in 1847 which was followed by a revised, second edition in 1878.

The *Initium* is written in octavo-size sheets, clearly printed in rather large Italian type on this paper. There are 506 pages in all with an index of chapters at the back; however, neither sources nor footnotes are given. The Latin style is uncomplicated, even terse, but graceful, and the English translation does not do it justice. At the beginning of the account, the words '*ex nonnullis fragmentis collecta, as Latinatate donata'* occur, and a different style of print indicates when the author is quoting directly from documents. Gaelic placenames and family names are spelt, for the main part, phonetically and are not latinised.[4]

Not every historical writer leaves the mark of his personality on his writing, but from the pages of the *Initium* there emerges a strong and unmistakeable pen portrait of O'Daly. He tells the story of the rise and fall of the Desmonds in an easy narrative form, relating anecdotes rather than acting as commentator on historical events. A well-informed and factual mind is at work; one certainly trained in logic and equipped with the objective outlook resulting from the writer's religious formation. Yet one thinks that this objectivity has been superimposed on a mind which was somewhat ingenuous, ardent and limited by family prejudices.

The work opens with the statement about its scope already referred to, and though O'Daly does not immediately give his sources, it is clear from a careful reading that he was not drawing from memory. He mentions the names of Philip O'Sullivan Beare, Geoffrey Keating and Caesar Baronius, and he says that he consulted their works. His other sources were 'ancient vernacular records', though he does not cite the documents. His account tallies with that of the Four Masters except where they deal with the Desmond rebellion and the years following it. Comparing his version of the Kilmallock affair with that of *Pacata Hibernia*, they agree in outline. O'Daly is then, according to contemporary standards, truthful.

Nowhere does he mention Russell's *Relatio*, published some seventeen years before his own, though an examination of the two works reveals that O'Daly follows Russell closely on many points, with one major exception: the religious issue. Of Russell very little is known. He dedicated his work to Richard Boyle, earl of Cork, and his sympathies, on the whole, were with the English administration. In a prefatory address, written from his house at Ballenrea, and dated 1 January 1631, he makes the statement that his father was 'an actor in the last part of this tragedy'. In the actual narrative he states that his father 'served Garret, the unhappy sixteenth earl of Desmond'. Hayman advances the opinion that he was probably the son of James Russell whose name is found signed to the 'Combination of Garret, late earl of Desmond'. He is quoted by Cox as 'Friar Russell' but Harris calls him simply 'Thomas Russell' and says he continued the history of the genealogy of the Geraldines, earls of Desmond to the year 1602.[5] Apart from its own intrinsic merit, Russell's *Relatio* is important in any consideration of O'Daly's *Initium*. O'Daly would seem to have been familiar with it; both accounts of the Geraldine rebellion are derived from eye witnesses and while they differ in presentation and emphasis, together they present a version of the Fall of the House of Desmond which contrasts with that of the Four Masters.

The first chapter of the *Initium* discusses a futile question of no historical value: whether the Geraldines were descended from Aeneas, hero of Virgil's *Aeneid*. He states, without naming a source, the origin of the Geraldines from 'that region of Hetruria where Florence stands'. Meehan, in his appendix, supplies the documents from which O'Daly presumably drew his information. He then proceeds to his main theme which is an attempt to trace the Geraldine succession as earls of Desmond. He admits the difficulty of tracing a true succession, but maintains that Gerald FitzGerald was the sixteenth or Great Earl Desmond. He admits 'a great discrepancy in the ancient vernacular records, some inscribing a James, a Gerald, a Maurice, as successor to the first Earl Maurice'. There is no reason to doubt that he had access to documents now lost or inaccessible. His father, Conchubar na Scoile, and his grandfather, CuChonnacht, were of the bardic class and acted as bards to the Desmonds. At some stage there was a bardic school near Kilsarkan. If Daniel O'Daly lacked the intensive training required in those schools, his interests lay in his father's profession. The library of Besançon lists among its manuscripts two genealogies of the O'Donnell family 'with a dissertation on the origins of that family by Fr. Dominicus a Rosario, 1627'.[6] Specialists in Geraldine history have pronounced him accurate, and at least two opinions cite the *Initium* and the *Four Masters* as the two most trustworthy written versions of the Geraldine succession.[7]

The most interesting part of the book from the historical point of view is the account of the decade immediately preceding his own birth. The *Four Masters* regards the earl of Desmond as having committed treason, and the version they give of his last years is prejudicial and harsh. Russell maintains that the earl's long capacity in the Tower induced a morbid state of mind amounting at times to a kind of dangerous fatuity, and working on this hypothesis, he writes an arresting and illuminating narrative which is borne out by the entries made from time to time on Gerald FitzGerald in *Cal. S.P. Ire., Reg. Eliz.* O'Daly is zealous for the honour of his patrons and treats the war from the Catholic angle, presenting it as a crusade for religious freedom, undertaken primarily by James FitzMaurice, and later, by the Earl Gerald. This presentation of facts is borne out by documents in the Vatican archives which corroborate O'Daly's statements in several instances. There is the acceptance by the Vatican of Desmond as general of the Catholic forces, and letters from the earl to the pope reporting the various stages of the war; one dated 6 November 1582 states clearly that he is ready to go on fighting for the Catholic faith but requests help from the pope; a still later one on 28 June 1583 asks the pope for a papal brief nominating him overlord of Desmond and states that he needs helps desperately.[8] The Desmond that emerges from the *Initium* and from Vatican documents is not the person whom Russell or the Four Masters put forward.

It may be asked if O'Daly exaggerated the claims of his patrons when he stated:

> of one thing I am certain, had the Geraldines lived, the Butlers and O'Briens would not now be in their graves or reduced to misery ... while the Desmonds were in the land, the English dared not persecute; when they were extinct, did not persecution date its birth?[9]

In one instance one might almost accuse him of being a dishonest sophist; in his version of the murder of Sir Henry Davells, partisanship has obscured his better judgement:

> Now it so happened that Henry Davells, of the county Cork, on hearing of the arrival of FitzMaurice and the Spaniards, retired into the county Kerry and took up his abode in the principal castle of the earl of Desmond in Tralee. At dead of night, John, who had been his gossip, entered the chamber, accompanied by his retainers and slew Davells, Arthur Carter and some others. This fact had been stigmatized and denounced as derogatory to the honour of John Desmond, yet I think unjustly; for Desmond only killed an avowed enemy, who not only sought to crush the cause of liberty, but did signal injury to John himself in the house of Lord Muskerry.[10]

Here O'Daly treats what was an atrocity too lightly. He implies that John of Desmond was justified in killing Davells on the grounds of expediency and revenge. Davells' only crimes, it would appear, were that he joined Sire Henry Carter, Provost-marshal of Munster in the march to Smerwick, and that as constable of Dungarvan he held jail delivery sessions in the Desmond palatinate.[11] If the slaying of Davells appeared such a heinous crime to contemporaries as Carleton, bishop of Chester, declared in his *Thankful Deliverance of the Church* (1630), then O'Daly, as defender of the Catholic party, should have assembled some evidence to substantiate his claim that John of Desmond was in the right.

138

Letter from Daniel O'Daly to Luisa de Gusmão
courtesy of the British Public Records Office
State Papers Foreign (Portugal), Vol 4, f 158

This over-zealous partisanship, evident in more than one case, may be remarked in his actions as a man of affairs. It is strange that the Irish friar could accept the domination of Spain over the Spanish Netherlands and even help to recruit Irish soldiers for it, while he championed so sincerely the cause of Portugal's freedom as to become a party to the French interest. Again there is his espousal of the Stuart cause, even as he made efforts to conciliate Cromwell's government to favour Portugal, and availed of Cromwell's ship to travel in as ambassador in 1656. O'Daly, the historian and the man, could defer to the doctrine of political expediency on occasion.

His style, when he is moved by strong feeling, at times descends into a kind of bombastic rhetoric. Possibly this tendency may be traced to the apocalyptic style of preaching which was fashionable in his time; or he may have been influenced by the flamboyant and inflated style of traditional Irish storytelling with its propensity to exaggerate what was praiseworthy:

> This sweet isle of ours yielded us in abundance, the purest gold and silver, lead, tin, iron, saffron and purple; fruits delicious to the taste; and antlered deer, warbling birds, countless fishes and shells replete with pearls. Barbary sent us gold and ivory, and Italy the richest produce of her looms. What if our climate did not ripen the vine? A gallant race grew strong on beer that did not intoxicate.

In fact O'Daly possessed the fiery imagination of the *file*, though he could on occasion be cool and calculating, but the gravity of a fine intelligence forced him again and again to take an objective view of matters that were near his own heart. This is instanced in his tolerant discussion of the qualities of the 'royal theologian', Queen Elizabeth, as monarch; and in his almost rueful observations on the 'dissensions of Ireland's children'. We will quote the first as exemplifying his objectivity:

Truly for my part, I recognise Elizabeth as queen of England and for her person I entertain respect, nor do I envy her, her fair fame; but in treating such matters as are ultimately interwoven with her public life, religion, veracity and honour counsel me to conceal nothing. It is not my desire to question her talents for they are great, but inflated, nor shall I venture even to dispute with one of her voluble sex on the right to make and unmake Latin adjectives; but the doctrine of the Apostle forbids me to bow to any female usurping the primacy of the Church ... nor was Elizabeth in the number of those who followed Christ, nor has she studied to imitate the meanest of them; but we must forsooth bow our heads and clap our hands since this royal theologian ascended the throne. I entertain respect for her as a temporal sovereign, for the Divine Teacher commands that I should be deferential even to a wicked one. Her right of ruling in temporalities I never questioned, by my allegiance shall never be given to her in the character of a usurper.[12]

O'Daly, then, in this first part of *Initium* was primarily an Irishman. He had a sense of the dramatic and a melancholy and philosophical turn of mind. Where his patriotic or clan prejudices were concerned he showed himself captious in his reasoning; yet that picture is not complete because he appears also to have possessed a fine intelligence, tempered and balanced by study and by religious discipline, which if it did not always dominate, at least held in check the ardent sensibilities of the man.

In the second part of the *Initium* he gives an account of the martyrs who died in the persecution that followed the downfall of the Desmond family, and from that time onward to the Cromwellian persecution he reveals himself as Father Dominic O'Daly, the friar among the immediate circle of his acquaintances and particularly among those of his own order. Of the martyrs whom he describes, six were know personally to him in Lisbon, and possibly he influenced some of them during his time as rector and vicar-general of the Irish foundation there. Father Terence Albert O'Brien, O.P., was associated with him in the early days of the ministry in Limerick. In 1644, at Rome, they received their degree as Master of Sacred Theology (S.T.M.) together and O'Brien was in Lisbon with O'Daly when news reached him of his new dignity as bishop of Emly. He caught the public imagination by his zeal as bishop during Ireton's siege of Limerick and O'Daly's account of Terence Albert O'Brien's last days is vivid, though restrained.[13] Father Tadhg Moriarty, whose reputation for sanctity has remained undimmed, was, like O'Daly, a Kerryman. Educated and ordained in Spain he came to Lisbon to teach in the college there for some time. Like O'Daly too, he chose the name in religion of Dominic of the Rosary.

We have noticed that where clan prejudice came into play, O'Daly as an historian was at fault. Might it not be that he fabricated the 'martyrdom' of his friends from pious legends? Reading the *Persecutions*, one is left with a sense of the poignant dignity which accompanied the deaths of these great men, and with the impression of cautious understatement rather than unpremeditated hagiography on the part of the author. His aim was first to lay before the reader 'the iniquitous laws by which the extirpation of Irish Catholics was to be effected', and then to give a rough outline of the persecution inflicted on them.

His list of authorities follows a certain order. Again he mentions O'Sullivan's *History* as an occasional reference. He cites Cecil's *British Justice* and Peter Malphaeus who wrote *Palm of the Faith in Ireland*, a work published in Brussels which enjoyed great popularity for a time. He drew upon a doctrinal work on martyrdom published by a Jesuit in Lyons in 1630, and he quotes from a *History of the British Parliament for 1643* by Coke. He was up-to-date in his general reading, for he quotes from a book published by Berkley in 1653.[14]

Having thus established his credentials for speaking on the subject, he proceeds to the documents and penal enactments promulgated during the reigns of Elizabeth and James. These he handles with precision, giving date and month of each penal enactment, and citing verbatim the whole of 'The Queen's promulgation against seminary Priests and Jesuits'. His reflections are logical and ponderous. For his brief descriptions of the manner of death of the men he mentions, it is almost certain that his main sources were eyewitness accounts, as twice he regrets that he had not 'as yet authentic documents concerning their martyrdom at hand'. He does not expressly mention his informants by name, but states vaguely, in connection with the insurrection of Limerick, 'those who were witnesses of them are here in Lisbon as well as elsewhere'.[15] One was Father James Douley, later to become bishop of Limerick. The other was a friar whom O'Daly knew since his early days in the Emly diocese, Father Fabian Mulrian. In the Rinuccini dispatches, Fabian Mulrian is given as the source of O'Daly's account of the Siege of Limerick.[16]

Much of the value of the *Persecutions* therefore depends on the proved integrity of the two informants. Father James Douley was vicar-general of the diocese of Limerick and escaped to Spain after the surrender of the city. A native of Limerick, he had studied with distinction in Paris where he had been elected Procurator of the German nation in the university in 1637, a mark of esteem from his fellow students. On his return to Limerick he filled the offices of chancellor and vicar-general. After his escape to Spain, he was attached to the retinue of the cardinal of Toledo, and it was most likely that it was during these years he met O'Daly to whom he related not only an account of the siege, but some of the extraordinary occurrences that took place during the blockade. These phenomena O'Daly recounts in detail, adding that 'Father

James Douley received information of the details'. Confirmation of what he narrated came from an unexpected quarter, a Cromwellian diarist who witnessed the globe of light wrote of the occurrence in almost the same words.[17]

Father Fabian Mulrian came from the barony of Owney on the border of Limerick and Tipperary; he was at one time the prior of the Cashel Dominican priory. A delightful encounter with him is given by Boullaye le Gouz in his *Tour of the French Traveller 1644*. 'During my stay in Cashel, the Revered Father Ryan, prior of the Dominicans, an Irish friar educated in France, invited me to dinner at his convent', and the traveller recounted how he and Ryan (or Mulrian) vanquished the Salamanca students in a philosophical joust.[18] He was known too to St Vincent de Paul, as a letter of gratitude to the saint from the master-general testifies:

> There is one consideration that especially urges me to give expression to my gratitude and that is all you have done for the establishment of a chair of theology in our university at Cashel … and for having done it at the instance of the Reverend Father Fabian Mulrian of our order who was deputed by the Provincial for that purpose.[19]

How accurate was Fabian Mulrian as an eyewitness? Again we can only surmise from a particular incident. His account of the death of Father Richard Barry on the rock of Cashel as told to O'Daly tallies with a circumstantial account of the massacre supplied by a Jesuit father who witnessed it. Mulrian also quotes a Father Cuillenan of the secular clergy of Cashel as a source for the death of the 1647 Inchiquin martyrs there. He himself wrote an account of the persecutions, but only a fragment is preserved in the *Comment. Rinucc.* From that excerpt, he would have Limerick subjected to perpetual interdict and deprived of episcopal status because the lay-section agreed so placidly to Ireton's demands.[20]

However, the account of the martyrs in O'Daly's book is disappointingly short and inadequate, occupying less than sixty of the 406 pages in the work. His failure to sketch in the biographical details of the several with whom he was personally acquainted was a regrettable omission. Too little is known about Father Tadhg Moriarty, Laurence O'Farrell and Father Vincent Dillon, all of whom lived in Lisbon and worked with him in the college.

'It is the cause, not the sentence that makes the martyr', remarks O'Daly. It is therefore all the more surprising that he does not enlarge on the doctrine of martyrdom which he must have studied and taught as a lecturer. It was not ignorance of the theology of martyrdom that prevented him from explaining the doctrine to his readers, and there are several allusions to the claims of true martyrdom and whether death is essential to martyrdom. Here he follows the *Summa* and there is a veiled quotation from Aquinas to be found in his discussion of the claim to martyrdom of a priest who fell victim to the plague contracted in the discharge of his duty.[21] Perhaps he assumed that his readers were already acquainted with the doctrine or that the men he listed as martyrs were entitled to be called by that name in the canonical use of the word.

The first part of his *Initium* may well be seen as a study of environment; in the second part, the *Persecutions*, that side of his character may be discerned which occupied itself with Ireland's religious needs. There remains O'Daly in his Portuguese setting. Again we are fortunate, for he has left one work, unpublished, which gives us a glimpse of him against his background.

Written in seventeenth century Portuguese, the *Papel* of Frei Domingos do Rosario was a disputation which he delivered in his role of friar-preacher. It was transcribed and the original is today in the National Library, Lisbon. It consists of sixty folio pages, forty-eight of these being O'Daly's presentation of the argument and his reply to his opponent's propositions. The disputation took place in the university of Coimbra, and full publicity was given to the occasion by the presence of the king. Father O'Daly's adversary was an Augustinian, Father Richard of St Victor, professor of Scotist philosophy at the university. Like O'Daly, he too was an Irishman and was a brother of the Franciscan Luke Wadding.

The disputation centred around the burning theological question of the day, the Immaculate Conception of the Virgin. For the Spanish and Portuguese, the devotion to the Virgin is one of the essential elements that characterises Spanish Catholicism, and the idea that she was free from sin as promulgated in the doctrine of the Immaculate Conception has a profound attraction for them. The mariological movement of the seventeenth century has its origin in countries untouched by the reformation; in Italy and especially in Spain. The protagonists of the movement were the first great Jesuit theologians: Salmeron, Suarez, who founded systematic Mariology, and Salazar who published his first great work on the Immaculate Conception in 1618. Between 1619 and 1630 the movement spread rapidly and reached its peak point between 1630–50. João IV, newly-restored king of Portugal, wished to compel the professors at Coimbra university to take an oath of belief in the doctrine of the Immaculate Conception because of his own personal devotion to that doctrine. Father O'Daly protested and a public disputation ensued. The date of the event is undetermined. Father Richard of St Victor was appointed professor in Coimbra university on 9 September 1643. Between 1642–44, Frei Domingos do Rosario was acting as regent of the Coimbra Dominican college, and during the same period a Limerick man, Father James Arthur, O.P., was *lector primarius* in the university. As the disputation centred around this Dominican chair in the university, it seems likely that it took place during those years.[22]

The Dominican's arguments were positive and gave evidence of a decided and even uncompromising attitude of mind. One notes a complete fearlessness in reproving the king, 'as a secular prince', for anticipating the decision of the Church in matters of doctrine, since the Immaculate Conception was not yet defined as a dogma. Though the *Papel* is cast in the form of a medieval disputation and is devoid of human passion, it contains a strong plea for liberty of conscience. Briefly, O'Daly's requests were twofold: that the king insist that only the known and approved doctrine of the Church be taught in the university; that the teaching of St Thomas Aquinas be followed in Coimbra.

In his reply, Dr Richard of St Victor, O.S.A., was brief. His main argument was that of expediency. João IV, he said, was enforcing the oath only on those who taught in the university to ensure that as teachers they were in good faith. He pointed out reasonably that liberty of conscience was not such as to allow persons to hold an opinion either incorrect or heretical.

Clearly the Dominican was in his element, as is evidenced in his counter-attack. He was nimble-witted and had the gift of being able to convey to his listeners the idea that his particular line of reasoning was right. Undoubtedly, the Kerryman had assurance of manner and was able to turn an opponent's point to his own advantage. If the king were to enforce the oath at the present time, he argued, it would sorely aggravate heresy. Furthermore, he viewed the oath as a three-fold attack on the liberty of the Church, because it anticipated dogmatic definition; it usurped the spiritual jurisdiction of the pope; and finally, no Dominican professor could take such an oath since each had taken one previously in the Dominican order not to teach doctrine contrary to that of Thomas Aquinas.

Here, it would seem, was the kernel of the Dominican's difficulty as regards the oath-taking in Coimbra university. Thomas Aquinas, surprisingly reserved and cautious in his treatment of the doctrine of the Immaculate Conception as Catholics understand it, seemed unwilling to reconcile the personal *'debita'* with the idea of a preservative redemption, which is the Scotist teaching of the doctrine.[23] O'Daly was careful to point out that however desirable the oath might appear, the doctrine of the Immaculate Conception was as yet 'only a pious belief'.[24] It is of interest that Father O'Daly subsequently refused a professorship in Coimbra university for himself or for one of the Dominicans under his jurisdiction.[25] In 1646, João IV dedicated the kingdom of Portugal to the Immaculate Conception.

So far we have traced the career of Daniel O'Daly, not in exhaustive detail, but selecting points with the object of throwing light on Irish-European relationships in a century when the connection between Ireland and Europe seemed most tangible from an intellectual point of view. This connection was due in some measure to the seminary movement on the continent which gave to Europe a series of gifted, even intellectually-brilliant, Irishmen. O'Daly, like his contemporaries, Father Luke Wadding and Father Peter Talbot, was Ireland's version of the counter-reformation man. It was the particular genius of Irishmen like O'Daly, Wadding and Talbot to be able to exploit their own talents fully, not just for their own personal ends, though these were not neglected, not solely for religious or patriotic motives, though these were an impelling force, but to use them in a multiplicity of activities which sometimes conflicted. While avoiding an imaginative reconstruction of an O'Daly mentality or personality, this study aims at presenting a many-sided character in some of its various and more arresting aspects. Talented and cultured, with generations of Irish tradition behind him,

Daniel O'Daly acquired a European outlook and mode of behaviour which made his personality a blend of idealist and Machiavellist.

As the historian is bound by a certain code of fidelity to the ascertained truth, she cannot create a synthesis wherein character seems to produce events. She is bound to analyse facts as they occur and to process backward from known events to the personalities that gave rise to them. Above all, the historian wishes to know the reason why an event happened, and more especially, the human element involved.

Is the historic O'Daly, then, at variance with the legendary Father Dominic of the Rosary who steals in and out of English state papers of the 1630–40 period, the 'very tall black man who speaks big'; the romantic friar who figures in the Irish novel *Brian Óg*? He was a lesser and more human person. Daniel O'Daly was in a certain sense enigmatic. For his contemporaries he had a certain mysteriousness which non-plussed them, an aloofness which avoided intimacy. In fact, he possessed that inscrutable suavity which is the mark of a successful Kerryman. On reading his letters to Mazarin during the regency period, one is aware of a certain bland equivocation beneath the courtly phrases. O'Daly wrote in Spanish, a language richly capable of conveying irony and polite mockery in phrases that resound with extravagant courtesies. O'Daly's last letter to Mazarin is dated 1 June 1650. It is on the subject of Cominges, the French ambassador, and is full of unctuous regrets and honeyed phrases. So smooth flowing are his subtleties that one would suspect the Irishman of laughing up his sleeve at both Mazarin and Cominges. It is a little masterpiece of inconclusiveness.[26] The resources of his pen were endless, and he must have derived a certain satisfaction from his many and varied concerns since he made no attempt to disengage himself from their toils. Yet, underlying his political activities and giving unity to them was his three-fold desire to serve his mother country, Ireland, his Dominican order, and his loyalty to the royal house of Portugal where João IV and Luisa de Gusmão had shown O'Daly such kindness. A letter of Luisa's to her daughter Catherine, queen of England in 1662, mentions the Dominican's death. His passing, she remarked, was mourned 'with general feelings of regret and in particular to my sorrow'.[27]

Hippolyte (Paul) Delaroche, 'Cardinal Mazarin's Last Sickness'
copyright The Wallace Collection

If the unfolding of Daniel O'Daly's career involves his being placed at the bar of the reader's judgement, then it is only fair to let him plead his own cause. 'There are many prelates in these Catholics countries', he wrote to Ormond in 1650:

(especially in Spain) my particular friends, whose assistance towards the advancement of that kingdom (Ireland) I doubt not to procure in a considerable manner if Your Excellency and the council think fit to send me an ample and authorised commission written in Latin wherein the state and danger of the Catholic cause may be largely expressed, which being sent me by the first convenience, will enable me to effect somewhat to the country's succor and speed ... I signify Your Excellency how his Majesty (Charles II) commanded me to deliver my mind plainly to him in all that I understood in the cause of Ireland, and I told him that the agreement and settlement of that kingdom consisted principally in the fruition of the privileges of a free kingdom and how it was against the natural law that a kingdom should be under another, but only dependent from their king immediately, accordingly to the condition of all nations.

On the margin is written Ormond's pained reaction:

Fr. Daniel O'Daly ... with his demands for a free Ireland, and this friar was rewarded by the king and queen and Lord Jermyn as having very good pretensions.[28]

NOTES
1   O'Daly, *Geraldines*, p. 22 (Meehan's translation).
2   De Marinis to O'Daly, 23 January 1651 (*Costelloe*, ii, 10 in Tallaght).
3   O'Daly, *Geraldines*, p. 5.
4   Cf., D. O'Daly, *Familia Geraldinorum*. My thanks are due to the National Library of Ireland for the use of its copy. T. De Burgo, *Hibernia Dominicana*, p. 544. D. O'Daly, *History of the Geraldines*, trans. C.P. Meehan (1878).
5   Russell's *Relation* is rather a mystery book. Harris claims that it was amongst the manuscripts of Sir James Ware, which afterwards became the property of the earl of Clarendon, and then passed into the custody of the duke of Chandois. In 1746, after his death, his collection was sold by public auction, Dr Rawlinson buying the greater bulk of the Irish Manuscripts which are now in the Bodleian Library. The remainder were purchased by Dean Milles and are now in the British Museum. Cf., Harris, *Writers of Ireland*, I, chapter XIV. Russell's *Relation* (No. 54 in the catalogue) is not to be found in the Bodleian or in the B.M., but a transcript copy may be consulted in Dublin City Public Library, Pearse Street, Dublin 2 (Gilbert Collection, 173). It is written in English. 54 may be the manuscript listed in Clement's Collection A 23 in the Victorian and Albert Museum, London. A valuable collection of original sources for Geraldine history may be consulted in *J. Hist. and Archael. Assoc. of Ire.*, 3rd

series 1868–9; and *Royal Hist. and Archael. Assoc. of Ire. J.* 4th series (1870–89), vols. I, ii.

6 See listing in *Cat. Gen. des Manuscrits. Gen des Bibliotheques de France*, xxxiii. 636, 'Bibl. De Besançon 119, ff. 47–56. Deux genealogies de la famille O'Donnell, avec une dissertation sur les origins de cette famille par Fr. Dominicus a Rosario, 1627'.

7 Letter of Dr Charles Ronayne on 'Hayman and Geraldine Documents', in *Journal of Cork Hist. and Archaeal. Soc.*, 2nd series, no 26 (1920), p. 79.

8 A.V. Nunz. D'Inghilterra I. Most of this file deals with documents concerning the earl of Desmond and the progress of the war. For letter of 6 November 1582, ff. 308–09; letter of 28 June 1583, ff. 330–331. Other sources in Vatican archives are Sec. of Briefs, vol. 47; Nunz. Di Spagna, 29, 30; Inghilterra IA, 2, 9.; in Vatican library, Cod. Ottobon 3209; Borghese III, 129D.

9 O'Daly, *Geraldines*, p. 230.

10 *Ibid.*, pp 85–7.

11 J. Begley, *The Diocese of Limerick in the 16th and 17th Cent.*, p. 86.

12 O'Daly, *Geraldines*, pp 152–3.

13 *Op. cit.*, pp 203–9.

14 *Ibid.*, pp 146–9.

15 O'Daly, *Geraldines*, p. 205.

16 *Comment. Rinucc.*, iv. 638, *et. Seq.*

17 J. Begley, *Diocese of Limerick in 16th and 17th Cent.*, pp 470–1.

18 Boullaye le Gouz, *Tour of the French Traveller 1644*, trans. Crofton Croker (1837), pp 17–23.

19 Cf., J. Leonard, 'St Vincent de Paul and M. General Tomasso Turco, O.P.', in *I.E.R.*, series 5, p. 129 *(Correspondence of St Vincent de Paul*, iii. 314, letter 1040, Paris 1920).

20 *Comment. Rinucc.*, iv, 652.

21 O'Daly, *Geraldines*, p. 220; *Summa* IIA, iiae, q. 124, a. 3, trans. Fathers of English Province, O.P.

22 National Library, Lisbon (Reservados), Fundo Antigo 3580. A.ToT, Chanc. De João IV, vol. 14, f. 169. P. Reichert, *Acts of the General Chapters O.P.*, iii. 89, 90, 163; for appointments of Father James Arthur and other matters.

23 E. Hugon, O.P., *Tractatus Dogmatici*, i, ii. 749 (5th edition, 1927).

24 National Library Lisbon (Reservados), Fundo Antigo 3580, f. 51.

25 Frei Lucas, *Historia de S. Domingos*, iv. 736.

26 O'Daly to Mazarin, 18 February 1658; 1 June 1659 (Correspondence de Portugal, iv. 143–4 in Ministry of Foreign Affairs, Paris).

27 Luisa de Gusmão to Catherine of Bragança, July 1662 (*Letters and documents of D. Luisa de Guzmão*, ed. H. Raposa, p. 438.

28 O'Daly to Ormond, recd. 28 August 1650 (*Carte Papers,* xxix, 506, add. 642, new paging in Bodleian).

NOTE ON ARCHIVAL MATERIAL

One of the major duties the historian undertakes is the evaluation of her/his sources. For the purpose of such an evaluation, sources are divided into two classes: primary and secondary. Primary sources, as the term is understood, fall into several classes which, for convenience, are generally divided as: (1) Manuscript material from ecclesiastical archives; (2) Manuscript material from the period; (3) State papers and public records. Because Daniel O'Daly was a member of a religious order as well as a diplomat, there are documents concerning his activities in all three divisions:

(1) *Ecclesiastical archives*

The principal collections of church archives and the most complete are in Rome. In 1611, Pope Paul V established a special deposit for the manuscripts known as the Archivio Segreto Vaticano, independent of the Vatican Library. Gradually, other manuscripts were added such as registers or copies of outgoing correspondence, as well as original reports of the nuncios and legates. The Vatican collection is divided into eight main groups which Karl

Fink has described in his indispensable *Das Vatikanische Archiv* (Rome, 1951). For modern diplomatic history the most important Vatican documentary collection is that of the secretariat of state. This contains the reports from the nunciatures and the instructions of the Vatican secretaries of state to the nuncios abroad. This deposit is not all-inclusive. Much material may be located in the private archives of Italian families, members of whom served as secretaries of state. Some of these private collections such as the 'Barberini Latin Manuscripts' and the Chigi collection have been donated to the Vatican and are maintained as private and separate collections located in the Vatican Library.

In 1622, the Congregation of the Propaganda Fide was set up to deal especially with the problems of mission countries. Plenary sessions of the congregation were held regularly to deal with matters such as the appointments of bishops, and the minutes of these sessions were recorded in volumes entitled *Atti* (or *Acta)*. A record of correspondence arising out of these minutes was kept, and is known as *Scritture*. It is a most valuable source of research as it contains an almost bewildering variety of personal reports and private letters from bishops, missioners and lay-folk, as well as reports from the inter-nuncio at Brussels. Besides the plenary sessions, Propaganda held meetings known as *Congressi* which discussed day-to-day activities, and these are filed in volumes relating to the different countries. *Letters* is the name given to the letters sent out by the Congregation to the different countries. The archives of Propaganda Fide are distinct from the various collections that form the Vatican archives.

The Dominican source material for this study was drawn from the general archives of the order in Rome, and from the provincial archives in Tallaght, Co. Dublin. In the general archives of the order at Santa Sabina, Rome, the registers and the correspondence of the master-generals are filed. The registers are a mine of information on the state of the order in the various countries at any given period. The acts of the general chapters of the order, occurring at regular intervals (every six years during the seventeenth century) supply names and dates and give an indication of the mind of the order on major issues. Each province of the order has its own provincial archives. Over a number of years, the provincial archives of the Irish Dominicans at Tallaght are being enlarged and stocked with transcripts, photostats, and microfilms of documents relevant to the history of the order in Ireland. These contain material from the Vatican archives, San Clemente, Rome, from Lisbon and Louvain. The registers of provincials and correspondence within the province are filed there also.

The history of the Irish Dominican archives during the unhappy seventeenth century is one of misfortune. By 1654, most Dominican priories in Ireland had been destroyed, and any documents that were salvaged were transferred to the Irish Dominican College in Louvain which then became the general archives of the province. There they remained until the Napoleonic wars when they were lost in transit from Louvain to Rome. The archives of Corpo Santo Lisbon were completely destroyed in the 1755 Lisbon earthquake. There is no complete published catalogue of the material in the general archives of the order in Rome, but Father Reichert, O.P. edited and annotated the acts of the general chapters (Rome 1910, six vols.).

(2) *Manuscript material from the period*
Because O'Daly was an ecclesiastic whose career as Portuguese diplomat brought him in touch with France, England, Spain and Rome, there are documents dealing with his mission in the state archives of those countries.

For a general description of these archives and their contents, I refer the reader to the useful *Guide to the Diplomatic Archives of Western Europe*, edited by Daniel Thomas and Lynn Case (University of Pennsylvania Press, 1959).

The principal storehouse of documents relating to the diplomatic history of Portugal are the Archivo Nacional de Torre do Tombo in Lisbon, the National Library and the Ajuda Palace Library, both in Lisbon, the archives of the Ministry of Foreign Affairs and the Evora Library. In the state archives of Torre do Tombo the career of Daniel O'Daly between the years 1639–62 is filled in by documents ranging from the books of chancery of João IV and Afonso VI, to the letters and instructions issued by the king to O'Daly as ambassador in Paris. In the Ajuda Palace Library, the minutes of the councils of state are kept in codices and for the period 1655–62 they supply full details of the Irishman's diplomatic and political negotiations on behalf of Portugal. From 1842 onwards, a systematic compilation of documents relating to France, Spain, England and the Holy See was inaugurated in Lisbon and gradually *Quadro Elementar des Relaçoes polit. e diplomat. De Portugal,* a monumental eighteen volume set, edited by V. de Santarem was brought out in 1842 (*et. Seq.*). In 1916, C. Bocages collected the documents connected with the Portuguese Restoration in a work called *Subsidios para o esstuda des relaçoes exteriors de Portugal.* Portuguese documents dealing directly with Rome are to be found in a sixteen-volume set begun in 1862 by Rebello da Silva and Jayme Moniz.

All treaties made by Portugal with other European states are contained in a collection made by L. de Castro (Lisbon, 1856) in a *Colleccaõ dos tratados, convenções contratos e actos publicos celebrados entre a coroa de Portugal e as mais potencias desde 1640.* In the National Library Lisbon the useful and massive *Fundo Antigo* may be examined. The name stands for a series of volumes consisting of notes and documents about the important buildings of Lisbon from the sixteenth century onwards. The section dealing with Corpo Santo and Bom Sucesso (No. 145) was written by an unknown Jesuit and is a contemporary account. It incorporated many of the documents relating to the establishment of the college. It also furnishes a full architectural description of the former building of Corpo Santo.

From the French archives, four sources at least have material dealing with the Irishman. In the archives of the Ministry of Foreign Affairs in Paris there is a magnificent file of correspondence dealing with the foreign policy of João IV. The reports of the Chevalier de Jant are kept in the Manuscript section of the Bibliotheque Nationale. I am indebted to Monsieur J. Porcher for locating that manuscript for me and to the microfilming services of the National Library of Ireland, Dublin. Cominges's dispatches are to be found in the British Museum (Harl.MS 4547) though of its nature, it belongs to the French archives. In 1886, the Vicomte de Caix de St Amour began to compile a collection of *Instructions* given to the French ambassadors after the peace of Westphalia. It is known as *Recueil*. Side by side with this, the *Lettres de Mazarin* and Michaud's *Collection* of Memoires give a fair idea of French diplomacy during the same period.

Of the many archives in Spain two yielded material for this study. In Archivo General de Simancas, the documents of interest for diplomatic history are conserved principally in the section called *Estado* consisting of the papers of the Secretariat of State. The records of *Estado* retain their old classification by 'negotiation', one for each county. A very important complement of the *Negociations* with Rome is found in the archives of the Spanish Embassy to the Holy See which are in the archives of the Ministry of External Affairs in Madrid. They are usually referred to as *Fondo*

Santa Sede and consist of the personal letters of the Spanish kings to their ambassadors in Rome.

One other small collection of documents from the Archives Generales du Royaume de Belgique proved useful, particularly the cartons relating to the financial assistance given by the state to the Irish Dominicans in Louvain from 1628 onward.

3) *State papers and public records*

In examining the English sources which refer to Daniel O'Daly, one gets the impression that the records about him are hostile. *The English Papers 1630–40* view his activities with suspicion, and, although from 1650 onwards, it seems clear that O'Daly was acting for Charles Stuart, yet, the references to O'Daly in the *Carte Papers* and the *Nicholas Papers* are full of distrust and doubt about his authenticity. For that reason, they are valuable because they provide the English point of view about O'Daly.

The period 1595–1662, which was the span of O'Daly's life, is well documented in Irish history. From Irish legal records, such as the *Fiants*, which were warrants for issuing 'letters patents' after the Geraldine rebellion, the background of the O'Daly family may be pieced together. In the National Archives may be found a Manuscript calendar of the Inquisition records for Munster, and from this, other details concerning the family may be gleaned. Another valuable document which supplies details of the O'Daly family and background is the *Desmond Survey Papers*. Like the Inchiquin records, the originals are lost, but manuscript copies exist in Kerry and Limerick. The *Survey* is an inventory made of the property of the earl of Desmond after the rebellion preparatory to the plantation of Munster. Of special interest are the scattered references to O'Daly's *History of the Geraldines* and to the martyrs he mentions in the appendix to his book which are found in the *Comment. Rinucc.*

In a class apart are the family papers relating to the O'Daly family in Portugal which are now in possession of the Pereira household near Lisbon who claim to be the descendants of Denis O'Daly, brother of the Dominican. The family pedigree of the family who trace their ancestry back to the arrival of the two brothers in Portugal is of particular interest; however, the official genealogy of the Familia O'Daly in the state archives of the Torre do Tombo was found to be more exact and served the useful purpose of checking information already traced in Irish legal documents of the Elizabethan period. When Father O'Daly was appointed bishop-elect of Coimbra, his relatives were automatically accepted into the ranks of the hereditary nobility of Portugal, and a record of the family was gradually compiled in the state archives.

BIBLIOGRAPHY

Daniel O'Daly is an enigmatic and controversial figure. His association with Mazarin makes him, *ipso facto*, suspect, as one tinged with Machiavellism. The earliest accounts of his life read like a legend, though, in the main, the basic facts are authentic. The archives of Corpo Santo were completely destroyed in the 1755 Lisbon earthquake; fortunately, some of the material there had been incorporated into several monumental source histories of the period written in Portuguese: Frei Lucas, *Historia de S. Domingos*, i–iv (1707–11); Frei Agostinho, O.S.A., *O Santuario Mariano* (1713); *Agiologio Dominico*, 6 vols. (1657–1712), begun by Joseph de Natividade, vols. i–iii, and finished by George Cardosa.

The two chief source for the history of the Irish Dominican province during the seventeenth century are J. O'Heyne, *Epilogus Chronologicus* (Louvain, 1706); T. de Burgo, *Hibernia Dominicana* (Kilkenny, 1762). O'Heyne's book, though it purports to give an account of Dominican figures and life in the seventeenth century is by no means trustworthy. The chief source book is de Burgo's massive compendium. It was first published in 1762, probably in Kilkenny, though its format and imprint have proved somewhat of a puzzle to bibliographers. In 1772, a valuable supplement was added. No second edition appeared. It has a special interest in view of the fact that de Burgo had access to both Lisbon and Louvain archives before they were destroyed, and painstakingly ransacked these and the Roman archives of the Dominican order.

In 1888, Mrs Morgan John O'Connell wrote *For Faith and Fatherland*, an attractive account of the life of Father Dominic of the Rosary; however, it integrates uncritical historical facts with a certain haphazard accuracy which leaves the reader bemused. No serious attempt was made to place O'Daly in his historical setting until the twentieth century. Professor Edgar Prestage of Coimbra and London universities published *The Diplomatic Relations of Portugal with France, England and Holland from 1649 to 1668* (1925) that gives an account of O'Daly's diplomatic career in France. This book was followed a year later with the Portuguese monograph *Frei Domingos do Rosario: Diplomata e Politico* (1926) which was a more developed study of O'Daly's mission to France. In 1934, Professor Damião Peres of Coimbra university did full justice to O'Daly as a diplomat in his *Historia de Portugal* (1934). The *Portuguese Encyclopaedia* (1947–48) includes a detailed account of O'Daly as a prominent figure in the Portuguese Restoration. O'Daly entries in the *Dictionary of National Biography* and the *Catholic Encyclopedia* (1907) emphasise his activities as an Irishman as well as a figure in the Portuguese Restoration.

MANUSCRIPT SOURCES

Archives generales du Royaume de Belgique, Brussels
Cartons, 1168, 2017

Archives general O.P., Santa Sabina, Rome
Ex Regeste M.G.O.P., IV (Nos 58–87)

Archives Propaganda Fide, Rome
Lettere, vols 1, 14, 294: Scritture 387

Archivio Segreto do Vaticano, Rome
Nunziatura di Francia, 99–113; 279; 309
Nunz. di Inghilterra, 1, 7, 9, 19, 30
Nunz. di Lisbona, Div. 11, Posiz. IX
Nunz. di Portugal, 22, 23, 155, 226, 227
Nunz. di Spagna, 30; 70–83; 101–113; 346
Fondo Borghese, Series 1, vol 939; Series II, vol 943
Fondo Pio, 275
Lettere di Principi, vols 65, 79, 83, 84, 85
Epistolas ad Principes, vols 53, 55, 56, 57
Miscell. Armario 1, vol 74; Armario II, vol 65

Archivo Nacional da Torre do Tombo, Lisbon
Chancellaria de João IV, vols 21, 22, 27
Chancellaria de Afonso VI, vol 24
Livro de Consultas e Repostas du Gov. de Castello, 1639
MSS Miscell., nos 170, 622
MS de S. Vincente, vols 12, 14, 22
Process of Inquisition, Maco 50, 821

Archives O.P., Tallaght, Co. Dublin
Costelloe Transcripts ii

Bibliotheca de Ajuda, Lisbon
Minutes of councils of state for years 1655–1660
Codices 49–x–13; 51–v–41; 51–vii–29

Biblioteca Apostolico do Vaticano
Barberini Latino, 8105; 8560–4; 8646
Chigi, F. VI.149; 0.1.12; Q.1.24; R.1.4
Nicoletti A, Vita di P. Urbano VIII, 9 tomes (Barb. Lat. 4730–8)

Bibliotheque de Besançon, France
MS 119: *Deux genealogies de la famille O'Donnell, avec une dissertation sur les origins de cette famille par 'Fr Dominicus a Rosario'* (1627)

Bibliotheque Nationale, Paris
MS de Chevalier de Jant, Fr. 5853

British Museum
Correspondence de Lieut. General, Le Comte de Cominges in Harl. MS 4547

Ministry of Foreign Affairs (Archives), Paris
Correspondance de Portugal, vol IV

Ministry of Foreign Affairs (Archives), Madrid
Fondo Santa Sede, Legs. 62, 70, 96

National Library, Lisbon, Sala Reservados
Fundo Antigo 145
Fundo Antigo 3580, Papel do Frei Domingos do Rosario
Colleacao 95 (Rare pamphlets), 290

Public Records Office, London
State Papers Foreign Portugal, vol IV

PAMPHLETS AND PRINTED SOURCES
(Pamphlets)
A Bloudy Fight in Ireland, Thomason Tracts E. 632 (9) in British Museum
Anti-Catastrophe (Lisbon, 1666), in Sala Res., National Library, Lisbon
Catastrophe de Portugal (Lisbon, 1669), *loc. cit.*
De Daena Sanchas, Notas e Documentas ineditos para biographia de João Pinto Ribeiro, National Library, Lisbon 14537
De Guzman Soares, *Ultimas Accões de Rey D. João IV, Nosso Senhor* (Lisbon, 1657), *loc. cit.*
Relecam Somaria e verdadeiro do estado presente do Reyno de Irlanda, tirada de muitas cartas de pessoas graves: e da informacoens de alguns homens de credito que irerao del' estes dias (Lisbon, 1644)
Ribeiro J. Pinto, *Discurso sobre as Fidalgos, e Soldados Portuguezes nao militarem em conquistas alhoes* (Lisbon, 1632), National Library, Lisbon

Printed sources (including contemporary or nearly contemporary chronicles)
Barozzi, N. and Berchet G., *Relazioni degli stati europei lette dagli ambasciate veneti nel. sec. 17.* 10 vols (Venice, 1856)
Caix de Saint-Aymour, *Recueil des instructions donne aux Ambassadeurs de France depuis les traites de Westphalie* (Paris, 1886)
Calendar of patent and close rolls of chancery in Ireland, Elizabeth, 19 year to end of reign. (ed.), J. Morrin (Dublin, 1862)
Calendar of State Papers, Domestic series, 1547–80
Calendar of State Papers, British and Foreign, vol 1

Calendar of State Papers Relating to Ireland, 1509–73, etc. 24 vols (London, 1860–1911)

Cardosa G., Agiologio Dominico, 3 vols (Lisbon, 1657)

Carvalho A., Corografia Portugueza, 3 vols (Lisbon, 1706–18)

Cherues P.A. and d'Avenal G. (eds), Lettres du Cardinal Mazarin pendant son ministere, 9 vols (Paris, 1872–1906)

Clarendon State Papers, 3 vols (Oxford, 1767–86)

da Silva, Rebello (ed.), Corpo Diplomatico Portuguez, 16 vols (Lisbon, 1862–1936)

de Burgo, T., Hibernia Dominicana (Kilkenny, 1762)

de Castro, L. B., Collecão de Tratados, convencoes e contratos celebrados entre a Corao de Portugal e as mais potencias desde 1640 ate o presente, 16 vols (Lisbon, 1856–78)

de Santaram, V., Quadro Elementar das relacoes politicas e diplomaticas de Portugal, 18 vols (Paris and Lisbon, 1842–59)

Ericeira, Conde de, Historia de Portugal Restorado, 4 vols. (ed.), A. Doria (Lisbon, 1945)

Frei Lucas di S. Caterina, O.P., Historia di S. Domingos, 4 vols (Lisbon, 1707–11)

Frei Agostinho de S. Maria, O.S.A., O Santuario Mariano, 4 vols (Lisbon, 1711–18)

Michaud, Nouvelles Collections de Memoires (Paris, 1857)

O'Daly, Daniel, Initium, Incrementum et Exitum Geraldinorum (Lisbon, 1655)

O'Ferrall, R. and O'Connell, R., Commentarius Rinuccianus (ed.), S. Kavanagh (Dublin, 1932–49)

O'Heyne, J., Epilogus Chronologicus (ed.), A. Coleman (Dundalk, 1902)

Stafford, T., Pacata Hibernia (ed.), S. O'Grady (London, 1896)

Warner, G. F. (ed.), The Nicholas Papers, 4 vols (London, 1897–1920)

NEWSPAPERS AND PERIODICALS

The Irish Monthly Mercury (Cork, 1649), B.M. E 952 (5)

Anais 7 (1942) Ciclo de Restauracão (Journal of Academia Portuguesa de Historia)

Archivum F.F. Praedicatorum, i (1932), xxx (1960), Journal of Instituto Hist. Dominicano, S. Sabina, Rome

Archivium Hibernicum, Catholic Record Society of Ireland (Maynooth, 1912)

Archivo Pittoresco, v (Lisbon, 1863)

Catholic Record Society, *Journal of Catholic Record Society of England* (Westminster, 1960)

English Miscellany, iv (1954), editor, M. Praz

Historical Manuscripts Commission, *Report of Franciscan Manuscripts* (1906)

Irish Ecclesiastical Record (Dublin, 1922), Series 5, xix.

Irish Hibernia, Societé Academique Hibernia, Fribourg (vol iii, no 5, 1957)

Irish Booklover, xiv, xvii, Dublin

Journal Cork Historical and Archaeological Society, xxvi, Series 2 (Cork, 1920)

Kerry Archaeological Magazine, vol 1, no 4 (Tralee, 1910)

Kerry Magazine, 1 (Tralee, 1854)

Lusitania Sacra, vols ii, iii (Lisbon, 1957–58)

O Instituto, 98 (Coimbra, 1941)

Proceedings Irish Catholic Historical Committee, no 3 (Dublin, 1957)

Proceedings of Royal Irish Academy, C.XXXVI (Dublin, 1921–24)

Revista Portuguesa da Historia, 3 (Coimbra, 1944–47)

The Irish Rosary, lvi, lvii (Dublin, 1952–3)

The Kerryman, newspaper files (August–October, 1927)

STANDARD WORKS OF REFERENCE

Cambridge Modern History, 8, 13 volumes (Cambridge, 1902–12)

Catholic Encyclopaedia, 15 volumes (New York, 1907)

Grande Enciclopedia Portuguesa e Brasileara, 24 vols (Lisbon, 1945–58)

Dictionary of National Biography, Sir L. Stephen and Sir S. Lee, 66 vols (London, 1885–1901)

Hill, D. J., *A History of Diplomacy in the International Development of Europe*, 3 vols (Longmans, 1914)

SECONDARY PRINTED WORKS

Ademola, A., *La Questione della Indipendenza Portoghese a Roma dal 1640 a 1670* (Florence, 1878)

Almeida, F. de, *Historia de Portugal* (Coimbra, 1918)

Andreas, W., *Staatskunst und Diplomatie der Venezianer* (Leipzig, 1943)

Anstruther, G., *A Hundred Homeless Years* (Blackfriars, 1958)

Arnauld-Henri, *Negociations de Portugal a la Cour de Rome*, 2 vols (Lisbon, 1748)

Aquinas, *Summa Theologica*, trans, Fathers of English Province (London, 1911)

Baron, V., *Libr Apologeticorum* (Paris, 1666)

Begley, J., *The Diocese of Limerick in the 16th and 17th Centuries* (Dublin, 1927)

Brady, W.M., *Episcopal Succession in England, Scotland and Ireland, 1400–1875*, 3 vols (Rome, 1876–7)

Boullaye Le Gouz, *Tour of the French Traveller, 1644*, trans, Crofton Croker (London, 1837)

Brazão, E., *A Restauracão* (Lisbon, 1940)

Brazão, E., *Uma Velha Alianca* (Lisbon and London, 1954)

Butler, W.F.T., *Gleanings from Irish History* (Longmans, 1925)

Casimiro, A., *Dona Catarina de Bragança, Rainha de Inglaterra* (Lisbon, 1956)

Cavalheiro, R., *1640, Richelieu e o Duque de Bragança* (Lisbon, 1942)

Cayolla, J., *A Restauracão e o Imperio Colonial* (Lisbon, 1940)

Cockayne, G.E., *Complete Peerage of England, Scotland and Ireland*, 8 vols (London, 1887–98)

d'Azevedo, L., *Historia de Antonio Vieira, S.J.*, 2 vols (Lisbon, 1918)

da Silva, R., *Historia de Portugal nos seclos XVII e XVIII* (Lisbon, 1869)

Davidson, L.C., *Catherine of Bragança* (London, 1908)

de Los Rios, J., *Historia de la villa y corte de Madrid*, 4 vols (Madrid, 1863)

Edwards, R.D., *Church and State in Tudor Ireland* (Dublin, 1935)

Giblin, C., *Collectanea Hibernica*, 1 (Dublin, 1958)

Gregorovius, F., *Urbain VIII in Widerspruck zu Spanien und dem Kaiser* (Stuttgart, 1879)

Hickson, M., *Selections from Old Kerry Records*, 2nd series (London, 1872)

Hogan, E., *Onomasticon Godelicum, locorum et tribuum Hiberniae et Scotiae* (Dublin, 1910)

Hoyos, P., *Registro Documental O.P.*, 2 vols (Madrid, 1961–2)

Hugon, E., *Tractatus Dogmatici*, 5th ed (Paris, 1927)

Jedin, H., *Dan Konzil von Treint ein ueberlick Die eaforchung seiner Geschichte* (Rome, 1948)

King, J., *County Kerry: Past and Present* (Dublin, 1931)

Lecler, J., *Toleration and the Reformation*, 2 vols, trans, T. Westow (Longmans, 1960)

Leman, A., *Richelieu et Olivares* (University of Lille, 1938)

Leman, A., *Urbain VIII et la Rivalite de la France et de la Maison d'Austriche de 1631–35* (Lille, 1939)

Martin, N.G., *La aportacion economica de Espana a la Santa Sede por medio de los espolios y vacantes durante la nunciatura de Cesar Monti (1630–34)* (Madrid, 1959)

Marañon, G., *El Conde-Duque de Olivares*, 9 ed. (Madrid, 1959)

Mattingly, G., *Renaissance Diplomacy* (London, 1955)

Meinecke, F., *Machiavellism*, trans, D. Scott (London, 1957)

Moran, P.F., *Spicilegium Ossoriense*, 3 vols (Dublin, 1874–84)

Mortier, R.P., *Histoire des Maitres Generaux del Ordre des Freres Precheurs*, 7 vols (Paris, 1903–14)

O'Connell, Mrs Morgan J., *For Faith and Fatherland* (Dublin, 1888)

Ogg, D., *England in the Reign of Charles II*, 2 vols (Oxford, 1934)

Peres, D., *Historia de Portugal* (Coimbra and Barcelos, 1934)

Prestage, E., *Diplomatic Relations of Portugal during the 17th Century* (Watford, 1925)

Raposa, H., *Dona Luisa de Gusmão* (Lisbon, 1946)

Ranke, L. von, *History of the Popes*, 3 vols (ed.), G.R. Dennis (London, 1908)

Reusen-Barbier, C., *Analectes pour servir a l'histoire ecclesiastique de la Belgique* (Louvain, 1899)

Revah, I.S., *Le Cardinal de Richelieu et la Restauration du Portugal* (Lisbon, 1950)

Routledge, F.J., *England and the Treaty of the Pyrenees* (University of Liverpool Press, 1953)

Tessier, J., *Le Chevalier de Jant* (Paris, 1877)

Von Pastor, L., *Storia dei Papi* (Rome, 1942–53)

India, 193, 227, 230

Indies, East and West, 125, 167

Infantado, Duke of, 178, 223–225, 241

Initium, Incrementum et Exitus Geraldinorum, O'Daly, Daniel, 245–252, 255, 259

Innocent X, Pope, 160, 215, 221–226, 241

Inquisition, 248, 274

Ireland, 7, 11–16, 20, 29–34, 39, 41–43, 46, 49–61, 64–77, 86–92, 98–99, 104, 109, 137, 149–159, 212, 231, 237, 246–247, 254, 256, 259, 262, 264–265, 271–273

Ireton, 256, 258

Irish Monthly Mercury, 149, 178

Irish scholars, 49, 246

Isabella Clara, sovereign of the Spanish Netherlands, 62–65

Italy, 13, 120, 190, 214, 254, 260

Jachinetti, 94–96

Jacobite, 151

James I, King of England, 37, 42, 57, 151

James II, King of England, 152, 175

Jannes, Peter, O.P., 86

Jant, Chevalier de, 128–141, 146–147, 228–229, 273

Jedin, 215

Jermyn, Lord, 157, 265

Jeronomite, order of, 86, 105

Jersey, 153, 160

Jesuit, 42–43, 55, 57, 63, 65, 88, 123, 126, 132, 136, 172, 203, 223, 230, 236, 256–260, 273

João IV, King of Portugal, 9, 16, 25, 48, 59, 70, 80, 100, 109, 114–147, 154, 157, 161, 165–172, 177–178, 182, 184, 186, 188–189, 193, 201, 208, 215–225, 229, 231, 233, 240–243, 260–266, 272–273

Joubert, Abbé, 248

Junta Nocturna, 187, 192, 221, 241

Kahvicon, 27, 30

Kavanagh, Donal an Spainneach, 98, 103

Kavanagh, Leonor, 98

Keating, Geoffrey, 247, 249

Kerry, 5, 7, 9, 20, 25, 27–37, 40–41, 48–50, 58, 61, 79, 252, 274

Kerry/Query, Knight of, 90–91

Kilcowan, 175

Kilkenny, 15, 150, 277

Killarney, 75

Kilmallock, 39–40, 249

O'Daly, CuChonnacht, 31, 87, 251

O'Daly, Denis/John, 29, 46, 87, 207, 275

O'Daly, Fr Daniel, Frei Domingos do Rosario, Fr Dominic of the Rosary, Hodal, O'Dála, Uí Dalaigh, 1–32, 35, 39, 45–80, 86–92, 96–114, 120, 123, 128–143, 147, 152, 154, 156–209, 223–278

O'Daly, Don Charles, 207

O'Daly, Maoilseachlainn Óg, 31

O'Daly, Phillip, 43

O'Daly, Tadhg Crookshank, 43

Odemira, Count, 187, 191–192, 199–200, 203–204

O'Donnell, Hugh Ruadh/Red Hugh, 31, 38, 40

O'Dubhthaigh, Eoghan, 49

O'Farrell, Laurence, 259

Ogg, David, *England in the Reign of Charles II*, 177

O'Heyne, John, 43, 54, 78, 277

O'Hurley, Bishop Dermot, 41

O'Hurley, James, Dominican provincial, 104

O'Hurley, Maurice, Bishop of Emly, 61

O'Keeffe, 29

Olivenca, 190

Ollamh, 29–30

O'Loughlins, 30

O'Neill, Hugh/Earl of Tyrone, 39, 68, 77, 137, 159

O'Queely, Malachy, Archbishop of Tuam, 61

O'Rahilly, T.F., 49

O'Sullivan Beare, Philip, *Historiae Catholicae Iberniae,* 35, 247–249, 256

O'Sullivan More, 61

O'Sullivan More, Eugene, 61

Old Irish, 40, 137, 150–151 159

Ormond, Earl of, 54, 60, 78, 137, 152–153, 156, 178, 264–265, 267

Ormond, Marquis of, 153–154, 157, 159

Ossory, Bishop of, 42

Ostend, 154

Our Lady of Limerick, 105

Owney, 258

Pacata Hibernia, 39–40, 49, 249

Palatinate, 32–33, 41, 50, 63, 252

Pallavicino, 215

Paloti, Cardinal, 227

Palm of the Faith in Ireland, 256

Pamfili, Cardinal Camilio, 221

Panziroli, 219–220, 241